PLAYING WITH DYNAMITE

Other titles in the
Forensic Psychotherapy Monograph Series

PLAYING WITH DYNAMITE

A Personal Approach
to the Psychoanalytic Understanding of
Perversions, Violence, and Criminality

Estela V. Welldon

Forewords by

*R. Horacio Etchegoyen, Brett Kahr,
& Baroness Helena Kennedy, QC*

Introduction by

James Gilligan

Forensic Psychotherapy Monograph Series

Series Editor	Honorary Consultant
Brett Kahr	*Estela V. Welldon*

KARNAC

First published in 2011 by
Karnac Books
118 Finchley Road
London NW3 5HT

British Library Cataloguing in Publication Data

A C.I.P. for this book is available from the British Library

ISBN: 978–1–85575–742–4

Edited, designed, and produced by Communication Crafts

To all my students from the "Golden Decade" —
from 1990 when the Course on Forensic Psychotherapy was
founded to 2000 before my retirement.
These students have become this country's
most accomplished clinicians, academicians, writers,
and researchers in this, the most difficult field
of psychiatric endeavours.

Most of them have been responsible
for the growth and expansion of the
International Association for Forensic Psychotherapy,
adding to the collective wisdom of practitioners everywhere.

CONTENTS

ACKNOWLEDGEMENTS

I have learned much from my teachers and senior colleagues in the field, my many contemporaries, patients, students, and friends.

I had the good fortune to study with, or to be influenced directly by, several historic figures in the fields of psychiatry, psychoanalysis, and psychotherapy, especially: Luisa Alvarez de Toledo, Horacio Etchegoyen, Adam Limentani, Joyce McDougall, Karl Menninger, Paco Perez Morales, Enrique Pichon-Rivière, Janine Puget, Salomon Resnik, Ismond Rosen, and Buby Usandivaras. I am indebted to the medical school at the University of Cuyo in Argentina, where I studied medicine for free; this training would have been impossible otherwise.

Without the crucial support of Professor Sir Michael Peckham, I would never have had the opportunity to develop the training in forensic psychotherapy under the auspices of the British Postgraduate Medical Federation at the University of London, which resulted in a diploma from University College London. Wendy Riley administered the diploma on behalf of the University of London with tremendous diligence and collegiality, and Bruce Irvine proved to be a very great help on the Steering Committee.

I also want to thank the members of the Forensic Women's group that met over many years at the Groucho Club. This group of pioneering colleagues and students made important contributions to my own thinking in the forensic field, and I thank them warmly for their creativity and support. In a wonderful, creative joint effort, the whole group, under the editorship of Cleo van Velsen and myself, produced together the *Practical Guide to Forensic Psychotherapy*. Its publication raised eyebrows among our male colleagues.

I owe thanks to many colleagues overseas whose work has enriched my thinking greatly, including: Mariam Alizade, Jacqueline Amati-Mehler, Giovanna Ambrosio, Simona Argentieri, Maria Amon, Luisa Brunori, Patty Capellino, Chiara Cattelan, Teresa Flores, Maurizio Freschi, James Gilligan, Julia Lauzon, Moíses Lemlij, Liliana Lorettu, Amedea Lo Russo, Norberto Marucco, Riccardo Romano, Maria Concetta Scavo, Candida Se Holovko, Athinas Tsoukalis, Amelia Vasconcello and Paul Verhaege, as well as the members of the Racker Group in Venice, namely Hugo Marquez, Marisa Petrilli, and Mauro Rosetti. I also extend my warmest appreciations to my cherished British colleagues, who are too numerous to mention and who, I trust, will forgive me for not listing each of them personally. I also thank the many organizations that have invited me to deliver lectures and papers (which helped to form the basis of the chapters in this book), among them, the Group Analytic Society of London for inviting me to deliver the S. H. Foulkes Memorial Lecture, and the Portman Clinic in London for asking me to deliver the Edward Glover Memorial Lecture. I also thank Oxford Brookes University for their wisdom when recognizing the field of forensic psychotherapy in conferring an honorary degree upon me, and to Bologna University. I have also given key lectures, which have developed my thinking, at meetings of the Committee on Women and Psychoanalysis of the International Psychoanalytical Association, at the Catholic University in Peru, in Buenos Aires, in Chile, in Sardinia, and in Rome and Venice, among other places. I also benefited from my teaching on the Diploma Course in Forensic Psychotherapy at the Portman Clinic, and at the Consiglio Superiore della Magistratura in Rome.

* * *

I have been most impressed by all my trainees at the Portman Clinic, and I feel that my work with emotionally damaged mothers has been especially validated by Carine Minne, who has followed, deepened, and extended this work in such a difficult setting as Broadmoor Hospital. I am looking forward to her eloquent, sensitive, and insightful work being published.

I am most grateful to many colleagues for their interest and constructive response to my book but am especially grateful to younger colleagues who not only read parts of the manuscripts at their earlier stages, but also gave positive criticisms on them, such as Anna Motz and Cleo van Velsen. Alex Goforth has provided much care, patience, and tenacity in pursuing references, and for being a good listener. Nigel Warburton has provided me with a link between contemporary art and the forensic field. Gregorio and Valli Kohon have kindly translated Horacio Etchegoyen's foreword from the Spanish into English.

My former student, and now friend and colleague, Brett Kahr, had first suggested this book to me back in 1994, and he has continued to encourage me over these last seventeen years. I am very proud to publish this book in the Forensic Psychotherapy Monograph Series which he edits for Karnac Books, and for which I have had the pleasure to serve as Honorary Consultant since its inception in 2001.

Oliver Rathbone, the Publisher of Karnac Books, kindly offered me a home for these papers, and I thank him for agreeing to publish my book. Eric King has proved to be the most patient, detailed, and helpful of copy-editors, making many extremely constructive contributions to the structure and style of the book.

So many loyal and loving friends have enriched my life and my work, and I am sure they know who they are. I thank my son Dan, my daughter-in-law Jo, and my granddaughter Isabella for their love and care.

E.V.W.
London, February 2011

SERIES FOREWORD

Brett Kahr

Centre for Child Mental Health, London

Throughout most of human history, our ancestors have done rather poorly when dealing with acts of violence. To cite but one of many shocking examples, let us perhaps recall a case from 1801, of an English boy aged only 13, who was executed by hanging on the gallows at Tyburn. What was his crime? It seems that he had been condemned to die for having stolen a spoon (Westwick, 1940).

In most cases, our predecessors have either *ignored* murderousness and aggression, as in the case of Graeco–Roman infanticide, which occurred so regularly in the ancient world that it acquired an almost normative status (deMause, 1974; Kahr, 1994); or they have *punished* murderousness and destruction with retaliatory sadism, a form of unconscious identification with the aggressor. Any history of criminology will readily reveal the cruel punishments inflicted upon prisoners throughout the ages, ranging from beatings and stockades, to more severe forms of torture, culminating in eviscerations, beheadings, or lynchings.

Only during the last one hundred years have we begun to develop the capacity to respond more intelligently and more humanely to acts of dangerousness and destruction. Since the advent of psychoanalysis and psychoanalytic psychotherapy, we now have access to a much deeper understanding both of the aetiology of aggressive acts and of their treatment; and nowadays we need no longer ignore criminals or abuse them—instead, we can provide compassion and containment, as well as conduct research that can help to prevent future acts of violence.

The modern discipline of forensic psychotherapy, which can be defined, quite simply, as the use of psychoanalytically orientated "talking therapy" to treat violent, offender patients, stems directly from the work of Sigmund Freud. Almost one hundred years ago, at a meeting of the Vienna Psycho-Analytical Society, held on 6 February 1907, Sigmund Freud anticipated the clarion call of contemporary forensic psychotherapists when he bemoaned the often horrible treatment of mentally ill offenders, in a discussion on the psychology of vagrancy. According to Otto Rank, Freud's secretary at the time, the founder of psychoanalysis expressed his sorrow at the "nonsensical treatment of these people in prisons" (quoted in Nunberg & Federn, 1962, p. 108).

Many of the early psychoanalysts preoccupied themselves with forensic topics. Hanns Sachs, himself a trained lawyer, and Marie Bonaparte, the French princess who wrote about the cruelty of war, each spoke fiercely against capital punishment. Sachs, one of the first members of Freud's secret committee, regarded the death penalty for offenders as an example of group sadism (Moellenhoff, 1966). Bonaparte, who had studied various murderers throughout her career, had actually lobbied politicians in America to free the convicted killer Caryl Chessman, during his sentence on Death Row at the California State Prison in San Quentin, albeit unsuccessfully (Bertin, 1982).

Melanie Klein concluded her first book, the landmark text *Die Psychoanalyse des Kindes* [*The Psycho-Analysis of Children*], with resounding passion about the problem of violence in our culture. Mrs Klein noted that acts of criminality invariably stem from disturbances in childhood, and that if young people could receive access to psychoanalytic treatment at any early age, then much cruelty could be prevented in later years. Klein expressed the hope that: "If every child who shows disturbances that are at all severe were to be analysed in good time, a great number of these people who later end up in prisons or lunatic asylums, or who go completely to pieces, would be saved from such a fate and be able to develop a normal life" (1932, p. 374).

Shortly after the publication of Klein's transformative book, Atwell Westwick, a Judge of the Superior Court of Santa Barbara, California, published a little-known though highly inspiring article, "Criminology and Psychoanalysis" (1940), in the *Psychoanalytic Quarterly*. Westwick may well be the first judge to commit himself in print to the value of psychoanalysis in the study of criminality, arguing that punishment of the forensic patient remains, in fact, a sheer waste of time. With foresight, Judge Westwick queried, "Can we not, in our well nigh hopeless and overwhelming struggle with the problems of delinquency and crime, profit by medical experience with the problems of health and disease? Will we not, eventually, terminate the senseless policy of sitting idly by until misbehavior occurs, often with irreparable damage, then dumping the delinquent into the juvenile court or reformatory and dumping the criminal into prison?" (p. 281). Westwick noted that we should, instead, train judges, probation officers, social workers, as well as teachers and parents, in the precepts of psychoanalysis, in order to arrive at a more sensitive, non-punitive understanding of the nature of criminality. He opined: "When we shall have succeeded in committing society to such a program, when we see it launched definitely upon the venture, as in time it surely will be—then shall we have erected an appropriate memorial to Sigmund Freud" (p. 281).

In more recent years, the field of forensic psychotherapy has become increasingly well constellated. Building upon the pioneering contributions of such psychoanalysts and psychotherapists as Edward Glover, Grace Pailthorpe, Melitta Schmideberg, and more recently Murray Cox, Mervin Glasser, Ismond Rosen, Estela Welldon, and others too numerous to mention, forensic psychotherapy has now become an increasingly formalized discipline that can be dated to the inauguration of the International Association for Forensic Psychotherapy and to the first annual conference, held at St. Bartholomew's Hospital in London in 1991.

The volumes in this series of books will aim to provide both practical advice and theoretical stimulation for introductory students and for senior practitioners alike. In the Karnac Books Forensic Psychotherapy Monograph Series, we will endeavour to produce a regular stream of high-quality titles, written by leading members of the profession, who will share their expertise in a concise and practice-orientated fashion. We trust that such a collection of books will help to consolidate the knowledge and experience that we have already acquired and will also provide new directions for the future. In this way, we shall hope to plant the seeds for a more rigorous, sturdy, and wide-reaching profession of forensic psychotherapy.

We now have an opportunity for psychotherapeutically orientated forensic mental health professionals to work in close conjunction with child psychologists and with infant mental health specialists so that the problems of violence can be tackled both preventatively and retrospectively. With the growth of the field of forensic psychotherapy, we at last have reason to be hopeful that serious criminality can be forestalled and perhaps, one day, even eradicated.

References

Bertin, C. (1982). *La Dernière Bonaparte*. Paris: Librairie Académique Perrin.

deMause, L. (1974). The evolution of childhood. In: Lloyd deMause (Ed.), *The History of Childhood* (pp. 1–73). New York: Psychohistory Press.

Kahr, B. (1994). The historical foundations of ritual abuse: an excavation of ancient infanticide. In: Valerie Sinason (Ed.), *Treating Survivors of Satanist Abuse* (pp. 45–56). London: Routledge.

Klein, M. (1932). *The Psycho-Analysis of Children*, trans. Alix Strachey. London: Hogarth Press and The Institute of Psycho-Analysis. [First published as *Die Psychoanalyse des Kindes*. Vienna: Internationaler Psychoanalytischer Verlag.]

Moellenhoff, F. (1966). Hanns Sachs, 1881–1947: the creative unconscious. In: F. Alexander, S. Eisenstein, & M. Grotjahn (Eds.), *Psychoanalytic Pioneers* (pp. 180–199). New York: Basic Books.

Nunberg, H., & Federn, E. (Eds.) (1962). *Minutes of the Vienna Psychoanalytic Society. Volume I: 1906–1908*, trans. Margarethe Nunberg. New York: International Universities Press.

Westwick, A. (1940). Criminology and Psychoanalysis. *Psychoanalytic Quarterly, 9*: 269–282.

FOREWORD

R. Horacio Etchegoyen

I had the privilege of writing the Foreword for the latest version in Spanish of Estela Welldon's *Mother, Madonna, Whore*, a book that has travelled the world, gaining a well-deserved eminent place in psychiatric and psychoanalytic bibliographies. Through the ideas developed in that book, we now know much more about the complex relationship between mother and child, and about the deep traces transmitted from one generation to another. Following this wise, audacious, and enduring book, there is now another—*Playing with Dynamite*—which extends and deepens the author's original insights.

This time, the talented author offers us a comprehensive study of perversions, encompassing the roles of both mother and father, expanding the understanding of the complex sexual life of human beings and its vicissitudes.

Chapter 1, on the true nature of perversions, carefully defines their diagnosis and psychodynamics. It is a wide-ranging, scholarly, and searching exploration, thoroughly covering other writers' work on the subject as well as her own contributions. Welldon never evades the complexity of the concept of perversion and its ramifications. The eternal conflict between morality and perversion is studied in depth, with a scientific approach that goes beyond what social morality and customs vainly try to circumscribe.

The author describes the diagnostic features of perversion, starting from the phenomenon of dissociation, which she prefers to call *encapsulation*. She believes that subjects suffering from perversion do not ignore the value of their actions, despite maintaining a deception, since the right hand *does* know what the left hand is doing, even though the subject cannot avoid it. It is a form of exciting imposture, where the ego and the superego allow themselves to be seduced for a while by the id, to then restart the whole process again.

A prominent feature of perversions, which Welldon notes with pristine clarity, is that while male perversions are aimed towards the outside world, perversions in women are mostly internal, attacking their own body and what is born from the body—that is, children. In this way, Welldon redefines female perversion. The dialectic between idealization and denigration of motherhood, first elaborated in her previous work, is affirmed and highlights its painful quality. A fundamental principle of Welldon's research is that, underlying all perversions, there is a mortal anxiety that the patient avoids at any price.

Chapter 2 of this valuable book refers to the perversion of transference. Welldon joins other authors to discuss this concept, not only in terms of its clinical value but also its therapeutic potential. The perversion of the transference is, for the author, a *malignant bonding*, that goes beyond sadomasochistic relationships, in which narcissism and aggression lead to the failures or abuses suffered by the perverse subject at the beginning of his or her life. In this way, perversion links one generation with both the previous and the next one.

Welldon constantly reminds us that the perverse mother is both excited and (temporarily) relieved by exerting power over her child in a diabolical game. In this macabre exchange, the father also participates with his destructive omnipotence.

Chapter 3 concentrates on the concept of female perversion and indicates that it is easier to make the diagnosis of fetishism in a man than it is in a woman, whose fetish is her own child. Taking up Winnicott's concepts of the transitional object and the capacity to be alone, Welldon points out the importance of remaining attentive to the possibility that a beneficial relation between mother and child can tragically become a monstrous, addictive link, in which the mother satisfies her own need to transform her infant into a thing.

The study in chapter 4 of Munchausen Syndrome by Proxy leads Welldon to return to the importance of the body in the tragic cycle of transgenerational abuse, a topic that she enlarges upon in chapter 5.

Chapter 6 studies the impact on children of witnessing domestic violence, and chapter 7 is concerned with group psychotherapy in which abusing patients and victims of abuse take part together, which allows them to share both pain and insight. It is Welldon's truly very original contribution, full of common sense as well as daring.

Chapters 8 and 9 examine the relationship of forensic psychotherapy to society and the courts. The theoretical and practical aspects of forensic psychotherapy are described in detail and illustrated through a rich vein of clinical case material.

Chapter 10 looks at the involvement of the Portman Clinic in forensic psychotherapy and the establishment of the International Association for Forensic Psychotherapy.

The three interviews interspersed throughout the book present an account of the author's trajectory from her native Mendoza, in Argentina, with a fruitful period at the Menninger Clinic, then eventually to London, where she has had a distinguished career at the Portman Clinic. Welldon was the force behind the creation of the International Association for Forensic Psychotherapy, of which she was the founder and first President and has now been elected Honorary Life President.

A truly admirable book and life.

Buenos Aires, February 2011

FOREWORD

Brett Kahr

For the last forty-seven years, Dr Estela Valentina Welldon has occupied a path-breaking place in the fields of psychotherapy, psychiatry, psychoanalysis, and mental health. A native of Argentina, she trained as a medical doctor and as a psychiatrist in Mendoza and at the Menninger Clinic in Topeka, Kansas, and then subsequently in group analytic psychotherapy. Welldon arrived in London in 1964 and began to work with psychiatrically disturbed offender patients such as murderers, rapists, paedophiles, and others who had committed grave crimes. Although many of her senior colleagues in the field recommended simply incarceration and punishment for offenders, she soon discovered that such patients, known as "forensic patients", would respond very successfully to psychological therapy, specifically psychoanalytically orientated psychotherapy.

After much painstaking work with these often overlooked or reviled patients, Welldon discovered that many members of the criminal patient population had suffered from horrific forms of abuse during childhood. This knowledge has now become widely accepted within the British mental health community, but during the 1970s and 1980s, few professionals bothered to study the early childhood histories of forensic patients with any degree of seriousness, and few dared to believe in such traumatic realities.

Working at the Portman Clinic in London, a specialist British NHS institution devoted to the psychoanalytic treatment of offender patients, Welldon not only undertook important work on the aetiology of sexual offending and violent offending, but she also pioneered new forms of therapeutic intervention, specifically group psychotherapy for offender patients, often placing perpetrators and victims together in the same group. Though shocking at first, Welldon discovered that only by having criminals and victims confront one another and engage with one another in this way could the parties begin to mourn the horrors that each had suffered. Once again, this revolutionary approach to forensic group psychotherapy has now become standard practice in many mental health care institutions.

Welldon not only worked with patients, but she also distinguished herself as an educator, creating the world's first training programme in forensic psychotherapy at the Portman Clinic, sponsored in collaboration with the British Postgraduate Medical Federation and the Medical School at University College London (UCL). She fought to gain recognition for this course, which launched in 1990, and which continued for a short while after her retirement. Welldon personally trained several generations of excellent mental health professionals in the forensic field, many of whom have since become world leaders themselves.

Using her knowledge of groups, and drawing upon her passion for the forensic mental health field, Welldon also founded a large, international organization, the International Association for Forensic Psychotherapy, which now boasts several hundred members worldwide, and which, in 2011, celebrates its twentieth anniversary as a scientific organization of excellence. The meetings of the International Association invariably attract the brightest and the most innovative multidisciplinary minds in prison reform, in the prevention of violence, and in the psychoanalytic assessment and treatment of dangerousness.

Welldon has written widely, and her landmark books include the now classic text, *Mother, Madonna, Whore: The Idealization and Denigration of Motherhood*, first published in 1988, as well as a highly readable book on *Sadomasochism* (2002). Her books have challenged the myth that only men commit sexual crimes against children. She broke new ground by calling our attention to the fact that many women secretly perpetrate incest and other forms of abuse on the bodies of their children, as well as upon themselves, and she linked this criminality and destructiveness to the women's own deprived and often tortured backgrounds.

Her new book, *Playing with Dynamite: A Personal Approach to the Psychoanalytic Understanding of Perversions, Violence, and Criminality*, is derived from a generous selection of some of her many literary gems, ranging from her study of the perverse transference, to the role of babies as transitional objects in perverse motherhood, to the impact of domestic violence upon children, to the treatment of incest survivors and perpetrators in group psychotherapy, to an analysis of the professionalization of forensic psychotherapy as a new field of clinical and academic endeavour. Written with characteristic vigour and verve, and in a style that betokens clear thought, her book constitutes a veritable education not only in the field of forensic psychoanalysis, but also in field of traumatology.

But quite apart from Welldon's professional contributions as an author and psychotherapist, her personality stands as a model to young and old colleagues alike. Not content to sit passively on the sidelines, Welldon has managed to mobilize her considerable charm, persuasiveness, intelligence, and, above all, passion, to enlist others to join in the cause. These essays provide a testament to the body of work that she has spearheaded, and which others have now taken to new depths and heights, always with her blessing and delight. As Series Editor of the Karnac Forensic Psychotherapy Monograph Series, it gives me much pleasure to welcome this collection.

Estela Welldon has inspired immense love and affection among her many students and colleagues worldwide. Her contribution to the mental health field as a clinician, as a researcher, as a writer, and as a teacher remains unique, and perhaps unparalleled. The forensic mental health field would be much the poorer without her myriad contributions. Her legacy will be one that endures for many decades, if not centuries, to come.

London, February 2011

FOREWORD

Baroness Helena Kennedy, QC

Ihave known Estela Welldon both socially and professionally for over thirty years. In many ways our friendship sprang from our shared interest in the human condition and our fascination with society's demands for normalcy, its ability to wrap sexuality in taboo and secrecy, as well as its desire to punish deviation. That conversation of our early days has become lifelong, richer and more diverse as time passes. It has also never been without wit and laughter.

As my law practice in the criminal courts took me into more complex and challenging cases, I drew upon Welldon's psychiatric expertise to help me unravel the underlying dynamics and pressures acting upon my clients. Many were women who were defying not just the legal standards of society but the expectations and beliefs held about what characterized good womanhood. They were women who stayed within abusive relationships, women who killed their spouses and lovers or their children, women who secretly disposed of babies or sexually abused them, women whose self-loathing made them accept degradation and humiliation, women who placed their men before the safety of their offspring, women whose cruelty and depravity shocked even court-worn barristers like me. Welldon's groundbreaking work shed light on all those behaviours in illuminating and sometimes explosive ways, confronting myths about female sexuality and conduct.

Welldon's book *Mother, Madonna, Whore* was a seminal work for professionals working in the fields of psychiatry, psychotherapy, and psychology, but it also had a powerful effect in the law, explaining the internal and external factors influencing the behaviour of criminal women. It explained female dysfunction, perversion, and offending behaviour to lawyers and judges who were traditionally sceptical about the contribution the psychological sciences could make to the criminal justice system. When I look back over the way the law has changed in the last decades, with a greater acceptance of psychiatric evidence and a willingness to understand the workings of the human mind, I think Welldon was undoubtedly one of the experts who helped create that shift.

The author has many proud achievements. Her expertise in sexual deviancy and perversion is recognized throughout the world. She is now an iconic figure in her field. I have also admired how she has nurtured so many young women in a very male dominated part of her profession; a whole generation of women forensic psychiatrists and forensic psychotherapists point to her as their inspiration and mentor. Many of them are experts who now give evidence in my cases. However, the cohort of her protégées is by no means confined to women. Her former students—men and women—all speak to her profound influence on their practice.

But one of her greatest initiatives has been the establishment of the International Association for Forensic Psychotherapy, which brings together specialists from all over the world to share experience and advance learning. At its annual conference, I too have drawn upon the wisdom and case studies of practitioners and researchers and marvelled at the brilliance of its inventor.

This new book draws together many aspects of Estela Welldon's life and work. However, in a life so full and multifaceted, no single volume can do justice to it entirely. What is absolutely clear is that this is a professional life lived and worked with commitment, insight, and depths of human compassion that are incomparable. Here is a psychiatrist who engaged courageously with ideas that discomfited the public and challenged preconceptions. This is a professional woman who has always, in her own way, played with dynamite.

London, February 2011

INTRODUCTION

James Gilligan

I can understand the feeling of pleasure and intellectual enlightenment that readers of this book who are already familiar to one
degree or another with Estela Welldon and her clinical, theoretical,
and educational work will experience, because that was my own initial
reaction to this text—and I had already known the author, and worked
with her, since 1993. It is very gratifying to encounter here the further
development of many of her most original and productive insights.
One of these is her groundbreaking theoretical understanding not
just of the psychodynamics of female perversions and violence, but
of the very existence of this category of psychopathology—a form
of destructiveness and self-destructiveness the recognition of which
had been seriously neglected, if not denied, by many psychoanalysts
prior to her opening it up for examination and analysis, the irony of
which is that this is a field one of whose whole *raisons d'être* is the
overcoming of denial. Freud may have taught us to see how much of
Oedipus there is in all of us, but it took Welldon to show us how much
of Medea there is in the mothers among us—including the Medeas'
own mothers. Apparently it has been easier for those in our profession
to face the castration anxiety that is a universal feature of our own
and our patients' psyches than to tolerate the even deeper terror of
recognizing that one of our most hallowed and idealized images—
that of motherhood—is so often the locus of the most horrifying
cruelty and sadism towards their own infants and babies and those
of other mothers—a horror that is often avoided by replacing both the
denial and the idealization with an equally unhelpful and distorting

denigration of these mothers. It is very appropriate that the book in which Welldon first formulated her approach to understanding this still daunting and disturbing problem, *Mother, Madonna, Whore: The Idealization and Denigration of Motherhood,* in 1988, was recently singled out by Pamela Ashurst in the *British Medical Journal* as a "Medical Classic" (which it certainly is, and deservedly so).

Another joy of the current book is Welldon's brilliant description and analysis of the emerging field of forensic psychotherapy, a field of which she herself was one of the main creators and developers. It is true that London's Portman Clinic, on whose staff she served as a consultant psychotherapist, had already been founded in a previous generation by Dr Edward Glover to serve as a base for the provision of psychoanalytically based therapeutic services to delinquents and other law breakers. But it was not until Welldon became the founding director of the first diploma course in this new sub-specialty at the Portman Clinic in 1990 that this new field actually came of age and finally had an educational mechanism capable of providing formal on-going training to each new generation of clinicians. She then followed that up with her second major contribution to the birth of this new discipline in the following year when she became the founding president of the first professional organization devoted to it, the International Association for Forensic Psychotherapy, which has continued to hold annual meetings and to serve as a catalyst for the development of post-graduate training programmes, consultative and therapeutic services to criminal courts, court clinics, and prison systems, and the writing and publication of research. Like a number of Welldon's and my own colleagues, I was privileged to serve as the president of the International Association for two years, but I am pleased that in recognition of her central and indispensable role in bringing this new organization to life, she still serves as its Honorary Life President.

But while I am writing this appreciation of her new book from the vantage point of one who has known, admired, and learned a great deal from Welldon over the past eighteen years, the people I really envy are those who will here be introduced to her personality and her ideas for the first time. For them, I would like to provide some indication of why this book, and the remarkable personality and life work of which it is the most recent product, is truly of historic magnitude and importance. As Dr Welldon points out in chapter 8, her "Introduction to Forensic Psychotherapy", the traditional, indeed age-old, response to those who commit acts of horrendous cruelty and violence (and even many of those whose offences against others are much less serious) has been to try to protect society and render the criminals harmless by punishing them, which currently consists of confining them in a prison, but otherwise neglecting and ignoring them. This is the approach that was championed by Prime Minister John Major when he said that what society needs is a little more condemning and a little less understanding.

But there are several reasons why that approach is a counterproductive, self-defeating, and self-deluding waste of time and money, which neither protects society nor renders the criminals harmless and which may in fact do more to stimulate crime and violence than to prevent them. First of all, that approach makes it impossible for us to learn anything of value as to why they committed their destructive acts—which the offenders themselves do not know, to begin with, and which we and they can only learn by engaging in serious, intense, and prolonged dialogue with them. And until we can learn what motivated their destructive behaviour, we have no way of knowing how we can prevent such behaviour in the future—by them and by other potential criminals who have not yet offended.

We know that, for several reasons, imprisonment is not an effective means of preventing violence and protecting society. First, there are simply too many criminals committing too many crimes, and we cannot lock them all up and keep them there for a lifetime or we would have to build hundreds of new prisons and subject hundreds of thousands more people to that form of social death. In addition to the fact that that would turn any nation into a police state, it would also bankrupt the government (even the most stripped-down prisons that do nothing but warehouse their inmates are horrendously expensive). And letting prisoners out after having offered them no opportunity to become able to understand why they have ruined their own lives as well as those of others merely results in what we see happening already: frustratingly high recidivism rates, with all too many discharged prisoners committing new crimes and returning to prison for new sentences. This is hardly surprising, given that prisons have always been known as "schools for crime" , which they demonstrably are—indeed, graduate schools.

The only feasible alternative to this manifestly failed approach to the age-old goal of crime prevention is the new field of forensic psychotherapy. That does not, of course, mean that we should not restrain people who are currently violent from harming others (or themselves), if necessary by depriving them of their liberty for as long as they continue to show a predisposition to behave in that way. Given the limitations of our current knowledge as to how to prevent violence, that is a tragic choice that we must sometimes make, though always temporarily. But there is a huge difference between restraint and punishment (by which I mean the gratuitous and avoidable infliction of pain above and beyond whatever suffering is unavoidably caused by the loss of freedom).

But there are three points that can be made about that. First, it makes all the difference in the world what we do with violent offenders once we have locked them up. If we follow the traditional practice, we would either neglect them or abuse them (or both). And that is a recipe for the degree of recidivism and future violence from which we already suffer. Which is why it is so important to take advantage of having a (literally) captive audience and make a meaningful programme of forensic psychotherapy available to those whom we have isolated from the community, so that when they return to the community (as they all should, sooner or later) they will not reoffend.

Second, it is time that we recognized that the modern prison system is an initially well-meaning social experiment (it was, after all, founded by Quakers like John Howard and Enlightenment reformers like Cesare Beccaria and Jeremy Bentham as a replacement for even more barbaric punishments, such as torture, mutilation, and execution) that has failed. Far from achieving the original goals of protecting the public and reforming the criminals, it has had the opposite effect. The only rational thing to do now would be to replace prisons with a whole new type of institution that would have two main functions: as a safe, secure therapeutic community, in which whoever was too violent to remain in the community would participate in forensic psychotherapy and whatever other types of therapy they needed (for substance abuse, medical conditions, etc.); and as a residential college or university in which the residents would be able to get as much education as they had the ability to acquire.

Third, it is important to recognize, as Welldon explains in this book and as I have witnessed repeatedly, that far from finding the deprivation of liberty to be a source of suffering, many of the most violent men and women experience it as a relief. In my own experience, what the most violent people I have seen feared most was their own loss of control, and they experienced an externally imposed set of controls as a source of safety and an escape from chaos—for themselves and everyone else. And once they have available the tools they need in order to remake themselves, such as psychotherapy and education, they welcome it. One of the San Francisco jail inmates with whom I worked said, "I should be in here for four years, not just four months, because I'm trying to change the habits of a lifetime."

As my colleagues and I demonstrated in the jails of San Francisco, it is possible, if you try hard enough, with an intensive multidimensional treatment programme lasting no more than four months, to reduce violent recidivism by 83 per cent, compared with an untreated control group of otherwise identical violent criminals. And as expensive as this program was, it actually saved the tax-payers $4 for every $1 spent on it, since the reduced re-incarceration rate saved far more money than the therapy cost (in addition to the fact that the public's safety was increased far more by this programme than by the traditional approach, and the fact that men who would otherwise spend most of their lives in prisons and jails had learned how to live successfully and non-violently in the community).

Now, one might think that with the success of this pilot demonstration of what you can accomplish with a serious programme of forensic psychotherapy—which was so unprecedented that it won a major national award (including a $100,000 prize) from a foundation administered by the Kennedy School of Government at Harvard, and as I said actually saved the taxpayers a substantial amount of money—any rational city or state or nation would be rushing to find out how to replicate it. Think again. The political unpopularity, at least in the United States, of doing anything constructive for and with men (and women) who have been identified as "criminals" is so great that in response to right-wing protests against "coddling" violent criminals, funding for the San Francisco programme has been cut (you might say that, like any good bank-robber, the politicians took the $100,000 prize money and ran), and other US cities interested in it were unable to allocate the funds needed to serve as the initial down-payment with which to replicate it in their jails and prisons, so that major requests to replicate our approach have come only from prison systems in other countries around the world (from New Zealand and Singapore to Poland).

What are the implications of this for the future of forensic psychotherapy? First, we need to recognize, as Welldon does in this book, that the public's attitude (and that of many of the politicians) can be, and sometimes is, just as irrational, self-defeating, and violence-provoking as that of the criminals they would rather punish than cure, and on whom they would rather waste money than save it. Certainly educating the public and the politicians about this sounds like a good idea; but perhaps we need to go beyond education (which assumes rationality) and think about how to adapt the principles of forensic psychotherapy (which assumes a mixture of rationality and irrationality) so that we could make it available and acceptable to the public and the politicians as well as to the criminals. (Welldon's predecessor in this field, the eminent psychoanalyst Edward Glover, wanted to bring psychoanalysis to the politicians. I would have to say that that still sounds like a good idea.)

Second, we need to recognize, as Welldon also does in this book, that the major innovation in forensic psychotherapy's approach to human violence, irrationality, and destructiveness is that it provides a method, one that has never existed until now, for advancing "beyond morality", so to speak, and replacing the quest for attaining "justice" by means of punishment (even when that approach is demonstrably self-defeating) with the medical attitude that we do not play God and presume to have either the knowledge or the right to decide who is evil and who is good, or who deserves punishment and who does not. Instead, like any clinician, we do not morally condemn our patients for being sick, we just try to diagnose their illness, treat it, and, to the degree possible, prevent it from recurring in them or occurring in others.

In other words, morality is not the solution, morality is the problem. If the public and the politicians would rather punish violent behaviour than cure those who are engaging in it, even though that only stimulates more violence, endangers them further, and puts them to even greater expense, one reason for their choice (or, at least, one means by which they rationalize it) is because they think in moral terms rather than in pragmatic, scientific, medical terms.

One problem with passing moral value judgments on those who are violent rather than attempting to learn how to understand them is that judging them morally does not help us in the least to learn what is causing them to become violent and what we can do to decrease the likelihood that they or others will behave in that way in the future. Another respect in which those popular public and political attitudes are similar to those of the very criminals against which they are directed is that criminals commit their crimes for exactly the same (moral) reasons that lead the public and the politicians to want to punish the criminals—namely, in order to attain justice. What we call crime is simply the form in which those we call criminal offenders are attempting to punish those by whom they feel offended (even if they sometimes direct that punishment onto scapegoats, if the original offenders are not as available or as vulnerable as those on whom they choose to take revenge for whatever offences they have suffered in the past).

In other words, just as we forensic psychotherapists need to overcome our own tendency to regress to moralizing attitudes in our response to the violent people with whom we work, so a central component of our therapeutic intervention is to help them to outgrow their own moralistic attitudes, which have provided them with the motivation and the rationale for committing their acts of violence. If only we could do the same with those members of the public and those politicians (and fortunately this does not include all members of either group) who would rather punish the criminals than treat them! But that will be a task for those who will replace old-timers like Welldon and me. That is why I am so glad that this book is coming out now, as I think that the depth of wisdom and experience contained in it cannot fail to be of help to those in the younger generation who will carry on the same quest for creating a more humane society that has animated Welldon's life and work.

An interview with Estela V. Welldon, July 1996

B RETT KAHR: *Estela, it's a very great pleasure to interview you, and I thought it would be useful if we could begin with how you came to the field of forensic psychotherapy, and really how you sculpted this field and made it your own. It would be very interesting for readers if we could ask you some questions about the influences in terms of your own personal life and in terms of the teachers you had—because I know you worked with some rather distinguished teachers in the psychiatric and psychoanalytic worlds—to see how you came to be the forensic psychotherapist you are today. So let's start at the beginning: you were born in Argentina . . .*

ESTELA V. WELLDON: I really don't want to believe that I'm the creator of forensic psychotherapy, or the person who has sculpted it either. I believe that the influence of my teachers has been essential to the interest or even passion that in a process of identification I've developed in this field, and in the way that I've contributed to the training of young people, people who are enormously courageous and extremely skilled in their own fields and who are then able to develop and to gain an awareness of unconscious mechanisms that had been unavailable to them before. . . . You asked me about Argentina, and I'm already talking about the present. It's difficult at times to fill in the gaps because it's not only a long life, but also a rich life, so I have to talk about the essential stages of my own training.

Firstly, I qualified as a teacher of children with Down's syndrome, and then as I was working with them I realized that I could do far more by becoming a doctor and psychiatrist, so in a way *I went into medicine in order to become a psychiatrist*. I had to endure all this medicine

1

to become a psychiatrist. I must add that I could only do my medical studies because at that time not only all universities in Argentina were free, but also a new medical school had been founded four years before in my own hometown. It was a pilot project with only 60 students a year, as compared to 2,000 in Buenos Aires, the capital. We had very stringent and rigorous selection exams. I've always felt a great debt of gratitude to my university since I've given so little or nothing in return for all that I received. The economic situation at home, with my parents struggling to realize their own ideals, was quite precarious. They were certainly unable to afford university fees, and I was blissfully unaware of what I took for granted. Indeed, I felt very fortunate to sell encyclopaedias from door to door, compared to many other students, such as the butcher's son, who had to work a night shift to provide for his parents before he could attend the daily university duties. I had assumed that university was free for everybody everywhere in the world!

Q: *Were your parents doctors?*

A: Oh no, they were children of very poor European immigrants, the first generation born in Argentina. From early childhood my father had to fend for himself, and he developed an enormous passion for the written word. His dream was to publish books, and his hero was Gutenberg. Through his sheer determination and tenacity he was eventually able to have his own printing shop and later a publishing house where he was the main craftsman. He was not good at managing finances, and it was my mother's main task to provide him with an area of complete containment and security where she was in charge of all practical matters.

Q: *What was psychiatry like in Argentina in the late 1950s? Was it analytic at all?*

A: There were many psychoanalysts, perhaps the largest number of psychoanalysts working in any country, but all of them were in Buenos Aires. Mendoza, my own town, is a mountain city located in the foothills of the Andes. Of course, with my one-track interest in becoming a psychiatrist I was pretty soon involved in psychological matters. In the Department of Psychological Medicine, third-year students tried to get a teacher with more psychoanalytic input. We were very lucky to get Dr Etchegoyen, who later became President of the International Psychoanalytical Association. Interestingly enough, *I think I was the first analysand in Mendoza.* Dr Etchegoyen arrived and became the professor, the dean, of a very active, interested group of people, as well as the psychoanalyst of most of us. So many boundaries had to be kept.

These boundaries were very firm and sometimes ridiculous, but very necessary. For example, my private sessions with him were at 6.40 a.m., and he was very much of the old school, shaking hands at the beginning and at the end of each interview. But then at 8 o'clock I had to be at work, and if I was two or three minutes late he would be very angry with me, saying that as a student of his I had to be on time.

Q: *So you had your analytic session with Horacio Etchegoyen and then went straight to being his student?*

A: Not just his student, but also his student assistant. In Argentina at that time, each university department had a paid job for one student, and many students used to apply for that one post. It was a formal procedure in which the application included both the CV and a *viva* with a patient. The job was for one year only, so new applicants would come forward every year. I got it for four consecutive years. So Professor Etchegoyen was also my employer, my boss.

Q: *And you published your first paper with him as well?*

A: That's right. We published it in Chile in 1959. In fact, before I got into analysis with him I went to see his former analyst in Buenos Aires, Heinrich Racker, who was meant to become my training analyst later. I talked to him about the difficulties of starting an analysis with the only psychoanalyst in my hometown, who was also my mentor and my boss. He said, "Do it, because it will be all about transference and countertransference." And I had to do it. Unfortunately, after finishing medical school and just as I was supposed to start my training analysis with Dr Racker, he died of cancer. That kind of situation has happened again and again in my life.

When I left Argentina, the Mendoza Psychoanalytic Society hadn't yet been recognized as a training institute, but now it has, and when I arrived at the Menninger School of Psychiatry, it was obvious that the training I had received in Mendoza was at an advanced level.

Q: *Before you go on to Topeka, let me just ask about the clinical experiences you had in Mendoza. What kind of patients were referred to the Department and what range of experience did you have with patients?*

A: People who go into medicine all over the world are very sceptical and cynical about unconscious matters. But we were extremely lucky to have a patient whom we could immediately recognize as suffering from a very serious post-traumatic stress disorder. The patient was a 30-year-old woman who talked like a 3-year-old girl. With that patient, Professor Etchegoyen did hypno-analysis, with all the medical students around watching, and brought her back to different ages. Eventually he brought her back to the exact time when she had been sexually abused, and it became extremely clear when she began talk-ing like a child of that age. The medical students could no longer bear a wall of resistance and deny the unconscious processes. It was extraor-dinary. Another clinical case that fostered analytic thinking and its application occurred in the teaching hospital. A 13-year-old anorexic girl, who had gone unsuccessfully through all the departments, was on the verge of dying because of her refusal to eat. She was in intensive care and was likely to die within the next two or three days. As a last resort, they decided to send her to us, the Department of Psychiatry, where I began to treat her with analytic psychotherapy. Eventually the treatment was very successful and the girl recovered.

Q: *Can we return to the first case you mentioned, about the woman who had been sexually abused? So much of your recent work has focused on women as perpetrators of abuse, at a time, even now in the 1990s, when most people don't believe it. What was it like to you in the late 1950s to hear about a case of sexual abuse? Was it published in the newspapers, or did this come as a shock when it emerged in the hypno-analysis?*

A: It was an extraordinary case that was used very positively for the understanding of unconscious processes. Was I shocked? No, because we'd already learnt most of the theoretical concepts with Professor Etchegoyen. But we were also aware that, as a professor, he had to compromise.

Q: *It's very unusual, because most English psychiatrists who trained in that same period claim not to have had an awareness of sex-abuse matters.*

A: I know.

Q: *I wonder whether Etchegoyen had a more enlightened department?*

A: I think it was due exclusively because he was an extremely coura-geous man who was very inspiring to us all. He was essential in my life not only as an analyst, but as a kind of inspiring force. And he made it clear that he had many expectations for my future as a profes-sional.

Q: *So you graduated in psychiatry in Mendoza and then you took up a resident post at the Menninger Clinic in Kansas. How on earth did you get from Mendoza to Kansas?*

A: Again, this had very much to do with Professor Etchegoyen. I was supposed to come back to our own department after my overseas training. And my applications to different schools of psychiatry in the United States were made with his encouragement. They were sent at the beginning of 1962 for the following year, since I qualified in Sep-tember 1962, but to our enormous surprise the Menninger accepted me for the same year. Our department was going through a difficult time, as other departments were envious of the prosperity and reputation Professor Etchegoyen had brought the department. I had to leave just when this situation emerged.

Eventually, I decided not to return to Argentina, not to return to Mendoza.

Q: *So Professor Etchegoyen recommended that you go to the Menninger Clinic. Had you ever heard of the Menninger Clinic? It was very well known in the United States, but was it known in Argentina?*

A: Not only did I know of the Menninger Clinic, but we also knew of Maxwell Jones and the Henderson Hospital. Such was the range of Professor Etchegoyen's knowledge. He wanted to know everything about everything.

Q: *So you were prepared to take on the principles of community psychiatry, social psychiatry, groups, and so forth?*

A: Exactly.

Q: *What a fabulous training you had! So you got to the Menninger Clinic in 1962, and, of course, at that time it was still being run by Dr Karl Menninger himself. Is it true that all his students called him Dr Karl?*

A: Yes, we did all call him Dr Karl.

Q: *What was he like as a man?*

A: Extremely affable and compassionate. Every Saturday morning he had what he called a colloquium that we were all "coerced" into attending. Not only was there a lot about crime and punishment to keep me interested, but also there were delicious doughnuts and coffee. He didn't allow anybody to smoke, but he wasn't against the pipe, so I began to smoke a pipe, just to be a bit controversial, as usual.

Q: *So there you are at the Menninger. Dr Karl had already written many books on crime and punishment, which was his great area of interest. Was that one of the pieces of writing that stimulated you into thinking about forensic matters?*

A: Yes. In fact, in Argentina I'd already begun working in borstals. But what I most remember of my first weeks in the United States is the great cultural shock to arrive there. It was really terrible . . . terrible. *The social situation in America was absolutely appalling.* And the fact that I was a young professional woman on my own astounded them. I was regularly asked, what, have you never ever been married? For me it was a matter of great pride, but for them it was a sign of inadequate behaviour. I was met with suspicion, and I felt not only misunderstood but offended by this sort of confrontation, which betrayed their culture of bias and prejudices. A similar situation arose when they learnt that

I wasn't a member of a particular church and I had received by mail an invitation to join a group of people who did not have any church affiliation.

When I arrived, I was delighted to be assigned to a wonderful ward, in a very nice building with air conditioning. All the staff except for the matron were black. I'd never encountered black people in my life before, and I just wanted to make it work. I always want to make it work. But I had a number of very disturbing experiences. One day, I told them I'd take them all for lunch at a local Mexican restaurant. They looked puzzled and I wasn't sure exactly why. I took them to the restaurant, and as soon as we arrived the Mexican guy said to me, "You're welcome to come here, but not the rest of your party".

Q: *Oh, my God!*

A: I hadn't expected this. I confronted the staff and asked them why on earth they hadn't told me before so we didn't have to go through this humiliation? They replied, "Well, you're the doctor so you're the one who determines things." I had such power that they wouldn't even dare to say anything.

Q: *They must have hoped that as the doctor you would have been able to magically get them in.*

A: No, I don't think so. In their minds they couldn't go against me. Later, we began to have meetings in my house, because, as black people, they couldn't invite me into their own meeting places. I used to have a one-room flat in a rather derelict area, and so, following the tradition, every Wednesday night I had a meeting in my flat for my staff. I cooked food for them and we discussed clinical matters about our patients and had theoretical seminars. One day, my landlord, who'd been very impressed and proud to have someone from the Menninger living in one of his little flats, came to me and said, "Dr D'Accurzio, please, I don't want to upset you, but we have to do something about your parties." I said, "What parties? I don't have any parties. I have working parties and we don't make any noise. Have the neighbours complained?" He said, "Look, please, I'd like you to stay in the apartment, but tell your staff to come through the back door". So I told him to keep the flat in his back passage. You see what I mean. That was injustice, social injustice, which has always been the main preoccupation in my life—much more than, say, crime and punishment, since social injustice is at the root of most violent and deviant behaviour.

Q: *It seems to me that there is an organic link between what happened to your black staff then and what happens to your forensic patients now, how the marginalized get further punished and further humiliated.*

A: That's right. The other shocking situation was that, while in my hometown then we were 50% women and 50% men in medical school, there were just a handful of women at the Menninger out of 70 people. This also was a source of problems. My lack of English produced another interesting situation because, as a single woman living on my own, I would devote all my time to my patients. I visited them on weekends and asked them to write about their lives—which was a good way for me to learn English. Some people only wrote one page, some wrote forever, which was quite an education about their mental state. I then checked my own English by asking them questions. But suddenly I was reprimanded because my colleagues complained that I was working too hard and their patients were complaining that they didn't have such a "good" doctor. I got into trouble again.

Q: *You were too interested in your patients?*

A: Well, I was also trying to learn English, mind you! Then there was the first American patient I ever had—a black woman from Alabama—I couldn't understand a word she said. I thought I had better take the next flight back to Argentina, but when I asked the rest of the staff, nobody had understood a word either, so I was greatly relieved.

Q: *I want to ask about the kinds of patients you saw at the Menninger, because Menninger's was known as a very fancy private clinic where all the Hollywood movie stars would go for their breakdowns. But I gather you didn't work with movie stars?*

A: I didn't work with movie stars. I worked with extremely disturbed patients. For example, we had a woman from a small island in the China Sea who appeared in all the newspapers in the Midwest. This one picture showed an enormous fridge, with an open door, full of food, and the caption said, "Woman kills her three children because of lack of food."

Q: *A perfect Welldon case.*

A: The fact is, while we waited for this woman to arrive in the ward, we worried that the other patients would be very aggressive towards her because she'd killed her children. But when the woman arrived she wasn't talking at all, wasn't communicating with anybody, and was in a completely psychotic state. All the patients were extremely nice to her, offering her cups of tea, showing the most amazing compassion, which came as a complete surprise to the staff.

The system at the Menninger was very strong in trying to work out symbols in a concrete way. For example, instead of giving electric shocks to our women with melancholia, they were made to clean the dirtiest areas. These were very wealthy elderly ladies who were made to clean dirty toilets or to sand down layers of paint. It was very difficult to get the nurses to make them do this, because nurses usually like to be nice to their patients, whereas they had to be absolutely awful to these patients, shouting at them. The patients had actually internalized an enormous amount of anger against themselves and their self-esteem was very low, so there were constant attacks on themselves—and that, in a nutshell, is melancholia. In this way, their outside world represented what the internal world was like, and when they could eventually say to the nurse in charge of their treatment, "Why don't you go fuck yourself!" everybody congratulated them because it was a great achievement.

Q: *And was it a helpful treatment?*

A: In the case of the young woman, she was thought to be emotionally regressing and unable to remember any English—it was the 1960s and the institutions had lots of money, so immediately a psychologist who could speak her own dialect was hired. It took him a long time to communicate with her. She had a very complicated history: the Americans had occupied her island and allegedly it was the only area left where families welcomed the birth of girls, because they were used as prostitutes by the age of 13 or 14. When this girl was born she was greeted with joy because she'd be able to help keep the family. However, when she began to talk about her early life to the psychologist, she indicated that from the age of 12 or 13 she was not behaving according to what was expected of her: she didn't want to go into prostitution. Then she came to know this black American soldier, but of course she knew nothing about colour differences. She married him believing she'd made the best life for herself. Then he was sent back to America, taking her with him, and as soon as they arrived a sense of despair came over her; she was isolated and ostracized because she was married to a black man.

Q: *So already in the early 1960s we have a case of female infanticide, of a mother using her children as part-objects, and this is in many ways a harbinger of all your later writings on female perversion and female violence. Did this case at the time stand out in your mind as a one-off, or had you already begun to develop the idea that there is this potential for violence and perversion in every woman in relation to her children?*

A: Well, I think that this was an extreme case. This woman had a psychotic breakdown, and perhaps it had begun from very early on. Violence is difficult to determine; it was violence against herself, and the violence in this particular woman was in killing her children—it wasn't about taking her revenge on her husband, even though he was responsible for her miserable situation in the States, which he was completely unaware of. But you can see how the children represented the parts of herself that were going to suffer in the future, and she wanted to eliminate this future suffering.

Q: *But what is extraordinary is that nobody could see the metaphor and the symbolism of the woman saying she had no food, and in fact the newspapers had to take it in a very concrete way, and say—look at this fridge, she's got lots of food.*

A: That's the way tabloids sell their papers, by being "concrete" and forgetting—actually not wanting to know—symbolism and symbolic implications, since this would make things far more complex.

Q: *So this was very much the golden age of the Menninger Clinic, when lots of people were coming from all over the world to train. Who else did you meet and work with, apart from Dr Karl?*

A: Indeed, I was very fortunate to have access to many important and inspiring people in the field, such as Margaret Mead, who used to do seminars there. We would have drinks in our homes, as poor as they might be, and she would be happy to come and enjoy the evening, and we learned an enormous amount from her teachings. It was also the time of Robert Wallerstein, Ralph Slovenko, and Joseph Sutton. I remember a three-day meeting on violence and criminology in which many experts—criminologists, anthropologists, lawyers, judges—were present. There were about fourteen of us, and some of us were lucky enough to be able to sit behind their chairs and just listen. The whole of the first day was spent discussing how the language from different fields could become one, and the impossibility of this task was so painfully evident: the legal, judicial, psychiatric, psychological languages were so different that seemingly they could never merge with one another.

It was also the time of Otto Kernberg, who was there with his wife Pauline, a child psychiatrist-psychoanalyst. I have a funny anecdote about how he was a surprisingly practical man for such a great theoretician. When I thinking of leaving the United States to go to England, I asked for his opinion and he said, "Estela, it is very simple. Just make two lists: the reasons why you should go and the reasons why you should stay. Then just look at both lists and see which one is longer!" Not much psychoanalytic subtlety about that, but lots of practical wisdom!

I also met Maxwell Jones, who came to give a series of lectures there, as well as different professors from Europe.

My English began to develop in funny ways, as you can see, but the idea was that I was the most sophisticated person when it came to psychological, unconscious situations. It created an enormous amount of rivalry, which in a way was quite good, but my lack of versatility in English was a handicap that people could use against me.

Q: *So you were at Menninger's in 1963 when JFK was shot—what kind of ripple did that cause in the Clinic?*

A: That again was another cultural shock for me. It was a very strange experience, one that I will never forget. It was a Friday. The residents, or Senior Registrars, had a very spacious room in which we could have our lunch together. You brought your own little bit of food and you each ate out of your own little packet. So we were all eating our own pre-packed lunches when this secretary from reception came running in, extremely upset, saying that President Kennedy had been shot. Some of us—I particularly remember a Cuban colleague—were very upset, but others were quite pleased. There was a man from South Carolina who said that it was about time it happened. I know that people want to believe that everyone's response was one of shock and bereavement, but that was not so.

Actually arriving in Topeka had been another cultural shock for me. It was a very small town, much smaller than Mendoza, and it didn't even have the wonderful views of mountains on the horizon. There was no cinema, no concerts, and no theatre. It was also a "dry" state, so you couldn't have a drink in any public place. Every two weeks the Menninger would put on a film, and I remember very well that that Friday it was *A Taste of Honey* and we'd all been look-ing forward to seeing it. In my own country, a film or any other sort of entertainment would immediately be stopped as a sign of respect. When I talked to some of my colleagues about trying to stop this film, they just laughed at me. So with two or three others we went to the place where the film would be shown and told the technicians to stop it because we had been told to stop the whole thing. In fact we had not been told, and we were behaving in a rather delinquent way. The technicians didn't seem to be surprised, but the ones who were surprised were my colleagues who arrived soon afterwards. Strangely enough, or perhaps aptly enough, the following morning in the colloquium, Dr Karl congratulated all of us for such a wise decision—because we'd shown an enormous degree of respect at President Kennedy's death. Of course he never learned the whole story. So some of us felt rather smug about it, and perhaps we had a few extra doughnuts that morning . . .

Q: *How long did you stay there altogether? Was it three years?*
A: No, two years.

Q: *Coming from a small town to an even smaller town must have been very stifling in many ways; you must have had ideas of roaming to somewhere more exotic, more culturally stimulating, which would give you more opportunities to try out your new ideas. How did London first present itself as a possibility?*

A: I was very tempted to come to London not only because of the psychoanalytic school but also because of the writings of Bion on group processes at the Tavistock Clinic. I very much wanted to leave Topeka, as the way of life there didn't suit me, but I was anxious not to upset Dr Karl because I was very fond of him and he had quite a soft spot for me. I told him that I would go to the Tavistock Clinic for one year only, to study group dynamics, and would then come back to the Menninger. He was somewhat disappointed, but immediately, in his very generous way, he offered to introduce me to Anna Freud. He wrote a letter to her to the effect that I was this young woman full of zeal and enthusiasm and all that. It was a very nice letter, and also very curious, because at the end he talked about coming to London and riding horses together with Anna Freud. I was quite perplexed, given their ages. But I never used that letter.

Q: *Why not?*
A: Because I was always very influenced by Kleinian ideas and I didn't feel I was doing the right thing by approaching Anna Freud. Also, I felt very strongly about making it on my own. But Professor Norval Morrison from the Criminology Institute in Chicago, who had also given me several letters which I never used, also wrote to the intended recipients of these letters, who then approached me. That was how I got to know Hugh Klare, who was then Chair of the Howard League, and it was he and Robert Andry who encouraged me to apply to the Henderson Hospital.

Q: *Did you not go to the Tavistock after all?*
A: I went to the Tavistock and I saw Martha Harris and Bob Gosling. The Tavistock was then in Beaumont Street, and Martha and Bob were extremely helpful to me. But suddenly I had another shock. In America, having a job as a psychiatrist was enough to pay for my own training and my everyday living. But when I came to England, with only $50, it wasn't the same at all. From America I'd booked a room in a B&B in Gower Street, thinking I'd find a job immediately. Jobs were offered to me, but I didn't want them, because they were not within the

psychodynamic field or with forensic patients. Another shock was that psychiatry in the UK was strongly divided—between psychiatry per se, meaning biological treatment, and psychoanalysis, almost exclusively dealt with privately, except for the Tavistock Clinic. Both ideologies were segregated into two different worlds, one represented by the Maudsley and the other by the Tavistock. It became very difficult after that first week, when I was thrown out of the B&B. Fortunately, Hugh Klare got in touch with me and directed me to the Henderson Hospital, where I applied for a position as a Registrar.

Q: *Tell me about the Henderson Hospital. It was already a well-known institution for therapeutic communities and community psychiatry.*

A: For me it was extraordinary because I'd already known about the teachings of Maxwell Jones in Argentina and had then met him in the States. But then he'd moved to Dingleton in Scotland.

A very curious thing happened with Maxwell Jones. He and Morris Carstairs, who was then Professor of Psychiatry at the Department of Psychiatry in Edinburgh, used to come to London and to spend some time together. At that time I had a one-room flat near Regent's Park. With the Carstairs we were like an extended family, and this was still the case even after his death. Morris sometimes used to stay in my place, though I'd never had Maxwell there. At that point I got a letter from Max asking if he could to come to stay one Friday night to talk about the therapeutic community. He slept in my bed, and I slept in a small bed, dreading that he'd wake up very early in the morning, as I knew he was an insomniac. Anyway, at 4 or 4.30 in the morning it was very dark and I heard noises and saw somebody. I thought, "Oh goodness me, this man has now woken up and would like to have a cup of tea." So I said, "Max", but—surprise surprise—the voice saying "Estela" didn't come from the chair, it came from the other bed! Somebody else was sitting in the chair. I always had the windows open, and it was a semi-basement. As soon as I'd said "Max" and Max replied, the person rushed off through the windows, leaving all the rugs behind. The amazing thing was that when I said I wanted to call the police, Max said, "Are you mad? Can you imagine what the journalists will do about this one, with us as experts in deviant behaviour becoming naïve victims! We'll appear in the tabloids on Sunday and everyone will assume that there's something going on between us, so we'll just keep this completely between ourselves!"

Q: *What did you do after that? It must have been very frightening.*

A: Well, I decided that it was very important not to leave the place, so

I stayed there but never left the doors and windows open again. I got a lot of anonymous mail delivered by hand, you know, pushed under the door, which was quite frightening, but it never happened again. So it might have been taking place for some time, but I never noticed because I was so deeply asleep.

My arrival at the Henderson, well . . . One can get engrossed in a life that's so rich every day that seeing friends socially later in the evening becomes rather pale and lifeless in comparison. It was like that at the Henderson in those days. There were a hundred patients, and it was extraordinary.

Q: *What kind of violent symptoms did they present?*

A: Some of them had "show-off" violence. In those days, very formal, old-fashioned psychiatrists from the Maudsley used to come every Thursday, and so the patients would put on a show in which they'd attempt to throw chairs at everybody and use the most terrible language. It was all really showing off, because the chairs never touched us. There was quite a bit of violence among themselves, but the place was very containing. In fact, the amount of containment among the patients was quite amazing, and they felt for the first time in their lives really respected and dignified. We patients and staff were assigned to different workshops, and, of course, being a woman, I was assigned to the homework workshop, which meant that we were in charge of cleaning the whole hospital. It was rather tiresome, and we looked forward to any crisis in order to get out of cleaning. When the new director, Stuart Whiteley, was appointed, I was ready to move on, but he asked me to stay because he did need someone and I think he felt he had to offer me something in exchange. At the time, my father was unwell and I had no money to pay for my trip back to Argentina, so he suggested I go home working as a ship's doctor. He said he'd done it, and I could go all the way to Argentina for six weeks for free. I said that six weeks was too long; nobody had been allowed to leave for more than two weeks: I'd already taken the issue to the staff meeting, and they had said "No way." I said that in that case I would take my request to the patients and the community meeting. So when the "doctors' spot"—a period of two minutes when doctors could talk—came, I was trembling and shaking a lot, and I said I'd really like permission to see my father, and wanted to work as a ship's doctor because I didn't have the money to pay for my ticket. To my colleagues' surprise, all the patients said, "Of course, Estela, of course, you go. You've got to see your old man." The previous decision was overturned and I was able to go for six weeks.

Q: *I'm very interested to know about the Henderson, because you did have some very violent patients. What methods were used? Am I right in thinking that there was no individual psychotherapy at the Henderson?*

A: Everything had to be done through groups. I really learned a lot from that, and *I began to trust group techniques more and more with this patient population.*

Q: *What was the rationale for no individual work?*

A: Because we could easily fall into countertransferential issues and be seduced by patients in a very manipulative way, which was the only way they had learnt to effectively survive. Also, the cohesiveness of the community was the paramount issue. I must say that this experience of dealing with angry communities has been very useful, because when I worked as a ship's doctor we had the beginning of a mutiny and I was able to use some of the techniques learnt in therapeutic communities.

I don't remember how it did happen, but one day I was invited to a cocktail party where I met an American journalist living in Italy with whom I began to talk about my work in the American Midwest in a maximum secure unit, where the most serious criminals were brought in for diagnostic assessment. He said I should get to know one of his friends, Kenneth Tynan, who was then writing a controversial review of Truman Capote's book *In Cold Blood*, a true account of two murderers in the Midwest. I was very new to London; I knew nothing about Truman Capote or who Kenneth Tynan was. At the journalist's request, I was introduced to Kenneth and immediately he sent me the galley proofs of the book with a request to write a psychological essay about the relationship between Truman Capote and the two murderers as portrayed in the book, as it would be very useful to have a professional involved. With great interest and excitement I began to read the book, not just as a reader, but with the view of writing an essay about their relationship. I asked him not to use my name, as the policy in the NHS at that time was if your name appeared in print, you could easily be struck off the medical register on the grounds of trying to canvas yourself as a practitioner. I was extremely worried about this, but he swore he wouldn't put my name in the newspapers. The long saga of the bitter fight between these two men who were using the book for their own ends appeared in the *Observer* in a series of articles called "The Guts of the Butterfly", a historical and critical review of the book and of the correspondence between Capote and Tynan. One day Kenneth rang me up and begged me to allow my name to be given, because Truman Capote doubted my existence as a psychiatrist, and I did eventually give my permission. So my name became very public at that point. I don't know if it's only with British audiences, but as soon as they read your name in a newspaper, you're invited to more dinners than you can accept. So it did give me access to people whom I might not have known otherwise.

Q: *Estela, the 1960s, when you were working at the Henderson, was a very exciting time in British psychiatry, when all the different treatments were being questioned and social psychiatry was coming in. I wonder, did you have contact with other therapeutic communities—with Ronnie Laing and Kingsley Hall, for example?*

A: Oh, yes indeed. In fact, a few of us were invited to Kingsley Hall for a most sumptuous meal by candlelight. Ronnie Laing, Aaron Esterson, and David Cooper were there as hosts, waiting for the local GP. The meal, which was exquisite, was spoiled by the smell of shit coming out of Mary Barnes's room, where we were taken so that they could display, with enormous pride, this room with paintings of shit on the wall. The smell was pervasive. It gave me a further confirmation about our own set of boundaries, including violence, with our patients at the Henderson. We struck up a sort of friendship with Ronnie Laing in which I felt there was a great deal of reciprocal respect. I always felt a bit in awe of him, and I think that funnily enough he felt a bit that way towards me. Of course, he was the revered anti-psychiatrist, and the 1960s were the right time for all questioning and challenging of assumed principles.

I met many different people during that time, as you say. For example, I remember going in 1967 to the first meeting of International Psychotherapy that took place in Wiesbaden. It was the first time I'd been to Germany. It was an extremely exciting meeting, with lots of revolutionary ideas from all corners of the world. By then I'd become fast friends with Maxwell Jones, Jurgen Ruesch, and Morris Carstairs. I was young and dynamic, quite popular, and I saw myself sitting at the same table with the three of them, going on this boat trip down the Rhine. These were the most important guys, and the talk over dinner was on the issue of censorship and the publication of *Last Exit to Brooklyn*. This trip also gave me the chance of meeting Franco Basaglia. He was the Italian psychiatrist who represented the anti-psychiatry movement. He was very political and influenced legislation related to mental patients in Italy. We immediately formed a very strong bond of friendship and professionalism, which lasted until his death.

After Wiesbaden I was invited to a very elitist gathering—perhaps one of the most important meetings I have ever been to in my life—which took place off the coast of Naples. There was a marvellously composed six-day meeting, with a different speaker on each day. I remember that Ronnie Laing had one day, Franco Basaglia had one day, and Nathan Ackerman had one day. It was wonderful. In the 1960s this kind of thing did happen. No one was worried about money, and we all had the chance to exchange ideas, to translate our work. I don't mean just literally but also during the evening at the bar. People were very excited by all sorts of projects. I also became quite close to Nathan, who was there with his daughter, talking about family therapy, which was just emerging in New York. I remember having dinner with them on my 30th birthday and Ronnie Laing joined us. I still feel that the conversation I had with him had profound effects on me. We talked about books, and he mentioned *One Flew Over the Cuckoo's Nest*. He advised me to read *The Death of Ivan Illich*, by Tolstoy. I found it fascinating—the idea of living truthfully all one's life and not bullshitting in any situation. It gave me a great sense of freedom in relation to our patients. It's very relevant to those patients who've been conning all their lives, and they know exactly when you're trying to con them, when you're not being totally truthful. To really face them with the truth is the only way of not patronizing them and being a real person to them. And they respond really well.

Q: *So you stayed at the Henderson for about three years, and why did you leave?*

A: Part of the training is to leave and go somewhere else, and I felt it was necessary to leave that community because, just as the patients are only supposed to stay for a year to make progress and not become institutionalized, I myself was really at the point of becoming institutionalized. *I was offered a very tempting post in a community day-hospital in London*, with some of the old staff from the Henderson. Although I must say it was quite difficult to leave the Henderson. I remember times when I cried on the way back, because I was emotionally very engrossed in the life there. It was hard to leave, but I did.

At Paddington Day Hospital I had the pleasure of being supervised by a great analyst, Ismond Rosen.

Q: *Tell me about your relationship with Ismond Rosen, because he had already published the first edition of his famous book on sexual deviation by that time.*

A: We had a few differences because by then I think that I'd been completely taken over by the community spirit of the Henderson and group therapy, and I was no longer so involved in strictly psychoanalytic treatment. He thought that at times I was too revolutionary, but we had an extremely good working relationship and mutual respect, and I became friends with him and his wife Ruth. I must say I learnt a lot about the treatment of sexual deviancy and criminality from him, and I'll always be very grateful for that teaching.

Q: *And from the Paddington you moved to the Portman?*

A: That's right. At the Paddington I had met my future husband. We got married and then worked together; he was a psychiatrist. He left the Paddington because he was very involved with terminally ill patients, and he worked in the very first UK hospice run by Cecily Saunders. I left the Paddington when I was pregnant. My husband died when our son was 9 months old. I was then in tremendous need of work, because I'd stopped working to have a big family. From one day to the next I had to earn a living, not only for me but also for my son. I was very fortunate to be called by the Paddington to take over from a consultant who'd suddenly died, and I took on that locum position. I went also to see a few people. One of them was Bob Gosling, who'd been one of my mentors in group therapy at the Tavistock, and he advised me to go to the Portman Clinic, where a clinical assistant position was available. He said they'd be very lucky to get me, and it would be a good place for me to develop my own training and skills in this particular area.

Q: *Had you heard of the Portman at this time?*

A: Oh yes. I'd heard a lot about the Portman Clinic. I was a bit in awe of it too, as I knew it was run exclusively along analytic lines, which I wasn't sure would allow me to develop work in group therapy. But I was very much encouraged by Bob Gosling, and I went to see a very charming man, a psychoanalyst, Lothair Rubinstein, who interviewed me and offered me the job. I was supposed to start in September 1971. It was with deep sorrow that I found, when I began work there, that Rubinstein had suddenly died of a heart attack during the IPA conference in Vienna.

Q: *Who took over as Head of the Clinic?*

A: Adam Limentani, who was also a very significant figure in my professional life.

Q: *He became a supervisor and a mentor for you, didn't he?*

A: Indeed, he did. He was a very special man, with an enormous amount of humanity, compassion, and wisdom. Each of my mentors seems to have brought something new to me, and all this I filtered, took in, and processed. I remember with great fondness my supervision sessions with him in which he always wanted to know something about my private life. That happened with several of my supervisors, and they also wanted to tell me a lot about their private lives.

Q: *And who else was at the Clinic apart from Limentani? Who were the early staff members?*

A: There was David Rumney, who actually wrote an account of the history of the Portman. Then two new consultants were appointed to the Clinic, Mervin Glasser and Pat Gallwey, who were both extremely influential in my own work in different ways, one being from the Freudian school and the other from the Kleinian.

Q: *What were your duties and responsibilities when you first arrived at the Portman? You were there as a consultant?*

A: No, I was a clinical assistant. So I didn't really have a proper job, but my work was highly valued. At the beginning I felt that I was the golden girl who was going to deliver the goods. My own insights about the patient population also impressed them. So at that point everyone was at least happy with me. Then a consultant, Dr Edwards, suddenly died, so there was a consultant psychiatrist position available. I decided to apply for it, with the encouragement and support of my medical colleagues. The administration wasn't so happy because they already had me working there on a lower salary! So they wrote me a threatening letter, saying that, in order to apply for the post, I had first to resign from my position as clinical assistant and in the end I mightn't get anything at all. I decided to go against that advice and went ahead with the interview. This is a situation I wouldn't recommend to anybody. It was in the days before equal opportunities, and on this particular occasion there were no equal opportunities at all. There were seven candidates for the job; I was the only woman and the only non-British-born candidate. But I was the insider. It was still difficult in the smoky room, with tepid coffee and my newly acquired name of Welldon. I was flabbergasted to be brought into this room with about eight or nine people, some of them university professors, all looking extremely serious and solemn. They asked questions that I found very revealing of their own problems. I must say Ismond Rosen was invaluable in that he was part of the panel and was very influential. The panel began to say that they knew from my records that I was a widow with a young child—this was 1975, my child was then 5—and how on earth could I apply for the job while having the responsibility of caring for a small child? I replied that the responsibility would be exactly the same as in the post I was already filling, but the pay would be higher, and that I didn't have any problems about working because I had to make a living for my son and myself. At that point a professor started to describe how his wife's mother had gone to work when his wife was a child and how much this had affected his wife's mental and emotional life. Ismond told me afterwards that he used this intervention in my favour, asking them, "Do you see how Dr Welldon is capable of making everybody talk about their own personal lives?" I got the job, even though there were many good professionals applying for it.

Q: *So you got the job at the Portman. What was your early caseload like? Did you have a full complement of forensic patients, sexual deviants and delinquents?*

A: Oh yes. I always felt extremely comfortable working with that patient population. In a way I just wanted to have the most difficult cases, but it was a completely different setting. From working in the community where we all looked exactly the same, then Paddington where we would scream at one another, then coming to a place where everyone was beautifully dressed and very formal, where everyone was called "Dr"—it was a big change in my life.

Q: *Can we hear a bit more about the basic philosophy of the time, because the Portman was unique in that it was the only analytic place in the world for treating perverse and delinquent patients?*

A: I believe that it's still exactly the same now, sadly so. It was founded in 1931 as the clinical arm of the Institute for the Study and Treatment of Delinquency (ISTD). It was set up by a few psychoanalysts with the aim of re-thinking the purpose of prisons and re-thinking what could be done better rather than just punishing criminals. The founders of this movement were extremely important, and I would say that it's not actually the professionals who define the Portman Clinic, but the patient population.

Q: *Estela, we now refer to these patients, thanks to you, as forensic psycho-therapy patients. When did the term forensic psychotherapy first come into vogue?*

A: It's a very ugly term, and not very up-to-date either, but perhaps it's the only one. The term is new, but I'm sure that it is exactly what the founding members of the ISTD and Portman Clinic had in mind when they created the place. And now the Royal College of Psychiatrists is to set up more training posts, and we're to offer more training from the Portman.

Q: *And obviously all the work and the groundwork that you did in the initial Portman courses and the Oxford Congress and the European meetings (see chapter 10) ultimately paid off, because in 1991 you became the founding*

Elected President and now Honorary President for Life of the International Association for Forensic Psychotherapy (IAFP). Can you tell me whether you're pleased with the way forensic psychotherapy is developing as a field, what you hope for it, what it hasn't accomplished, what your aspirations are for the discipline?

A: Firstly, let me tell you that *I feel proud of my own students*, who have done such wonderful work in different parts of the UK, where they often have to improvise facilities for their patients. I am also extremely moved by the fact that they feel responsible for the welfare and treatment of offenders in this country, in very different and difficult forensic settings. I feel this is very necessary, especially considering the views of our Home Secretary, Michael Howard [in 1996], which we have to counteract with the very courageous, inventive, and resourceful experiences of all my students.

Q: *Let's go back to your patients at the Portman, because I think there are a lot of myths surrounding forensic patients. One is that they're all men, not women, and another is that they all come from the lower classes and aren't educated. I know your work has really tried to challenge that.*

A: Yes, it's very revealing, especially working with groups, because people come together from totally different backgrounds. I can see an enormous amount of intolerance from the lower classes. Some of them, like shoplifters who feel absolutely justified in shoplifting because of their poverty, have a total lack of understanding about upper-class patients who are in the same group and who suffer from different predicaments, from depression associated with suicidal ideas to severe perversions. The general assumption that "good education" precludes any emotional problems is not only a prejudice of the upper classes, but it's also adopted by the lower classes. This takes me to a very revealing incident.

I was invited by friends in the mid-1990s to dinner at the Athenaeum Club, where I'd already been many times. It's very much a men's club, but it was a "ladies' evening". The people who invited me were not in the profession, but they told me they thought the topic of the evening was very much my "cup of tea", but they couldn't remember the subject or who was speaking. We arrived, and to my surprise and delight there was Professor John Gunn speaking about the treatment of sexual offenders. I thought this was quite a subject for the ladies' evening! There were some psychiatrists and many people from the judiciary. The chairman told us the "instructions" for the evening: that we would listen to the lecture after dinner and everybody (including the ladies) would have the chance to talk for two minutes, and ask only one question. Professor Gunn gave an extremely good lecture about offenders, but left the audience with a feeling of helplessness about their treatment. I felt that I had the golden opportunity to offer more insights about the internal world of people who offended. So I put my hand up, and I could see that perhaps Professor Gunn was not too happy to see me trying to make a contribution. Knowing I only had two minutes I tried to express the view that these problems happen to all different social classes. People assume that the upper classes don't need any treatment because they've had a very good education, and sometimes this very much hinders their being helped professionally, and we lack compassion about people in very high positions. I said that sometimes there's a poor understanding of a situation, as we'd had not so long before in the case of someone occupying a very high office, the Director of Public Prosecutions. No one had thought this person could be in need of help, and he had to resign his job. His wife had later committed suicide. When I said this, everybody was absolutely silent; my contribution received such a cold reception that I couldn't understand it. I sat down and my friends ignored me. I was sitting next to a very nice lady, who was a part-time magistrate, so I asked her what I'd done wrong. She said, "My dear, my dear, he's a member of the Club."

Q: *Well I'm not surprised you got a very icy reception, given that the DPP was a member of the Athenaeum Club, but I suspect that your remark would have caused a lot of ripples in any case, as you cut very close to the bone by suggesting that these kinds of pathologies can affect anyone regardless of class or sex. In doing justice to all the aspects of your professional career, I know that there's another area which is very important to you, and where you're able to use your forensic knowledge. Not many people know about this area of your professional work, namely that you do a lot of consultancy to various television and film companies to help check out the veracity of their characters. Can you tell us how you got into that?*

A: I've always felt very much at ease and relaxed with people from the theatrical world, and they find me rather theatrical—I don't know exactly why! I've struck very deep friendships with such people. Through the American journalist I met his parents, who later became sort of adoptive parents for me. They were Ella Winter and Donald Ogden-Stewart: he was a very famous film scriptwriter in Hollywood, responsible for many great scripts, among them *Philadelphia Story* and *The Keeper of the Flame*. She had been a left-wing activist working as a correspondent in Moscow and was an avid art collector. I had met them in my very early days in London and used to go to them every Sunday for lunch. After lunch, they had a salon where I met many interesting people from the media, such as Katharine Hepburn and Ingrid Bergman, the Chaplins, and also left-wing intellectuals such as Leonard Boudin, the American civil rights lawyer. It was through him that years later I met Helena Kennedy, a young, passionate, exceptionally intelligent Scottish woman advocate, who still is my intimate friend. Another friend, very influential for my future life in the enjoyment of the arts, was Patrick Woodcock. He was a GP treating all the theatre and media people. I remember when he took me to a performance of *Hay Fever*, with Noel Coward at the old Old Vic. We went backstage to his dressing room and Patrick introduced me as his girlfriend, a psychiatrist from Argentina. Noel Coward—I could see the charm exuding from every pore of him. He said, "Nina from Argentina", and he just went on singing this, and asking Patrick where he was taking this young lady for dinner. Then he offered his Rolls Royce and his chauffeur to take us there. It was a very special experience.

Q: *How did you first get involved in script consultancy?*

A: Well, as I was in contact with these people socially, they began to feel they could ask me about how to portray certain situations. This is how I began to act as a consultant on their scripts. It's much easier to do that than to do a court report, I tell you. It's very interesting to advise people how to set up situations and to think about what background the characters might have come from. Sometimes characters like the mother or father never actually appear, but they're important in the creation of another character in the play.

Q: *So you give it psychological veracity?*

A: That's right. And after I make my alterations or suggestions to the script, the people doing the film find it more credible, and they get more funding for it.

Q: *I know that you're also very involved at the moment in doing court work. Can you tell us how you function as a psychotherapist in court?*

A: That's a very new venture and an important challenge in my life. After the publication of my book *Mother, Madonna, Whore*, I was often invited to give lectures on women's problems. I'd always avoided appearing in court for many reasons. One is that it affects the work situation with patients, because you can be called to court for the whole day. Another is about the fear of being exposed, of being grilled by cross-examination, which is always difficult. But then I was asked by a guardian *ad litem* to do an assessment of parenting abilities and risk assessment. I wanted to refuse, feeling rather a coward about this, but I felt that if I didn't do it, who would do it? So *I was compelled to do assessments of women with children* whose caring ability one questioned because of their own early faulty mothering. Some professionals hadn't been aware of the internal world of women who are inundated with early memories which, despite their own conscious efforts not to let it happen, interfere with their "normal" mothering process. So I took this on; I gave myself a kick and I thought I had to do this before I retire: "I'd better grow up before I retire."

I've devised a system of seeing a mother six times for an hour and a half each time and writing a careful and well-thought-out report. It makes my life hell in a way, because wherever I go there is the idea that a mother can't bring up her own children and they have to be adopted, and this weighs very heavily on my conscience. I strive to write a report almost as a kind of exorcism, to deliver the goods in such an accurate way that I feel I'm doing the job in a thoughtful manner. There is the popular prejudice that judges don't listen to anybody else and would never be prepared to consider unconscious motivations, but I always felt that they would be only to willing to listen to clinicians and learn from their own experience. And I was delighted that after I put a proposal during an annual meeting of the Advisory Group to the diploma course (see chapter 10) for a "judges' residential weekend", to learn about unconscious motivations of offenders, this was taken seriously and was immediately put into action by Tony Lloyd, now Baron Lloyd of Berwick, and a residential weekend was made possible in Windsor in 1991. Later on Matthew Thorpe, now The Rt. Hon Lord Justice Matthew Thorpe, another member of the Advisory Group, followed suit as a family judge and began to convene a series of weekends for the family justice system with the same format, involving Portman Clinic staff.

Q: *As we approach the end of this first interview, I wonder if I can ask you what advice and encouragement you have for young workers who are entering the forensic field today?*

A: I believe that they're already inspired and I'm extremely impressed with their dedication to their work, although sometimes they don't know exactly what they're doing and have very few facilities and little support from other workers or from their own institutions. I'd like to emphasize how much we can achieve, and how much these young people are needed in these times of political uncertainty and financial burden. I'd say that the tabloids are full of bad news, but we never acknowledge the good things that are achieved. Even though only the most extreme cases are reported in the tabloids, there are some other cases where people are able to achieve an enormous amount in their forensic work. I feel that the message has to be: work hard, but work with facilities for supervision, and talk to one another.

CHAPTER ONE

The true nature of perversions

History of the term "perversions"

Freud, using instinct theory, classified sexual perversions into two groups, according to the sexual object (e.g., in paedophilia) or its aim (e.g., to inflict or experience pain, as in sadomasochism). Perversion is different from a classical neurotic or psychotic condition, although the three terms have been interlinked in the history of psychoanalytic thinking. Freud's famous axiom that the neuroses are "the negative of perversion" (1905) was later taken up by Glover (1944), who under the influence of Klein suggested that perversions were the negative of psychosis. This view was supported by Melanie Klein's followers, who saw perversion as a defence against psychosis.

Gillespie (1940, 1956; Gillespie, Pasche, Wiedman, & Greenson, 1964) supported Sachs's view (1923) that splitting of the ego resulted from the conflict between the ego and the id and considered the activity of the superego to be a fundamental mechanism in perversion. Gillespie (1956) thus developed the Kleinian viewpoint, as the above mechanism was of paramount importance in understanding the association of perversion with psychosis. Klein's (1932) theories centred on the relationships between mother and baby in the first year of life. Greenacre (1968) and Sperling (1959) also acknowledged the importance of a disturbed relationship between mother and baby in the creation of perversions. The nature of this early relationship and the better understanding of the dynamics of the ego thus started to replace instinct theory in the understanding of perversions. Pre-oedipal

factors and the role of early disturbances in the mother–child relationship are also stressed by McDougall (1984). Mahler (1963) examines
symbiosis and separation/individuation stages in normal infant development and postulates their failure as causal in perversion. Khan's
(1979) view is that perversions have a specific structure of their own
related to an inability to establish a sense of intimacy. Stoller (1975)
furthers this view and attaches major importance to the pervert's need
to hurt, humiliate, and hate the object. Etchegoyen (1978) considers
perversion to be as much a defence against psychosis as its cause, and
that on occasions it may be the psychosis itself. Chasseguet-Smirgel
(1983), Greenacre (1968), and Arlow (1971) highlight the role of sadism and control of aggression in perversion. Kernberg (1991) describes
perversion as "the recruitment of love in the service of aggression—the
consequence of a predominance of hatred over love". Richards (2003)
accurately points out that "perversion has an antisocial connotation, in
that it is sexual pleasure that coincides with inducing pain in oneself or
another person". She is one of the analytic authors who defines some
(five) attributes of perversion, some of them coinciding with my own
list, and takes a rather optimistic and also realistic view of treating
patients *suffering* from perversions.

The subject of understanding perversion has become in the last few
years a favourite in the field. We have benefited from many outstand-
ing contributions from the psychoanalytic perspective in general and
from the intersubjective field in particular. Most of these writings have
included the emotional quality of the therapeutic relationship between
the psychoanalyst and his or her response to patients and have offered
clinical cases to provide evidence for their theoretical explanations.
Some authors have also used mythology, literature, and works of art in
the quest for understanding a concept that invariable and unwittingly
changes according to cultural, historical, ethical, moral, and certainly
judgemental issues. There has been a constant and consistent flow
of contributions in this area, from the "classic" authors such as Stoller (1974), Khan (1979,) McDougall (1978, 1986), Chasseguet-Smirgel
(1984), Malcolm (1970), Meltzer (1973), Etchegoyen (1977), Joseph
(1994), to more recent ones—among others, Michael Parsons (2000),
Arlene Kramer Richards (2003), Alfonso Sanchez-Medina (2003), Juan
Pablo Jimenez (2004), Ruth Stein (2005), and Ofra Eshel (2005).

In a challenging paper, Eshel (2005) explores the Greek tragedy
The Bacchae, specifically in relation to King Pentheus and his mother
Agave. Pentheus, disguised as a woman, joins a celebration over
which Agave presides. She does not recognize him, and he is torn to

pieces and devoured by her. After the killing, when she recognizes her own son, she is overtaken by grief and madness. According to Eshel, "Severe perversion is no longer rooted in an oedipal world, but rather in the world of Pentheus, which has its beginnings in transvestism and voyeurism, continues on to exhibitionism, and goes as far as sado-masochistic violence and cannibalistic murder" (p. 1080).

Features of perversions

Devereux (1954) emphasizes that from the intrapsychic point of view, the purpose of foreplay is to increase tension and to cathect the part-ner, whereas the purpose of perversion is to release tension and to decathect the partner; from the object relations point of view, normal sexuality is characterized by true object cathexis in which the partner matters as an individual, is not used as a means to an end, is highly cathected, and is valued in the subject's and the partner's sexual grati-fication, whereas the so-called passionate love relationships between perverts lack these characteristics. A pervert does not perceive the object of his love as a "total" human being, but as a part-object.

For Khan (1965, p. 402), the pervert cannot surrender to his sexual experiences, but retains a split-off, dissociated, manipulative ego-con-trol of the situation, which is both his achievement and his failure in intimacy. It is this failure that supplies the compulsion to repeat the process. Although the pervert arranges and motivates the idealization of instinct which the technique of intimacy aims to fulfil, he himself remains outside the experiential climax. Hence, instead of instinctual gratification of object-cathexis, the pervert remains a deprived person whose only satisfaction has been of pleasurable discharge and intensi-fied ego-interest.

Essential to the understanding of the complex psychopathology of these patients are the elements of sadism, aggression, and hostility. For example, Stoller refers to "erotic hatred" and states that "At the core of the perverse act is desire to harm others". Another noteworthy char-acteristic is a strong, compelling urge for immediate action: though the pervert knows that this action is wrong, he is unable to resist the impulse because it offers immediate relief from unbearable anxiety. Such heightened drive intensity is often based on childhood sexual traumas such as seduction and deprivation, singly or in combina-tion. Glasser (1979) discusses the "core complex", in which there is a deep-seated and pervasive longing for an intense and most intimate closeness to another person, amounting to a "merging", a "state of oneness", "a blissful union". This is never realized, partly because whenever such a person has the opportunity to be emotionally close to another, he experiences a threat to his identity and withdraws.

In DSM-IV (APA-1994) the category "perversions" was changed to paraphilias (*para*: deviation; *philia*: attraction), defined as: "Arousal in response to sexual objects and situations that are not part of normative arousal-activity patterns and that in varying degrees may interfere with the capacity for reciprocal, affectionate sexual activity." Despite the inclusion of the quality of the object-relationship, no attempt is made to give a developmental perspective. Furthermore, neither definition offers a clear or distinct explanation of the sexual outcome reached by the affected person. I believe that this is because there are many individual sexual responses, as varied as in the so-called norm. This outcome is even more difficult to elicit in women, since they have a wider range of sexual responses than do men. I would therefore propose that the needed outcome for both sexes is that of a sexual relief, which brings about a transitory state of satisfaction from an increasing sexual tension.

It is revealing that the DSM-III-R (APA, 1987) listing of paraphilias omits both zoophilia (bestialism) and necrophilia. This may denote a trait associated with the "culture of complaint" (Hughes, 1993) in that the omissions may have to do with the inability of victims to voice being abused!

According to Stein (2005), perversion occupies a unique position and a controversial category in psychoanalytic thinking today because it is a complex notion that resists simple definition and eludes stabilization because of historical and cultural changes and shifts in psychoanalytic sensibilities. In my view, perversions are complicated and complex phenomena that are a challenge to our intellectual abilities and emotional responses because they are paradoxically based.

Perversion is neither the negative of psychosis nor a defence against psychosis or a psychosis itself (views held by Glover, Klein's followers, and Etchegoyen), but a defence against the dreaded black hole of depression hiding away suicidal ideations or just plain suicide. For example, it is self-destructive in that patients take many serious risks from which they also experience or derive a great sense of excitement, and it acts as reinforcement that they are still alive. What Ogden (1996) calls flirting with danger I prefer to call dancing with death. When death takes place, is that an accident? Or is it—especially so during psychotherapeutic treatment—a well-concealed desire to die in order to avoid extreme painful awareness of an almost-death in early experience. This may be linked to Winnicott's (1974) notion of the fear of breakdown as the dreaded event, an event that has already occurred but has not yet been experienced. Following this, I would argue that perversion is a manic defence used against depression, not as a mental category as appears in the DSM but as a psychodynamic concept.

Where Eshel concentrates on the perverse aspects of Pentheus, I shall concentrate on Agave—that is, on his mother's actions. Clinicians familiar with women who have hurt and damaged their children in different and varied ways are used to being witness to the women's tremendous sorrow, emotional pain, and despair following those actions, which are now experienced as though somebody else had taken over. The sentence "If only I could turn the clock back" is a constant reminder of their pain, shame, and remorse.

Eshel (2005) regards perversion as a defence organization—through splitting, externalization, and compulsive sexualization—against a violent, devastating, unbearable, deadening early past situation. She uses the term autonomous solution, borrowed from biology, to explain a process of massive dissociative splitting into two disconnected parts, alien to each other, as a means of psychic survival. One part continues functioning in the world, surviving by inertia, emotionally impaired, lacking and dull, lifeless, and alienated from the inner core of its experiences. The other part—the self that was offered to be devoured—is stuck in that devouring state, suicidally attracted to whatever wounds and preys, to whatever embodies and actualizes (at times, to the point of total actualization) the dark violence, the devastation, devourment, sadism, and imperviousness, both within the psyche and in self–other relations.

Does morality have a place in perversions?

What on earth has this to do, if anything, with morality? Nothing, nothing whatsoever. It is so archaic, so primitive, that even if on the surface the perversion appeared to be so self-destructive—of course, in many ways it is closely associated with the death instinct—it also secures our patients' survival. We have to keep in mind that judgemental responses are of no use and are the expression of intellectual laziness. We have the duty, if and when working with these patients, to have a much more enquiring and open mind, and to feel privileged to be the recipients of primitive fantasies that will enable us to learn more about the dynamics of the deviant mind. For example, a patient of mine, a female prostitute involved in the mafia world, tells me with great pride that she is such a good mother that some years ago while still pregnant and left abandoned by her bank-robber lover, she succeeded in securing a responsible, conscientious father, someone able to create the "fear of God" in her previous irresponsible lover to such an extent that any possibility of him reclaiming his paternity would be pre-empted. Her choice was not one we would automatically have forecast—the chosen putative father was a better, more "prestigious" bank robber than the ex-lover. A far cry from our own expectations!

Paul Verhaeghe (2004), whose book *On Being Normal and Other Disorders* has become a sort of alternative DSM-IV, eloquently argues that: "Perversion is unquestionably one of the most difficult of the clinical categories as far as both research and treatment are concerned" (p. 397). He warns us that in order to be able to study perversion as such, we have to overcome at least three difficulties, of which the first is an ever-present moral reaction. He reminds us that whereas we can liberally talk about our patients "as a 'good neurotic', and probably even a 'good psychotic', the idea of a 'good pervert' is a contradiction in terms" (Verhaeghe, 2004, p. 398). Dany Nobus (2006, p. 15) asserts that this is key to the ongoing utility of the category which itself has come to stand for the preparedness within the psychoanalytic discipline to be challenged and to be dislocated at clinical, theoretical, and epistemological levels.

As Simona Argentieri asserts:

> The pervert, today as well as yesterday, is not someone who concedes himself an extra pleasure, but a sick person who, with great difficulty and many rigid restrictions, tries to reach (often at the expense of others) that minimum of pleasure compatible with his pathology; what he does is less significant than what he cannot do. A compulsive impulse forces him to periodically discharge his internal tension, experienced as an unbearable threat of implosion, through sexual acting-out. There is never true fulfilment but only a superficial sensorial outlet that, because it is not a real relationship with the other, constructs nothing inside. [Argentieri, 2007, p. 70]

A psychodynamic definition of perversion

Jimenez (2004), in a most comprehensive article about perversion, clearly asserts that theoretical constructs in psychoanalysis have affected the concept of perversion, reiterating the confusion of Babel and resulting in its lack of clarity, and reminds us that at the 1995 IPA Congress in San Francisco, Amati-Mehler stated in the panel "Perversion and Psychic Reality" that "every time the word 'perversion' is used, we would need a conceptual and clinical redefinition".

I fully support this view; hence my intention here is to combine a phenomenological approach with psychoanalytic understanding. This combination of approaches means diagnosing symptoms both by their form and by their content in order to make an accurate diagnostic appraisal of what we understand by perversion. My aim, it should be noted, is not to categorize people but to categorize conditions or disorders that people suffer from. It may be useful to think of a constellation of symptoms appearing in perversions which will enable us to classify a condition with clinical clarity devoid of ethical/judgemental innuendoes.

As I stated previously (Welldon, 1996), perversion is a condition in which the person afflicted does not feel free to obtain sexual genital gratification through intimate contact with another person. Instead, he or she feels "taken over" by a compulsive activity that is subjectively experienced as inexplicable and "bizarre" but provides a release of unbearable and increasing sexual anxiety. The activity usually involves an unconscious desire to harm others or him/herself. Perversion, as used here, is a clinical and psychoanalytic term and carries no moral connotations.

> But in Sade, as in all perversion, and to a certain extent in the *Kama Sutra*—despite the declarations of liberty—there's no freedom for the participants to escape the limited repertoire of roles their fantasies assign them, or to be altered by one another—the other doesn't exist. Pleasure is more contentious, difficult and subversive, both emotionally and politically, than these authors want to see. [Kureishi, 2011]

It is preferable to use the term perversion rather than deviation, since the latter implies only a statistical abnormality. Fantasies about bizarre or perverse actions do not qualify as perversion. True sexual perversion always involves the *actual* use of the body. In talking about sexual fantasies, it is essential to mention Brett Kahr's book *Sex and the Psyche* (2007). This is the most comprehensive survey of sexual fantasies ever to be researched and written about. The reliable outcome is that nine out of ten people have sexual fantasies, mostly pretty gaudy ones—and Kahr thinks the remaining tenth are crippled by shame, guilt, or repression.

Kahr focuses on traumatic experiences in the past. Fantasies are a way of rewriting childhood history, with an important element of repetition ever present, accompanied by an illusory sense of control and mastery whereas, in the original trauma, they felt defenceless and at the mercy of others.

In her remarkable book, *Mad, Bad and Sad* (2008), Lisa Appignanesi recounts the history of the study of the female mind over the past two centuries and tells the historical background of Celia Brandon, one of the first British patients whose case notes diagnosed her as having "Freudian" problems, perhaps because she showed an exceptional understanding of her own condition and sexuality. She was brought up by a brutal aunt who physically abused her from the age of 3 years; this abuse came back later, following a miscarriage, as sexual fantasies in a delusional system with memories of her childhood, with auditory hallucinations punishing her for the "dirty" fantasies in her memory.

By definition, perversion embraces some specific and characteristic features that correspond to a dysfunction of the sexual component of personality development. In some cases, perversions may be encapsulated from the rest of the personality so that on the surface the person *appears* totally normal (Hopper, 1991). This is because perversion involves a deep split between genital sexuality as a living, or loving, force and what appears to be sexual, but it actually corresponds to more primitive stages of development that are dominated by pregenitality.

The diagnosis of perversion

Listed below is a cluster of psychodynamic and phenomenological features that could work as a constellation specific to perversion. For its accurate diagnostic appraisal, at least four of the characteristics would be required to be present:

1. *Encapsulation.* I believe that encapsulation is a more accurate term than splitting or dissociation, since the person knows what is being hidden. The person has enormous fears of being found out in this self-imprisonment, but the self-imprisonment is also combined with an intentional self-deception. In this I am arguing that the "right arm" knows what the "left arm is doing". This has been called by other authors splitting, etc., and most recently by Eshel (2005) *autotomous solution.*

2. *Compulsion and repetition.* This involves a compulsive and repetitive action that is subjectively experienced as bizarre and is incomprehensible, but which provides for the release of the unbearable increase of sexual anxiety (from ego-dystonic to ego-syntonic under the increasing pressure of the sexualized anxiety).

3. *Body engagement*. Fantasies about bizarre or perverse actions are not enough to qualify as perversion. True sexual perversion always involves the use of the body. The "body barrier" means that the individual must use the body for the perverse action.

4. *Part-object relationship*. Instead of the ability to have a whole "object-relationship", there is only a "part-object relationship". I use the word "object" as opposed to subject, and a part-object relationship when the individual finds it impossible to see the other person, or "object", as a whole and complete separate being.

5. *Emotional interference* in the achievement of a loving and sexual relationship—making hate vs. making love.

6. *Dehumanization of the part-object*, which exists only and whimsically to provide a temporary sense of libidinal gratification.

7. *Sexualization*, which has replaced the capacity to think, hence:

8. *Symbolic meaning eludes patient's consciousness*. Although the person is only too painfully aware of the compulsion to repeat the action, he is profoundly unaware of its unconscious meaning. "Symbolization is empty of meaning, and in some extreme cases it appears as truly bizarre" (Kohon, 2010). According to Kohon, the "main characteristic in 'symbolic impoverishment' [his term] is that drives are thought of as *if* they were actions".

9. *Fixed script*. Characteristically there is a complete restriction on the choice of a sexual scenario, which usually has a fixed and repetitive "script". The person does not know why he needs this specific scenario and not any other for his sexual release. The symbolic unconscious links become apparent, if ever, during psychodynamic therapy.

10. *Hostility*. The person is oblivious to the hostility that causes it: he is deeply unconscious of whom he hates and on whom he wants to take revenge. This hostility includes humiliation, directed towards his partner or himself.

11. *Extreme fears of being "trapped" or engulfed.*

12. *Need to be in complete control.*

13. *Deception*, with an "impostor-like" quality, which is partly responsible for a therapist's strong countertransference response of being trapped in "conspiracy" or in collusiveness by the patient. This again seems to be related to the notion of being a part-object and not a real person: a false self as opposed to a true self. This results in his need to be in complete control and his complete incredulity

of being loved by anyone, hence the internal need to present as another person in disguise; it clearly represents a very low sense of self-esteem.

14. *Private–public issues* intertwined with a real/illusory sense of power. We are all aware of the "famous" figures who suddenly succumb to their "destinies" and are exposed to public scandal and general shock. I have called this common phenomenon "From fame to shame".

15. *Risk-taking*. This is closely associated with the death instinct. There is a constant, irresistible pull towards situations that put the individual's life at risk. Dancing with death (Welldon, 2009) is a metaphor for seeking serious danger.

16. *Inability to mourn.*

17. *Manic defence against depression*. Faced with such trauma, individuals use denial as a defence mechanism in order to ward off psychic pain. Every form of risk-taking could be construed as a manic defence.

There are internal processes that draw some of these individuals to professional situations of power, despite or due to the fact that they know they are placing themselves in a most vulnerable position, painfully aware of suffering from perversions. What sort of internal motivations lead to a person taking a *public* position, in which he could

---

Key points in the psychodynamic assessment of perversion

- Lack of freedom in the object choice
- Part-object not whole-object relationship
- Compulsive and repetitive action
- Encapsulation
- Action experienced as bizarre
- Release of sexual anxiety vs. creation of intimacy
- Making hate instead of making love
- Fantasies are not enough—"body barrier"
- Deception or "impostor-like" quality
- Inability to mourn
- Manic defence against depression

easily feel vulnerable and subjected to threats of blackmail? These elements of danger may actually be functioning as added risk and excitement factors and could easily trigger off a life–death situation. Such individuals may be in those positions as a result of a very sadistic superego that has taken total power. The experience of "near death" actually works as a reassurance of being alive.

Perversion implies a private lie that tantalizes, allures, and teases in an agonizing way. In my opinion, deception is not only at the core of perversion but is also its distinguishing feature. Deception requires a degree of collusion or complicity from others, which is different from cooperation. The understanding of deception offers insights into the differences between psychosis and perversions. For example, in psychosis, a delusional audience is created and the presence of others is not necessary. In perversions, object relationships and the use of sexuality, even though they may be damaged, damaging, faulty, or extremely precarious, are still desperately needed. In other words, in deception the presence of an audience or public is essential. The infantile wish for a captivated audience requires at times an admiring response or, in the case of "flashers", one of shock and fear. In either case, the performance is created as a protection against the dreaded black hole of depression and the possibility of a psychotic breakdown.

Even in those perversions that are not punishable by law, such as in transvestism, the existence of a need to repeat together with duplicity and double moral standards may precipitate further excitement at the service of the superego. The fear of being caught, with the fantasized ensuing humiliation, creates an unparalleled and overlapping position of both risk-taking and excitement, which adds to the erotization of death as the last sentence. In fact, when caught, despite enormous losses of all sorts, these individuals experience a great sense of relief at not being able any longer "to get away with it". The true nature of whatever brings them much agony, pain, and suffering is now in the open and they have the possibility of being "judged" as they really are.

People involved in sadomasochistic practices frequently present this attitude, taking great pride in trying to demonstrate they are actually in control and derive a great sense of sexual pleasure. They claim that for the first time they are "free".

Many clinical cases from the past come to mind, such as a policeman who is a flasher, a nun who has stolen money from the authorities, a policewoman who has committed fraud, a medical doctor who indulges in acts of violence and harassment with his junior colleagues.

This difficult field is discussed further in chapter 8. It is impossible to cover all dimensions, but throughout the book there are vignettes from my clinical practice which I trust convey some of the flavour attached to the forensic patient. I know these individuals are difficult to assess and treat, but they offer such a challenge, which includes, unexpectedly, a sense of privilege of being at the worst times recipients of their "awful" confessions and at others containers for their fantastic acts of psychic survival.

The psychodynamics of perversion

In perversion, sexual anxiety appears as a result of conflict between the id and the superego, in which the id titillates the ego with a bizarre fantasy that does not obviously appear as sexual. The id puts pressure on the ego to be partly, or temporarily, corrupted by its increasing needs. The ego, supported by the superego, fights against the acting-out of the fantasy since it is felt to be incompatible with the ego's sense of integrity. Thus, anxiety increases and immediate action is demanded. Eventually, under the increasing pressure from the id, the ego is corrupted and succumbs to the "acting-out". The action has become temporarily ego-syntonic, thus allowing the perversion to take place. The goal is reached by the release of hostile sexual anxiety. The hostility is related to revenge for an early trauma associated with early gender humiliation and/or tremendous fears of not being in control when facing the imagined loss of the primary object or most important person. However, the sense of well-being achieved is of short duration. It is immediately afterwards superseded by feelings of guilt, self-disgust, shame, and depression. The "acting-out" is again experienced as ego-dystonic, and the circular motion starts once more, as shown in Figure 1.1. Other aims involved in the perverse acts are the regulation of self-esteem (Rosen, 1979) and the taking of risks (Stoller, 1975). Success constitutes a shocked response from the victim reassuring the pervert of his or her dangerousness; failure arises from a repetition of the early humiliation.

Review of the early literature on female sexuality and female perversion

The symbolic equivalence of penis and baby was created in Freud's description of the girl's resolution of the Oedipus complex by accept-

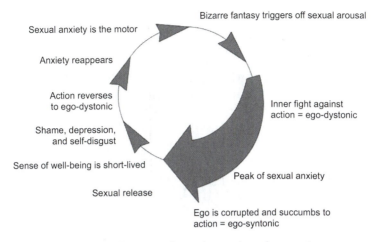

FIGURE 1.1.   The internal circular motion of perversion.

ing castration and resigning herself to have a baby by her father as opposed to have a penis. Freud himself thought that female sexuality was a "riddle" and asked his women colleagues for enlightenment about their own sexuality. The response of his female colleagues was overwhelming. It was most unfortunate that their voices were not heard as voices of legitimate self-assertion, but instead were taken as voices of dissent. Horney (1924, 1926, 1932, 1933), Muller (1932), and Barnett (1966), rather than simply seeing the little girl as lacking a penis, wrote about her experiencing vaginal sensations and impulses that made her feel feminine from the beginning. From her own clinical experiences with adult women, Greenacre (1950) developed the view that vaginal awareness is present in females well before puberty.

Other workers in the field still refer to the disagreements over female sexuality between Freud (1905, 1931, 1933), Abraham (1920), and Jones (1927), but their female contemporaries' ideas were treated with ignorance or patronizing indifference. Other women colleagues made important contributions in supporting Freud's views—for example, Riviere (1929), Brierley (1932, 1936), and Payne (1935). During the last twenty years important theories about female sexuality and perversions have been advanced by some female colleagues—for example, Chasseguet-Smirgel (1984, 1985) and McDougall (1986)—and are taken seriously by our profession. Kaplan (1991) redefines female perversion as a "psychological strategy" failing to fulfil the criteria of perversion as clinically defined.

Conceptualization of female perversion: the body as the torturer

As I argued in *Mother, Madonna, Whore* (Welldon, 1988), there is an important distinction between male and female sexual perversions. In both men and women the reproductive functions and organs are used for perversion; the man uses the penis to carry out his perverse activities, while the woman uses her whole body, since her female reproductive–sexual organs are more widely spread. Their different psychopathology originates from the female body and its inherent attributes, including fecundity. As early as 1968, it was noted that the neglect of this area in psychoanalytic literature could be regarded as "an aspect of the universal resistance to acknowledging the mother's filicide drives, undoubtedly the most dreaded and uncanny truth for us to face" (Rascovsky & Rascovsky, 1968, p. 392).

The psychopathologies most frequently associated with women are syndromes of self-injury associated with biological/hormonal disorders affecting reproductive functioning: for example, anorexia nervosa, bulimia, and forms of self-mutilation, where the absence or presence of the menses can act as an indicator of the severity of the condition; self-abuse; some forms of prostitution; and the sexual and physical abuse of children, including incest with children of both sexes (see Figure 1.2). Ethel Spector Person has coined two terms—"the body silenced" (meaning the lack of sexual desire) and "the body as the enemy" (meaning hypochondriacal symptoms)—in a study of beating and sadomasochistic fantasies in women (Person, 1994; Person & Klar, 1994). I believe that a fitting term for my female patients' specific predicaments in relation to their bodies and babies could be "the body as the torturer". This term would signal the compulsive unconscious urges these women experience towards their bodies, making their bodies function as the effective torture tool in victimizing themselves and their babies. Victims can experience an addiction to trauma that induces self-destructiveness. Anna Motz (2008) describes vividly the way in which self-harm is a defence against intimacy, binding a woman to her own body to the exclusion of the other. She makes a connection in women "cutters" between the cutting of the skin and the creation of a barrier between therapist and patient: "Women locate their sense of identity in their bodies, which may be their most powerful tools of self-expression. For many women, painful experiences are literally inscribed on their bodies" (Motz, 2008, p. 250).

Not only can painful experiences of different degrees be present in

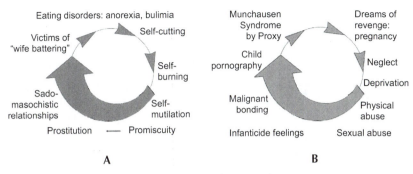

FIGURE 1.2:   Female perversion:
(A) against her own body; (B) against her own baby.

the body, but a different intensity of dissociation with the body itself may be present, with her own body or with the baby's body such as in Munchausen Syndrome by Proxy (see chapter 4). However, it never reaches the frozen quality and the alienation of one's own body so well described by Salomon Resnik in *Glacial Times* (2005). At other times, the partner is unconsciously designated as the torturer.

Dissatisfaction with the female body

It is likely that young women who have experienced early emotional deprivation, and who have failed to learn self-assertion during adolescence, will become increasingly dissatisfied with themselves and their own bodies. This is often manifested during adolescence in eating disorders such as anorexia and bulimia, promiscuity, drug abuse, self-cutting, or self-burning. These are the precursors of abusive behaviour to others and constitute part of the psychological profile of the female abuser. Ambivalence towards the female body, and towards the mother, lies at the heart of the cycle of abuse. As they grow older, these young women may find enormous internal difficulties in achieving healthy, satisfactory, mature emotional relationships. Instead, they might easily enter relationships with men or other women with whom a sadomasochistic pattern emerges. It is extremely difficult for these women to extricate themselves from these relationships because the dance with death operates in such a compelling and irresistible way.

If and when they do manage to give the relationship up, they do so only in order to start a new relationship, which in no time acquires the same characteristics as the previous one. This happens because the brutish partner represents an internal part of herself, the partner becoming the embodiment of her own self-hate. She might now no longer need to attack her own body in various ways, because her partner has been unconsciously assigned to perform this role. Heterosexual intercourse with sadistic characteristics becomes the rule. Though on the surface the woman is submissive, compliant, and passive, revenge is being harboured in daydreams, dreams, and fantasies. Dreams of a pregnancy are engendered, with different psychic connotations—for example, falling pregnant as an expression of revenge against the man who is so undermining and contemptuous. Or, if left on her own, feeling isolated and despondent, the woman might want to have a child to keep her company and to provide her with unconditional affection. She is quite unaware that, left to her own devices, she might easily fall into abusive actions against her baby, since she is unable, psychologically and otherwise, to deliver all that is required from a "good-enough" mother. Such motivations are not usually taken into account by those who assume that motherhood is a sign of healthy and mature development. I never cease to be amazed at the extent of the denial of the perversion of motherhood and the lack of acknowledgement and recognition that some women on becoming mothers can damage and hurt their children.

I was invited in November 2010 to a symposium held by Itinerari Psicoanalitici in Verona about "The Bad Mother". Whilst there I came across a comprehensive and fully informed book on this subject, *La Mamma Cattiva* [The bad mother], which until then was unknown to me and has never been translated into any other language. The book is devoted to the phenomenology and anthropology of filicide and gives examples from the mythical literature. The cover of the first edition states that its aim is to expose all types of hypocrisy surrounding the idealization of parenthood. The new edition (Carloni & Nobili, 2004) includes many different clinical manifestations of filicide. The authors address the denial of this painful predicament that is often only recognized too late, when irrevocable damage has already been inflicted. According to Nobili, society's usual response to a mother detected because of harming and even killing her child is: "She never showed any signs that she would be able to act in such a terrible way."

The matricidal wish has been studied by Amber Jacobs. *On Matricide* (Jacobs, 2008) is in a way the counterpart of the ideas put forward 20 years ago in *Mother, Madonna, Whore* and of the theories prevalent at the time, the outcome of the denial of a conceptualization of female perversion and even more so if this was associated with the ideal-ized version of motherhood. The classic book that dispels the myth of motherhood and all its religious, sociological, and historical trappings is *Alone of All Her Sex* by Marina Warner (1983).

The mothering process

Psychoanalytic authors from Margaret Mahler (1963, 1979) onwards refer to the mothering process in the production of future perverts. Most agree that the mother–child relationship is of paramount impor-tance in understanding the genesis of perversion, but recognition of the perversion of motherhood itself is absent. Furthermore, little is said about the real pathology of those mothers, and one is left uncer-tain as to whether the authors consider the "cruel", "sadistic" mother to be a fantasy of their patients, or an accurate assessment of these mothers. Perhaps the essential problem is that Freudian theory treats perversion as the product of oedipal anxiety. As Paul Verhaeghe says, supporting my own theory in Lacanian terms: "This is wrong; the anxiety is about the maternal superego. It was the First Other who was in control, and the perverse scenario is explicitly aimed at reversing this situation" (2004, p. 411). Again, when referring to the importance of post-traumatic stress disorder in the psychoethology of perversion, he asserts: "The pervert's basic distrust is of the Other, and therefore of every other. To have been abused by someone who was supposed to be protective means that later on the victim will distrust everyone" (p. 411).

This terrible predicament of being cheated by the person who is supposed to take care of us and be responsible for our well-being is clearly and cannily demonstrated in artistic expressions of the tricks we face everyday and still find so difficult to come to terms with. Juan Muñoz provided an extraordinary insight in a retrospective show at Tate Modern in London, where he put us in touch with violence, disaster, and our encounter with the other within ourselves. Perhaps the most subtle way he demonstrated this binding situation of safety/danger was a deceptively simple piece of art—a handrail, with its own distinctive twist. In the words of the catalogue:

> The presence of the human figure is strongly implied: the banister is something for the hand to grip, a means of safety and guidance while negotiating a tricky staircase or passageway. But it was pre-cisely this feeling of reassurance that Muñoz wanted to undermine.

First Banister (1987) includes an open switchblade, hidden from view
and waiting to slice the hand of anyone who holds the rail for support. [Tate Modern, 2008]

This is exactly what happens to the infant who implicitly trusts and
relies on mother for his own negotiations with life. If in trusting this
to happen he encounters the opposite, his survival is now at stake
because his mother, through her own human frailty, is providing him
with a life-undermining situation.

The new piece by Turner Prize-winning artist Martin Creed is entitled *Mothers*. Phil Miller (2011) appropriately calls it "The Mother of
invention". The power of motherhood has never been in such blatant
and obvious evidence as in this work.

This is not Louise Bourgeois, with her threatening spiders, effectively conveying the maternal elements of being both slightly dangerous and simultaneously protective. It is also a far cry from Muñoz's
First Banister, in which the danger is almost imperceptible and apparently innocuous, silent and unpredictable, hiding away its potential
dangerousness.

Creed's work is described by Miller as:

A huge, metal, revolving sign, bearing the legend "Mother", it fills
an entire large room at the Hauser & Wirth Gallery in Savile Row,
London. With a central steel beam that is 12 and-a-half metres long
and two-and-a-half metres high, it revolves steadily and dangerously, with an audible metallic groan, about more than two metres
off the ground. It is both sinister and somehow amusing in its scale.
It weighs several tonnes and cost £100,000 to make, and it would
seem more at home atop a mountain, or large building, rather than
fitted perfectly into a darkened gallery space.

Interestingly enough, this was supposed to be a piece for a German
airport and was to have consisted of both a Mother and a Father. There
is no mention of the reasons for the change leaving only Mother, but
this makes a big, important statement. Martin Creed candidly admits
that:

I don't really know how Mothers came to me other than thinking it
was a word that could be done really big. Working on this piece has
made me sick, literally sick. On my way to some meetings about it
last year, I remember thinking, "Oh my God, do I really want to do
this? What the fuck am I doing?" I think that mothers are difficult
in general, so maybe that's why it was such a difficult work for me.
I think the relationship between the mother and child is the most
difficult and powerful of all human relationships. . . . In this rela-

tionship the baby is literally part of the mother and is not separate, and then the baby comes out and has to be separate. It is the most difficult thing to do. I think to actually be a mother is very difficult and to have a mother is difficult.

In other words, mothers are important but also very dangerous. Never underestimate the power of a mother. The huge metal spinning sign, although supported by a vertical column, is no longer symbolically placed in a phallic, vertical, erectile manner as in the "old" times. This piece is in a horizontal position depicting perhaps a female figure but spinning non-stop, so the danger is not at all abstract—it is there for everyone to take risks with its differing spinning quality and different speeds.

We may also have to start thinking in terms of the effects of pregnancy. In both male and female perversions, the object of attack and murderous envy is mother's body. These attacks are usually perpetrated in symbolic ways, but on occasion the actual body is attacked in concrete ways. This is even more clearly evidenced and experienced in the most sadistic way against the pregnant body.

In psychoanalysis it is commonly acknowledged that a particular symbolism is also present in incidents where breaking and entering takes place but not for financial gain. The incidents usually involve a few youngsters who, once they have broken in, indulge in all sorts of behaviour such as taking food from the fridge, making a mess of the home and its contents, urinating, defecating. They leave the house in complete disarray, but to the humiliated and angry owners' further bewilderment nothing has been stolen.

Richard Davies asserts that "If we think of the client as the 'powerless' child whose internal experience is that of a sadistic mother who keeps him there to hurt him, then we have a view of somebody who, when with the female worker or the volunteer, feels powerless against their sadism as he sees it" (2007, p. 230). This is a most appropriate observation; however, I believe that the professional's gender is irrelevant since, in the client's internal world, regardless of the gender of the professional involved he or she will be experienced as the sadistic mother.

These break-ins are sadistic actions against the mother's body, symbolically represented by the house they have trespassed against. The pregnant body is more than the sum of its parts: it represents the embodiment of fulfilled desire, the sexual longing for the other, and the completion of that union represented by the new being. However, we are also familiar with the fact that pregnancy triggers violence and that pregnant women are much more prone to physical abuse from their male partners and also from strangers (Aston, 2004; Bacchus, 2004; Foy, Nelson, Penney, & McIlwaine, 2000; Mezey, 1997; Royal College of Midwives, 1999; Stark & Flitcraft, 1996; Taft, 2002).

This is the primal scene par excellence, and it leaves vulnerable, immature individuals in a most curious predicament. Even the men responsible for the pregnancy may be subject to powerful and opposite emotions. Consciously they are proud and excited by their own potency in having impregnated their partner. But in their unconscious minds a paradoxical operation may be at work, and some return to the position of being the humiliated and excluded child. Drawing on her psychoanalytic experience with violent patients, Perelberg (1999) proposes that violent acts have underlying specific phantasies or unconscious narratives that motivate them. She expands Freud's ideas by linking violence to a core phantasy of the primal scene, involving the pre-oedipal mother, in contrast to Freud's emphasis on oedipal phantasies. Perelberg proposes that in affective or self-preservative violence, the person's unconscious phantasy of the primal scene is of violence and the relationship to the pre-oedipal mother is engulfing and also violent. These beliefs have developed in the context of a pathological intrusive early symbiotic relationship with the mother as described above. The violent act is therefore an attack on the mother's body, the mother being experienced in phantasy as being in possession not only of the child's body, but also the child's intellectual and affective experiences.

James Gilligan (1996; see also 2009) states that any violent act is always preceded by the subjective feeling of being humiliated. This feeling of humiliation arises when early traumas are being re-enacted in full, such is the power they had when these men were powerless and defenceless children. It is the same for women if their partner leaves them: they have been injured emotionally, and at times also physically, and experience a great sense of humiliation. They can easily act this out against their defenceless, powerless children. So the cycle of violence and abuse is perpetrated forever.

Differences between male and female perversions

The main difference between a male and female perverse action lies in the "location" of the object. In men the act is directed at an outside part-object. In women the act is usually directed against themselves, either against their bodies, or against objects that they see as their own creations—that is, their babies. In both cases, bodies and babies are treated as dehumanized part-objects. (Welldon, 1988).

It is interesting to note that even though women's exhibitionism could superficially appear to be the equivalent of men's, this is not so. It is well-known that male exhibitionists have the compulsion to "flash" only to women—and women who are unknown to them—whereas women suffer from this compulsion only with other women to whom they feel a close attachment. This is yet another remarkable difference between the genders (Welldon, 1988). This finding is confirmed by Richards (1989) when she describes a woman's perversion that consisted of her repeatedly and compulsively making obscene phone calls to her mother and other female protective figures. Hollender, Brown, and Roback (1977) report a comparable situation regarding genital exhibitionism in women, and their explanation is that "in psychoanalytic terms the male's problem is genital (phallic), whereas the female's problem is pregenital". Bak (1953) dismisses female perversion since, in his view, perversion is a reaction by the boy to his mother's lack of a penis.

In comparing the erotic differences between men and women, Stoller (1991) asserts that men's propensity for fetishizing contrasts with the opposite desire in women for relationship, intimacy, and constancy. The problem is that if women fail to obtain these wonderful "feminine" qualities in their relationships, they could fall into perverse behaviour. Fantasies of revenge against their partners could then materialize in motherhood using their children as dehumanized, fetishistic objects of which they are in complete control.

In one of my therapeutic groups comprising both victims and perpetrators of sexual abuse, the entry of a male perpetrator produced an extraordinarily unexpected reaction from some of the female patients. On admitting that he had been using his 6-month-old baby for the purpose of masturbation by rubbing the baby against his genitals, women began to admit to similar feelings, talking openly about their feelings of being "turned on" by little babies, their "soft skin" and "milky sweet smell".

The view that female fetishism is the *exact* equivalent of that in men (Raphling, 1989; Zavitzianos, 1971, 1982) is seriously challenged by Gamman and Makinen (1994). These authors provide a new theoretical representation in a comprehensive study of female desire, though their definition of female perversion does not fall in the classical clinical definition.

Some of these differences are independently corroborated by Matthews (1993) and Bentovim (Bentovim, Kolvin, & Trowell, 1993). Bentovim *speculates* about the reasons why women make up a small proportion of abusers despite the fact that girls are abused four or five times more commonly than boys. He postulates that during their socialization girls tend to internalize their response to abusive experiences and develop low self-esteem, together with self-mutilation or anorexia nervosa, whereas abused boys externalize and project their experiences of abuse.

Women seem to suffer more from their own abusing actions, to be more aware of the deep psychological wounds and long-term consequences they produce, to take more responsibility for them, and to ask for professional help, which, unfortunately, is not easily available to them.

These differing characteristics in women—a degree of responsibility, experience of psychic pain, flexibility in their "choice" of perversion, and the attachment displayed in female perversions, which is absent in their male counterparts—may account for the better prognosis in women.

Table 1.1 summarizes in simple form the main phenomenological psychopathological features in male and female perversions.

Treatment implications

Dangers may be encountered if a prospective patient is not ready to take on either psychoanalysis or any other psychotherapeutic intervention, partly due to the influence that the acquisition of insight into what lies beneath the perversion may have on the patient. Since behind every perversion is a non-resolved mourning process, its awareness may produce either a serious depression with suicidal ideation or a psychotic breakdown. We could say that the perversion acts as an active avoidance of emotional suffering, and that is why they (the perverse patients) are so resistant to face any psychotherapeutic treatment that will challenge them and eventually provoke the mental agony that insight inflicts in them.

People suffering from perversions take many serious risks from which they also experience or derive a great sense of excitement that acts as reinforcement that they are still alive. This flirting with danger clearly describes the unconscious mechanism at work that may appear in the countertransference processes when the analyst/psycho-

Table 1.1. The main phenomenological psychopathological features
in male and female perversions

Male perversions	Female perversions
Aimed at an outside "object" or person.	Aimed at themselves or at objects of their own creation.
Onset usually at an early age.	Onset at variable stages, with earlier psychopathology such as self-abuse, promiscuity, and sadomasochistic relationships.
Inflexibility and habitual chronicity in the action.	More flexibility than their male counterparts.
Lack of freedom in the object-choice.	Some degree of changeability in the object-choice.
No emotional or physical attachment to the object or "part- object".	Some degree of emotional or physical attachment.
The action does not usually involve heterosexual intercourse.	The action frequently involves heterosexual intercourse for fantasy purposes and as a means of producing the perverse scenario.
Interference at all times with all other areas, including volition, thought processes, and affects.	Interference at times of emotional crisis with other areas, including volition, thought processes, and effects.
Desire to harm others, sometimes not obviously apparent to themselves.	Desire to harm themselves and/or their babies.
Persist through life.	Appear and fade away at different stages of life.
Unrelated or not significantly related to present stress conditions.	Significantly related to other distress conditions.
Lack of concern of consequences inflicted on their victims.	Awareness of the consequences inflicted on their victims.
Poor prognosis.	Variable prognosis

therapist feels unwittingly titillated, mesmerized, and seduced by the patients' psychopathology.

Therapists at times feel overwhelming invaded in "a perverse pact" and "deeply and perversely implicated in this game" (e.g., Jimenez, 2004; Moguillansky, Szpilka, & Welldon, 2007; Ogden, 1996; Stein, 2005). It is possible that this timing may be seen as the "good-enough" therapy to guarantee a level of psychic safety for the two parties involved in individual therapy. The other option available under the NHS is group analytic therapy, which has enormous advantages for this patient population (see chapters 7 and 9).

When people with perversions become patients, they can be drawn into acting out, negative therapeutic reactions, and reversible perspective. As Etchegoyen (1991, p. 764) reminds us, these three phenomena are deeply associated, since they create obstacles to the gaining of insight in order to ward off the psychic pain that insight invariably produces. I support Bonner's (2006) hypothesis that Bion's (1961) concept of reversible perspective is crucial to the understanding of perversion; this mechanism is in fierce opposition to acceptance of an interpretation leading to a dynamic inner transformation, and to the gaining of insight. The individual is actively trying to defend himself against the unbearable psychic pain that this transformation will inevitably produce in him. We are familiar with these prospective patients who during evaluation and when offered psychodynamic treatment would rather face a prison sentence, since they know that the latter will be far more endurable.

Carine Minne describes in painful detail and tremendous sensitivity the process of analytic psychotherapy with a female patient who had killed her child and how any move towards improvement would be followed by resistance against treatment, manifested by psychotic regression, self-harm, or flying into manic "improvement". In her words:

> In my view, there is a link between these positions in terms of her dangerousness. In the situation of remaining unaware, she remains a chronic risk to her babies, actual ones or symbolic representations of them. The pathological mother–child dynamic remains intact. In the situation of getting to know herself and being helped to deal with this knowledge, the risk to these babies diminishes but, without treatment, the risk of dangerousness to herself rises. Both these dangerous attitudes could be considered suicidal, indirect or direct. [Minne, 2009, p. 199]

According to Jimenez (2004), "the analytical situation creates a new social reality as a field of intersubjective agreement between analyst and patient, that is, as tacit acknowledgement that both of them, patient and analyst, belong to the 'same world'." I agree with Jimenez that at the beginning there is an inevitable collusion and it will require a second hearing, but I would argue that within the perverse transference the worlds populated by analyst and patient are not the same, although it may be assumed by the analyst to be "the same world". There are two distinct worlds, and that is why the second hearing is essential for the understanding of that fabricated, illusory world of self-deception. This is because we have unwittingly fallen, to the patient's disadvantage, into his or her collusive world of deeply ingrained defensive mechanisms. It is only when we are able to see through this well-constructed scaffolding that the patient feels recognized and acknowledged in his or her true colours: naked and really seen. At this crucial juncture, through the elaborated work of the interpretation of the transference–countertransference, it is possible for the "false self" to be revealed. Patients may now be involved in the quest to reach, in a slow and erratic way, their own real selves.

There is a growing general consensus regarding the crucial importance that interpretation of transference and countertransference (e.g., Etchegoyen, 1977; Jimenez, 2004; Ogden, 1996) phenomena has in the psychoanalytic treatment of patients who suffer from perversion. Needless to say, this particular psychoanalytic approach, born from object-relations theory, has been consistently endorsed and applied at the Tavistock–Portman NHS Clinics Trust since the inception of the Portman Clinic (see chapter 10).

I have noticed from relevant publications that there are at times differences in the outlook regarding the definition of perversion and its adequate treatment. These differences seem to stem from the fact that most publications are from colleagues who work mainly, if not exclusively, in the private sector, whereas my findings are from the public sector. In summary, these differences may be due to multiple factors. I believe it is important to emphasize not only the regular practice of NHS providers to have regular multi-professional meetings to discuss in detail the psychodynamic findings of interactions during sessions, but also the frequency of sessions, which is very different in both practices. It had been customary to see our patients just once weekly due to NHS funding, although some of them have been seen two or three times a week, but the general rule is once a week. This characteristic, which may in the first instance appear to be rather limiting, may be instrumental for patients who feel so threatened by being confronted with much psychic pain. Sometimes, once weekly is as much as they (and we!) can take, and they use the rest of the week to digest interpretations that include harsh and unpalatable truths about themselves, keeping constant "dialogues" with their therapists that take place in their heads.

CHAPTER TWO

Perverse transference
and the malignant bonding

It was Etchegoyen (1977) who first introduced the concept of "transference perversion", characterized by the erotization of the therapeutic relationship with a peculiar type of narcissistic object-relation. The patient permanently tries to create a delusional subject–object unity, provoking excitement and impatience in the analyst. Etchegoyen also made us aware that these processes must be uncovered in order to solve potential problems dealing with the dissociation of the ego, subject–object confusion, and the transformation of desire into ideology.

Ogden (1996) has provided another dimension to this hypothesis, asserting that the patient uses sexualization as a way of protecting him/herself against the experience of psychological deadness. Hence the compulsive erotization is used to create an illusory sense of vitality. This is the start of my thoughts on the escalation of the perversion "acted in" during the transferential process with the psychoanalyst to the most severe and difficult type of relationship to understand.

I have chosen to start with these two authors' principles since I mostly adhere to them when thinking or working with patients affected by perversion. For example, and to start with, the interpretation of the negative transference is crucial, not only in us understanding them but also in their own being of feeling understood. This vital element could never be overstated, particularly when it is well-known that clinicians drawn to this particular psychopathology often have "rescue fantasies". (See what happens later on in the account of Lord Longford trying to rescue Myra Hindley and her utter contempt for him towards the end of their relationship.) They would rather be "do-gooders" than confront patients with their own most negative feelings, such as hatred and revenge. These patients are able to read between the lines and to elicit better than anyone else the emotional responses they create. Therapists who may feel ashamed about their sense of impatience and frustration may try to conceal them with an even more "benign" or "kind" response, which will be not only useless but also utterly despised by the patients—such is the patients' own degree of awareness they have about emotional responses they produce; such is their own long, deeply engrained "training" from conception/birth at not only feeling, but also being in reality, rejected, abandoned, and humiliated by their carers.

I very much agree with Ogden's concept of the compulsive erotization against deadness being used to create an illusory sense of vitality. I have been alert to patients' attempts, by using manic defences, not to succumb to their own sense of dread depression.

The malignant bonding

The quality of enmeshment and engulfing does not only involve the perverse couple; their relationship continues to bond at the expense of sadistic and sexual acts perpetrated together against dependent persons, such as their own children or other immature individuals who fall under their control and dominancy. Not only are there notorious cases from the media, but I have also been able to corroborate these in my own clinical findings, which I have termed the concept of "the malignant bonding".

"Malignant bonding" is a different condition from either erotic-sadomasochism or "relational perversion" (Filippini, 2005; Pandolfi, 1999), although at times it could be the outcome of the progression or escalation of a sadomasochistic relationship. Filippini (2005) makes some relevant points regarding the connection between narcissism and perversion and the type of object relationships, if any, the narcissistic person has. She also makes a distinction between sadomasochism and relational perversion. The author takes as her starting points and discusses in depth Racamier's (1992) concept of "narcissistic perversion" and Pandolfi's (1999) concept of "relational perversion". Filippini postulates that maltreating behaviour, in fact, originates from the encounter of particularly non-empathic relational styles that are typical of certain personalities, but she is exclusively concerned with the man as a perpetrator and the woman as the victim (although Filippini is aware that the opposite, though rare, does occur). I am not referring to this particular psychopathology, which of course I have often seen during my clinic practice. I am concerned with the activities of the couple together in most self-destructive actions, which are directed to the outside and, by their mutual participation in them, can add to their own perverse bonding an extremely exciting and erotic quality. Furthermore, this can be initiated and even stimulated not only by the man but also by the woman in the couple. We are no longer talking of who is the victim or perpetrator within the couple. They have both become partners with equal participation in the designing and execution of their actions against their own severe very early traumatic experiences. In fact, as already observed in chapter 1, the difference between male and female perverse actions lies in the "location" of the object or target: whereas in men it is usually directed towards the outside, in women it is either against themselves, against their bodies in self-destructive patterns, or against objects of their own creations—that is, their babies.

Narcissism

André Green's concepts of positive and negative narcissism are relevant to the understanding of these very primitive modes of behaviour. In the positive type—"the cathexis of the self being fed, at last partly, at the expense of the object cathexis" (2002, p. 637)—*egoism*, selfishness, and self-sufficiency are to the fore. The second, negative type "is the form narcissism takes when combined with self-destructive drives" (p. 644). It is a tendency towards annihilation, which manifests itself as emptiness, self-hatred, and denial of castration. In particular, he posited the origin of masochism and sadism in the destructive drives deriving from the death instinct (Freud, 1924). We are able to observe this in women who attack their offspring. The situation becomes more complex to understand when it involves a couple; so far, all findings are from heterosexual couples, although it quite possibly applies to homosexual couples too. The couples to be described exhibit the negative type, in which no separation or individuation is envisaged, such is the process of massification (Hopper, 2003) between the two. This pathological union of both persons suffering from a perversion resulting from very early and repeated traumas requires, for their psychic survival as one, sadistic actions of the most cruel type associated with libidinal charges directed towards the outside world in the concrete body(ies) of children. These children represent the split-off traumatic introject of the traumatized parents. Parents or couples react with fight and flight or dissociative behaviour towards the "threatening child". Amon and Bihler's (2007) discussion of children from traumatized parents gave much enlightenment to my own ideas of the malignant bonding still in working progress. According to them, there are two different groups of traumatized parents. The first group never open up about "family secrets". The second group are openly obsessed with their trauma and talk about it all the time; there is an externalization of the parents' traumatized parts of their personalities projected onto the child. Thus the child is forced to identify with this parental projection. There is a reversal of the container–contained relation, and it becomes transgenerative. This becomes a transgenerational transmission, and there are severe difficulties regarding separation and individuation.

If we are able to follow Amon and Bihler's reasoning created by their clinical findings, it is easy to understand why these children fail to abandon their traumatized parents and are unable to express aggression and so easily become their prey for further abuse.

It seems to me that the malignant bonding may be corresponding to the first group of parents, those who never talk about their "family secrets"; the repetition of the sadism involved in their actions becomes the actual remembering of what happened to them before. But now *they* are in the "triumphant" position: not only is there a role reversal as to when they were infants; they are now in complete control of the primary scene, no longer outside it but just like puppeteers in their joint effort to re-enact early painful experiences with those helpless children, who see their involvement as their own way of survival. But this is not enough to reassure them that they had survived horrific physical and psychic damage to themselves. As soon as they are no longer in the concrete scenario of their sadistic but "necessary" actions, their sense of control of the victim gradually becomes illusory and fades away. They wonder: were they in control or were they the victimized children dispossessed of all power? Thus they have to remind themselves that they *had* been control. Hence the use of devices to listen and watch to once more create an illusory sense of being omnipotent in their minds, that, yes, they are now the executors.

There is a lot to learn from observing behaviour that involves domestic violence, including verbal, physical, and sexual abuse, not discounting paternal, maternal, and sibling incest. There are serious consequences arising from these different but related sorts of behaviour, not only on their direct family members but also on the following generations.

Early severe trauma as a "matcher" of couples

It is fascinating, although at times very difficult, to get to know what makes a couple "tick". We have to observe and explore how couples originate, how they meet and pursue their relationships in unconscious ways that may become conscious only later on, when they seem to have been consolidated, and only then do the enormous conflicts emerge that have been hidden away. How many times have we all been witnesses to occurrences of incestuous actions from parents to children, a father or mother who him/herself has been an early victim of child abuse. In the family dynamics in which usually the father is the perpetrator, the mother/wife has so far been "blissfully" unaware of this particular scenario; however, when later on she is confronted with the harsh reality of the abuse, she has flashbacks, and a memory of having been herself sexually abused as a child emerges with pervasive power from within.

It is as if a magnet was operating in both partners at the moment of their initial meeting, which was felt be so bonding that it was equally irresistible and dangerous and as such very exciting—so exciting that falling in love was inevitable since the "radar" was in full functioning order and the polarizing aspects of the two was felt to be the perfect combination for a perfect coupling. But this "felt" sensation of "equality"—or, better said, "sameness"—was no longer enticing when the union became legalized and, as such, no longer taboo. Of course, I am not talking here of conscious, rational behaviour. This couple, these two different persons, have felt, as from the moment of their first meeting, in almost automatic pilot mode, very close and united together but not knowing exactly why. However, this great sense of wonder starts fading away when the union is felt to be in some way "contrived" or coercive from within. Now, the taboo element is no longer present and the sense of excitement is gone. What happens next? The pursuing of the transgressing has become the compelling element, and as such the using and exploiting—including sexual abuse of children—may start. There is an irrepressible need to continue succumbing to these transgressive actions because, just as with pornography, it makes them feel alive. They feel really dead inside themselves, and their own way to make sure they are still alive is by exerting this enormous sense of power and control over their children. This power has an added element of libidinizing the interaction between the couple.

Rosenthall (2009) describes a similar clinical finding, a perverse type of couple relationship in which the couple attempt to join together to manage "sheer unconscious terrors, some of which were neurotic, while others had a psychotic quality . . . at times, this seemed to contain the threat of unbearable experiences that could be psychotic in nature" (p. 209).

Cases from the media

There are two famous and notorious cases in England of the "malignant bonding"—Myra Hindley and Ian Brady, and Fred and Rosemary West—and they come to my mind when thinking of the interactions between both partners and their harmful actions produced by both together against children.

In order to pursue my own findings, what I would like to emphasize is the strong reaction of disbelief that the women in question could have had anything to do in any active way in the horrid actions against the children. Everyone—from the lay public to all professionals, including experienced judges—tacitly assumed that, if at all involved, these two women were responding to bullying and threats from their male partners.

The first case goes back to 1964 and was dramatized and screened on October 2006 for television by the BBC under the title *Longford*. Lord Longford was a very compassionate, although rather naïve, kind, eccentric English aristocrat, who took care of all the most difficult and at times impossible law cases, in the belief that he could not only understand better but also help those he saw as victims of miscarriage of justice. He was a strong believer in hope and change, even in the most intractable cases. He became famous for his intense interest and activity surrounding Myra Hindley after she was sentenced. This is the woman who, with her partner and lover Ian Brady, took children on many different occasions to the moors in northern England, and together they subjected the children to all kinds of acts of torture, including sexual violence and rape, eventually killing and burying them there. Lord Longford, although being in active service during the war, was stunned by the enormity of Hindley's crimes, which "made even him pause to draw breath for a moment". At their first meeting at Holloway, she asked him to facilitate meetings with Brady, who was serving his life sentence in a men's prison.

Longford, who was initially very much against such meetings, was eventually persuaded by Hindley and agreed to do as she had requested. From then on, and for the next 35 years, Longford continued to argue her case. Such were her formidable powers of persuasion.

The crimes committed by Hindley and her lover, Ian Brady, shocked the nation and became the benchmark by which other acts of evil came to be measured. It is revealing that while, to start with, Hindley was never thought to be an active party in these horrific actions, after seeing evidence of her being active the media view of her changed 180 degrees and she was then depicted by the tabloid press as "the most hated woman in Britain".

On 6 May 1966, Hindley and Brady were jailed for life after a 15-day trial. The killings soon became known as the "Moors murders", and it was made even more notorious by the tape-recording played at the trial of one of their victims pleading for her life. Hindley's active involvement in the case was now unquestionable, since the young girl was directly appealing to Myra for her release. Later on, while in prison, Hindley admitted to her active influence in all crimes. In 1994, Hindley wrote that she was "wicked and evil" and had behaved "monstrously". And again: "Without me, those crimes could probably not have been committed."

When they had originally met, Brady had a minor criminal record with stretches in borstals and prison, and, while inside, he began his fixation with Hitler and the writings of the Marquis de Sade.

Myra left school at 15, learned how to type, and within three years went to work at a small chemical firm. There she met Brady, who was working as a stock clerk, and fell in love with him. Once they became lovers, Hindley was prepared to do anything Brady asked.

At her trial, evidence was produced that she had been subjected to threats, violence, and intimidation by him.

Again, prejudices were to the fore when, two days after the original trial, the judge who sentenced Hindley said: "Though I believe Brady is wicked beyond belief without hope of redemption, I cannot feel that the same is necessarily true of Hindley once she is removed from his influence."

No one, including Lord Longford, was emotionally capable at that time of seeing a woman—in this case, Myra Hindley—as being both the prompter and promoter of the malignant bonding with Brady. But, of course, who could suspect that a woman whose capacity for pregnancy and bringing up babies is the one who may be the perpetrator? Why the reluctance on his part to consider this possibility? The BBC programme suggests that it may be because he was already, in transferential terms, caught in the same process of malignant bonding with Myra. Interestingly enough, in the film, the person who almost succeeds in his breaking up this relational perversion was his wife, Elizabeth. But Elizabeth Longford's opposition weakened over time. In December 1976, she finally agreed to accompany her husband to Holloway. Surprising as it may seem, she and Hindley became firm friends. This may be further evidence of Myra's enormous powers of seduction and persuasion, and as such it becomes a potential *ménage à trois*, with her as part of the parental couple, with her husband placing Myra as being the "sick baby" unable to wake up from the drug-induced, almost catatonic situation. In the film, different and varied possibilities of malignant bonding of a very perverse nature are shown. Hers and Brady's first—which, of course, is what excites the others, who are unconscious of the nature of this interest.

The West family represents the most famous case of family abuse, which includes the physical and sexual abuse, torturing, and eventually killing of their own and other children. Such actions, sadly and most unfortunately, are not isolated and exclusive examples. And if this appears to be extreme and beyond the boundaries of what we are supposed to know and to be familiar with, let me tell you that this is not so. There are couples and families afflicted by this perverse behaviour who live at close quarters with us. Perhaps the degree of their perverse actions is not as extreme as the Wests', but it does require acknowledgement and professional expertise to deal with. Sachs (2008) says that "parents who feel compelled to see their children tortured or dead have an extremely traumatic history themselves", which leads to "the inevitability of further trauma, generation after generation" (p. 132).

In the last few years we have read in the British newspapers about different couples who while performing their "duties" as babysitters have physically and sexually abused children in their care. In February 2006, an incident was reported in the *Guardian* in which a couple had repeatedly raped a 3-month-old baby. Not only that—they even took videos of all the rape scenes, performed by both partners, man and woman. More recently, on Saturday 27 March 2010, a story appeared in the *Guardian* under the headline of "Couple Face Life Terms for Murdering Boy in Their Care". The boy, aged 3 years, had 70 injuries to his body. He had been neglected, abused, and beaten by a 19-year-old woman cousin of his mother and by the woman's boyfriend, aged 25. The baby's mother felt unable to cope with the baby's demands and paid the couple for taking care of her baby.

I know these public cases are accounts of most horrifying and sadistic happenings, but I want to make you aware of these awful possibilities that may or may not come your way, as an incipient awareness is essential in order to detect these happenings from very early on. In the history of psychoanalysis, there was a reluctance to take claims of sexual abuse as real, and instead these were considered to be phantasies. But today it is no longer possible to persevere with that position since the reality is present in flagrant ways. This is a subject taken up with sensitivity and accuracy by Ann Scott (1996).

All these public cases, and the ones I am familiar with, share a terrible predicament: the strangled, panicky, unbearable pain experienced by their victims is being recorded. Technology has afforded the most sophisticated means to do so—from recording just the voices of those innocent children, as in the 1960s, to the making of home videos, now with digital cameras. And today different images such as these can be downloaded from the internet.

There is thus a compulsive need to repeat again and again to themselves—the perpetrators—the tortures inflicted on the innocent victims. I find this feature a most distressing one, and I am reminded that Freud in *Beyond the Pleasure Principle* (1920) linked the destructive impulses and this need to repeat, to re-present, to double, and to supplement results in either identifying with another or finding it impossible to determine which of the two she herself is. When perpetrators make and record not only their own actions but also the confused, disturbed, painful, and frightened reactions of their victims, is this used as identification with their own childhood? Is it to do with their need to make themselves feel all-powerful and in complete control of the torture inflicted because they need this "reassurance"? Is the listening/watching also associated this "addiction" with early sexual abuse and the need to form sadomasochistic relationships of which they have the monopoly of power? It could also be, speculated pragmatically, a home-made pornography so that the sexual excitement of the torture could be re-created on future occasions, as a sexual trigger to masturbate to.

Frequently the children involved are not even their own, just as happened with the cases described above, particularly the notorious case of Hindley and Brady. Not only did they torture and kill the children involved in their rampage of seducing, grooming, and taking children away, but they also recorded their victims' anguish, pain, and suffering while they were being tortured, to listen to on repeated occasions. Why this need to re-enact this barbaric, primitive, irrational behaviour? This is an extreme situation, but we also have equally or even more perverse behaviour in the case of the Wests. The West family tortured and killed some of their own children as well as others and kept the corpses within the walls of their own home. What should one make of this couple who had to use their own family to create their own intimate, close, family genocide and holocaust within their own home walls? After this indescribably awful discovery, it was most alarming to recognize the compelling element it provided others, with the gruesome and ghastly curiosity of looking at the "forbidden". How many people went to visit the Wests' "home"—to see what? This reached such alarming proportions that a council decision was made to destroy the site.

But what is the extent to which a couple can let themselves go in order to elicit a sense of excitement so pervasive, so unreal, but so enormously effectual to make them feel all-powerful, omnipotent, being able to create, destroy, and macerate lives. What is the extent of their feeling so empty, so vacuous, so dead, that in order to recreate a new life they had to pursue those horrific actions? And for our own interest here, what on earth put these two together? What was the chemistry/love/attraction that drew them together to start with and later on lead them to these joint, combined actions of reproduction, which in our view could be the product of a mature relationship. After all, surely what we expect from couples, when they develop and evolve in their relationships, is for them to pursue parenthood as a concrete symbolism, if this is allowed, as evidence of a healthy resolution to have children, to grow a family. But then to torture, to abuse and finally to kill them and bury them within their own confines?

CHAPTER THREE

Babies as transitional objects:
another manifestation of perverted motherhood

I saw a man who had requested a consultation with a female psychiatrist. The first time he came he asked me directly and emphatically: Are you Jewish or Catholic?

Although the question did not take me by surprise since patients or prospective patients would like to "know" all sorts of information regarding their therapists, the tone of the question conveyed a sense of urgency and despair that made me feel it was necessary to take into account the unconscious deeper layers behind this question. As usual, I explained that, though the factual information could be easily imparted, this would immediately pre-empt access to other immensely significant areas unknown to himself that could give us important clues to his present predicament.

This was a married man in his mid-forties with four children who had referred himself with the following letter:

"I have lived with a condition for most of my life which manifests itself in the form of transvestial or transsexual behaviour and feelings. While I am able to suppress these feelings for a good deal of the time, there nevertheless comes a moment when I can cope no longer—as has happened now . . . and for the first time self-mutilation seems to be logical. . . . *I desperately need someone to help me* decide upon the best way in which I could free myself of my now unremitting torment. . . . The symptoms that I am experiencing at the moment fall into two quite distinct categories, i.e. mental and physical. Mentally, I feel that I am a woman in the cliché situation

of having to masquerade my way through life simply because I am not as perfect as I want to be. .... I can quite see the clear possibilities of a 'change'. To this end I have now almost cut myself off emotionally from those around me—and so the conflict rages, as I question: to whom does my first loyalty lie, my family, all of whom are and will be able to make lives of their own, or to myself, with one precious life only? .... On the physical side, the tension can only be relieved by wearing anything other than men's clothes. ...
More obvious symptoms, on the physical side, that is, are: morning sickness, vomiting through the day, loss of appetite, feeling shivery, aching in the small of the back and the most obvious sign that tell me when I am about to 'go under' again—that my breasts become tender and sore—and it is at these times that the sensation of my nipples touching against my woolly jumper makes me just want to scream ..."

And so on. From his own description of his problem, we can vividly experience his enormous despair and sense of despondency and desolation.

He told me of his bizarre and complicated early childhood. He was the younger child in a family of two, with an older sister. When he was a year old (during the war) he was sent to stay with one of his aunts for "reasons of safety". His early recollections had to do with feelings of being lost. He remembered his time with his aunt as an extremely confused one. She was a warm and kind woman, but suddenly at the age of 3 years she made it blatantly clear to him that unless he complied with all her wishes, she would withdraw her love. The conditions she imposed included not only wearing girl's clothes, but behaving like one. He still remembers with trepidation that period of his life. At the beginning he tried to go against his aunt's whims, but soon he realized that the consequence could be complete isolation. After all, he had already been given away by his own mother, from whom he received a few postcards but never a visit. He then started to comply with everything required of him. After an initial period of resistance during which he felt awkward, uneasy and on the alert lest others should notice his being a "fraud", his mood changed and he acquired a growing sense of self-confidence while wearing girl's dresses. Actually, to his own surprise he began to thoroughly enjoy this "imposed" cross-dressing when everyone took it for granted that he was a girl.

His aunt had had a daughter, who had died at a very early age, and this was followed shortly after by her husband's death.

She now decided to send her nephew to an all-girls' school and taught him how to behave like a girl; for medical visits she would come to London and have him examined by a doctor friend of hers. At the age of 12, he convincingly looked like a girl. On the occasion of a family member's wedding, he was made the bridesmaid. He became the object of the most extraordinary scandal when, during the ceremony, his real mother—who had not seen him since she had sent him to live with his aunt—suddenly realized that this beautiful "girl" who was accompanied by "her" aunt was in fact her son. Amid screams and shouts he was taken away by his real mother, who not only severely punished him but proceeded immediately to send him to an all-boys' school. There, his suffering, torment, and humiliation became so great that eventually his mother decided to send him back to his aunt, but things were never to be as they had been before. He now had to suffer his aunt's denigration for his "maleness". I prefer not to go any further into this case here; what has been said is sufficient to convey the horrors that the two women, in their role of mother, together inflicted on this poor boy from infancy to adolescence.

But what about his first question to me?

His father and mother were Jewish, but the aunt (married to his father's brother) who brought him up since the age of 1 was the only Catholic member of his family.

He had been surrounded by all sorts of "maternal" perverting attitudes throughout his early life, from both his mother and his aunt. The fact that I didn't give him any information about my personal life—in this case, my religious affiliation—gave us the chance to explore his trepidation in his own search for who he really was. Had I been Jewish, would it have implied for him that I wanted him to *continue* to be a male? But, if, on the other hand, I had been a Catholic, would he have felt forced to go ahead with *his* transsexual wish?

Would he have felt free enough to wonder about the intricacies of his own gender identity? or indeed to look into his own sense of anger and confusion created by the two women carers in his early life? He had been messed about, forced to take up being either a boy or a girl, not only to please both women but also to secure not only his psychological but also his physical survival. In an earlier work (1988), I argued that motherhood plays a key role in the etiology of perversion and that for some women motherhood could provide an excellent vehicle to exercise perverse and perverting actions towards their children. These actions are directly related to these women's own experience of mothering going back at least three generations.

There are few psychoanalytic studies dealing with the particular psychopathology of perverse relations between mother and child. However, among them, those of Melitta Sperling (1959, 1963, 1964) are helpful in providing further understanding of the findings I am putting forward. The observations in these studies include childhood experiences in the lives of pervert patients, in which the relationship between mother and child is described as the perverse type of object-relationship and considered a genetic factor in the pathological ego and superego functioning of the child.

Nevertheless, it is disappointing that even though Sperling refers to a "perverse type of object-relationship" and takes mothers of transvestite boys into analysis prior to taking the children, she never again refers to perverse motherhood. Even when Sperling is advocating the treatment of mothers of perverse attitudes in their motherhood, she refers instead to "maternal functions [that] were highly valued". For my part, I believe that those patients were abusing their position of power as mothers, and that they were exhibiting what I would call perverse maternal attitudes.

In comparing the erotic differences between men and women, Stoller (1991) asserts that men's propensity for fetishizing contrasts with the opposite desire in women for relationship, intimacy, and constancy. The problem is that if women fail to obtain these wonderful "feminine" qualities in their relationships, they could fall into perverse behaviour. Fantasies of revenge against their partners could then materialize in motherhood using their children as dehumanized, fetishistic objects of which they are in complete control. Stoller himself in his clinical work with male-to-female transsexuals describes how his patients treated him as "their mothers treated them; as things, as appendages, rather than as separate people". He also defines the specific task required from a mother with a growing son in order for him to be acknowledged as a male and to fix the sense of maleness and pride in his own masculinity. This outcome will not be reached when an intense process of symbiosis takes place between mother and infant. Mothers of future transsexuals do not facilitate a process of separation and individuation in their sons. On the contrary, they treat the baby boy as their missing phallus and as the "happy completion of their formerly inadequate body" (Stoller, 1975, p. 158).

Joyce McDougall asserts that Winnicott's concept of the baby's "capacity to be alone" is easily endangered because of the mother's own anxieties and unconscious fears and wishes. This makes the baby need to constantly seek his mother's presence and according to

McDougall creates an "addictive relationship to her presence" and her caretaking functions. This condition, according to her, is actually created by the mother who is in "a state of dependency with regard to her infant"(McDougall, 1995, pp. 186–187). The infant left unable to identify with a containing figure will appeal, in times of internal turmoil and despair, to addictive objects, which she calls "transitory objects". These, unlike transitional objects, fail in providing a consistent sense of well-being because they utilize somatic attempts rather than psychological ones in dealing with absence. It is particularly relevant in this context to remember this patient's self-referral letter, in which he vividly described not only his psychic pain but also the production of physical symptoms.

I would call his particular predicament a case of "super-imposed" transsexualism. In doing so, I am supported by Stoller's assertion that true transsexuals never have episodes of masculinity, whereas my patient had a long-standing happy marriage that had produced four children, grown-up at the time of his consultation. His wife telephoned me then to let me know that her husband was a *"real man"*, indicating that both were able to enjoy a happy marriage, including a fulfilling sexual life. I consider that the reason for his consultation had to do with a mid-life crisis, when he saw himself as an ageing, unattractive man with a receding hairline and an enlarged abdomen; he was in terror of being rejected and left alone because of his physical appearance, just as he had felt when living with his aunt.

We do not have any access to this patient's mother's motivations for sending him away and neglecting him to the point of not visiting him.

About his aunt's motivations' for her bringing him up as a girl, we could speculate that she was trying to replace her dead daughter, perhaps deeply absorbed in pathological mourning. Darian Leader (2008) eloquently and comprehensively explores mourning and remarks on the fact that "when we lose a loved one, we have lost a part of ourselves. And this loss requires our *consent*. We might well tell ourselves that we have accepted a loss, but acquiescence and true consent are fundamentally different" (p. 149). Furthermore, this aunt may appear herself to have accepted the death of her little girl, but I think in trying to turn her nephew into a niece it was obvious that her bereavement had not been worked through, and this was responsible for a future tragic life of my patient. More evidence of this can be found in the life of Didier Anzieu, described recently by Naomi Segal (2009).

My clinical work has shown me the dangers of a quick "replacement" pregnancy. By this I mean that at times we treat women as if they were factories for producing babies. Many people, including health workers, inappropriately advise bereaved families to proceed in conceiving a new pregnancy. Even a cherished pet is not usually replaced after its death before its owners have had some time to overcome their feelings of grief.

We have learnt from Stoller (1968) that one of the very important components in the production of the child's core gender-identity is the infant–parent relationship, in particular the psychological aspects of the oedipal and pre-oedipal relationships. The mother's acknowledgement of her child's sex plays an extremely important part in establishing and confirming its core gender-identity.

In talking of early infancy, Winnicott (1953) establishes important differences between "transitional objects" and fetish. Whereas the transitional object is part of a normative process and is eventually given up and "relegated to limbo", the fetish dates from infantile experience in the transitional field and has the persistence of a specific object or type of object from those early days.

In Winnicott's (1953) terms, the "transitional object" is used by the pervert to be invented, manipulated, used and abused, ravaged and discarded, cherished and idealized, symbiotically identified with and de-animated all at once. This is exactly what I believe takes place in the perverse mother's mind and through her manipulation of her baby from which she derives a momentary sense of sexual relief from her increasing sexual tension and anxiety. In other words, the baby becomes for such a mother her "transitional object", as proposed by Stoller (1968).

Granoff and Perrier (1980) make a similar comment on the type of perverse relationship a mother establishes with her baby in which the baby is first identified as her missing phallus and then becomes her "toy" or "thing"; this they see "as analogous to the part-object relationships of fetishistic perverts" (p. 85, my translation).

Winnicott (1965) said that babies achieve their "true self" through "good mothering". However, this is more easily said than done, since mothers are also the children of their own mothers, with their own range of early ordeals and traumas.

My hypothesis based on my clinical observations is that mothers who exhibit these perverse tendencies towards their children do so within the first two years of their infants' life. They are likely themselves to have been the recipient of deficient mothering in their early years, as will have their own mothers before them through at least three generations. Perverse mothers use their babies as "transitional objects" or actually as fetishes to gain relief from sexual tension and anxiety. Such pathological intimacy is a special form of abuse that has far-reaching transgenerational consequences.

CHAPTER FOUR

Is Munchausen Syndrome by Proxy another case of female perversion?

Notwithstanding my large clinical experience of dealing with mothers who exhibit the most damaging and perverse attitudes towards their children (Welldon, 1988), I found myself in a state of disbelief and shock when I was asked to prepare a psychiatric court report on Mrs H. Such was the horror of Mrs H's actions that they left me astounded, confused, and unable to think. Mrs H was suspected of pulling and removing, from birth, her two babies' finger- and toenails. At the time of the enquiry, they were aged 21 months and 10 months. A case of Munchausen Syndrome by Proxy (MSBP) was suspected, and an assessment of her parenting abilities with the confirmation of this diagnosis and her suitability for psychotherapy was needed.[1]

During psychiatric assessments, mothers usually display strong emotions about the possibility of their children being taken away and try very hard to give a "good impression" of their maternal abilities. This was not the case with Mrs H, who appeared throughout all our meetings to be completed devoid of any feelings—flat in her affects, detached and dissociated. Not even when she said "the most important thing in my life are my children and I want them back with me" did she show any signs of affection.

Another unusual feature in this case was that the removal of her children's toe- and fingernails appeared to be a cold, planned revenge, showing a strong sadistic quality. In contrast, previous cases involved mothers who had become impulsive, out of control, and aggressive during the course of their mothering duties. There were no precedents of this kind of behaviour, except in acts of torture.

Whereas at the beginning she denied harming her children, she eventually told me that not only had she done so, but that also, while harming them, she was effectively able to convince all professionals involved—GPs and paediatricians—that the children's suffering was the result of skin diseases. I consider that, in some ways, she must have felt seriously distressed about being able to deceive all the professionals, because she *knew* that those actions were extremely harmful to her children and to herself because she was getting away with it when she was in urgent need of professional help.

These actions, which could easily and vividly evoke the Medea complex, cannot be solely and simply explained as a vengeful strategy against an "uncaring" husband. I believe that her strong sense of revenge was born in early infancy and was directed, symbolically speaking, first against her own mother for abandoning her at age 4 months and later against her father for sexually abusing her from the age of 6 years. These explosive negative feelings had been enacted in a combination of neglect and abuse towards her own children from their birth, culminating in the most unthinkable sadistic behaviour.

Compulsions to enact as opposed to experience feelings are linked to early traumas where mother–baby bonding breaks down at early stages of the baby's emotional development.

Being the receptacle of much early neglect and abuse had seriously impeded her mothering function. It looked as if a challenge of disbelief had been created within her when she was confronted with the evidence of being able to produce healthy babies. She could not accept any intrinsic goodness because it would have implicitly implied a recognition that she was intact despite the injurious psychological harm inflicted by her own mother. It was then that she proceeded to inflict on her healthy babies endless suffering and serious bodily damage. When I began to regain my capacity for thought, I speculated that by taking away growing and protective structures such as nails, leaving fragile, raw skin exposed to continuous physical harm, it might be the way she experienced herself: a raw object exposed to so much suffering that she had to rigidly protect herself with detachment and strangeness to avoid experiencing her own unbearable pain. I have described female perversions as either self-abuse or child abuse, which then becomes a dual process involving mother and baby. When I first encountered MSBP, I questioned its inclusion in my definition of female perversion, since it appeared at first sight to involve three persons: mother, child, and medical practitioner whose clinical judgement is being corrupted or perverted by the mother's persuading him (usually it is a he) that her baby's physical ill health is caused by fictitious illnesses.

For a time, I considered the possibility of including MSBP as a type of maternal perversion since the process is symbolically a dual one, as the mother is in complete identification with the image of a seriously ill baby. I even thought that despite protestations about the adequacy of the term "by proxy", it was wittingly or unwittingly the most accurate way to designate this extremely severe psychopathological syndrome. At the time of the publication of *Mother Madonna Whore* (1988), awareness of MSBP was limited, and there were some doubts in my mind as to whether this was yet another manifestation of what I had defined as perverse mothering. After years of clinical experience, I had to acknowledge the existence of feelings and activities among women that could or must be called perverse, even if the mental mechanisms are different from those found in men. In brief, in both genders the reproductive functions and the organs attached to them are those used for perversion: the man has the penis to carry out his perverse activities, the woman the whole body. In general, the hypothesis is that female perversion is very different from male perversion, because the aim is directed towards themselves, their bodies, or what they perversely regard as an extension of themselves, their babies (Welldon, 1988). This is in contrast with men, where the target for the sadistic action is directed to an outside object. The object in women is highly cathected physical and emotional attachments. This characteristic, again, is in contrast to men who do not experience emotional or physical investment.

In fact, I believe that the important differences between males and females could help us in the prediction, assessment, and management of female dangerousness. These could be used in a positive way to promote further understanding and prevention of these particular conditions.

From my clinical observations, I have identified distinctive features that differentiate MSBP and perverse mothering (Welldon, 1988). There are some common traits in the mothers' histories, but the differences in the mothers' attitudes and actions are important. The perverse mother may neglect or physically or sexually abuse her child. She is concerned and experiences anxiety, but she is secretive about her actions and scared of being caught.

Instead, cases of MSBP always require a third party (a professional), are always premeditated, cold-blooded, and show complete detachment, and are always presented as seeking help. Another significant difference is the mother's complete denial of the harm inflicted on the child. The mother will also commit at least one of four actions: smothering, poisoning, fabrication of seizures, or fabrication of other symptoms. Perverse mothers are often young mothers with a history of eating disorders and/or self-harm. In contrast, MSBP mothers tend to be older and present with somatizing behaviours and/or a history of illness. The ways in which the babies are treated also differ: the actions of perverse mothers usually involve older babies, who may present in future with serious personality disorders. In cases of MSBP, the babies are usually much younger, and they may in future have physical illness, sometimes leading to death.

The professional attitudes are also different: in maternal perversion, the patient is usually completely isolated; her problems are met with disbelief and lack of awareness. The patient is usually amenable to treatment, if offered; the assessment of parenting abilities is relatively easy in long-term assessments. Cases of MSBP usually involve many medical staff and hospitals, with the focus placed on the baby's physical illness. The mother usually resists treatment, and assessment of parenting abilities is difficult.

Perversion of motherhood is the end product of serial abuse or chronic infantile neglect. This condition involves at least three generations in which faulty and inadequate mothering perpetuates itself in a circular motion, reproducing a cycle of abuse.

Note

1. Munchausen Syndrome by Proxy is also now referred to as Fabricated and Induced Illness (FII) or as Factitious Disorder by Proxy (FDP).

CHAPTER FIVE

Bodies across generations and cycles of abuse

This chapter explores women's specific struggles in the fulfilment of the function of mothering after having been the receptacle of much early abuse, at times going back many generations. The long-term consequences can in the first instance lead to acts of self-harm such as eating disorders, substance abuse, self-cutting, and self-burning. Later on these can be superseded by sadomasochistic relationships with violent men, whose attacks might come to represent the women's own self-hatred towards their female bodies. This perpetuates and reiterates the early abuse. Some of these women might get pregnant and have babies, and then a process of identification with the aggressor can take place in which the victims may become victimizers of their own children.

Having a baby gives a unique reassurance to some women that their bodies and their reproductive functioning are still intact. Also, having babies may be the only way for some to communicate and express their own emotional needs, which have not previously been properly addressed nor recognized in themselves. The complexities of the body–mind relationship become crystal clear in observing the female *body* responding adequately to the physical demands of the pregnancy, but there is *emotional* inability to respond adequately to the newly born or growing baby's demands.

I wonder at the paradoxical and somewhat unfair position that young girls with most deprived and abused childhoods have to face. That is, whereas they are able with their bodies to produce babies, they are unable with their minds and emotional resources to mother babies. This discrepancy happens regardless of their conscious commitment to take proper care of their babies. This determination suddenly and unexpectedly fails to deliver, and hence it inflicts harm either to themselves or to their babies.

What is the purpose for some emotionally severely damaged girls of a repetition compulsion to have more and more babies? Perhaps to create an illusion linked to the pleasure principle, which then becomes in itself a self-destructive quest. McDougall tells us in *Theaters of the Body* (1989, p. 28) that "The body, like the mind, is subject to the repetition compulsion", and she also reminds us that Freud in *Beyond the Pleasure Principle* (1920) linked this manifestation to the destructive impulses, and this need to repeat, to re-present, to double, and to supplement results in either identifying with another or finding it impossible to determine which of the two her self is. I have observed exactly this phenomenon in my clinical observations working with psychologically damaged women.

One of the few ways for these young women to make sure that they are still able to produce something beautiful from inside themselves seems to be to reproduce a new baby, who will also represent basic and primitive nurturing needs they have experienced all through their lives. In other words, the babies are unconsciously being used as the evidence of their inner goodness. This emotional reassurance is short-lived and at times breaks down, especially when confronted with external pressures brought up first by the new baby's demands and later on by social agencies concerned about the safety of the baby. At these times, deep and primitive anxieties regarding their own functioning as "good-enough mothers" emerge powerfully. These are evoked by their own mothering experiences, which were felt to be either inadequate or absent, including neglect and abuse. This creates a sense of loss: what appears initially to be an inability to mourn for that important loss proves to be an unconscious "chronic mourning" for a good-enough parental figure. If detection of the real problem is recognized and professional help is offered to the young mother, she will react defensively as if attacked; internally, she will feel relieved that her inadequacies have been found out and that assistance will be available to her, in contrast to what happened to her own mother. The problem is that her baby has become the focus of concern and not herself—in other words, the attention is transient, short-lived, exclusively geared to her own pregnancies or babies. Revealingly enough, authorities are up in arms when a woman gets pregnant again. A new pregnancy is experienced by the women as the only way to get any help. But there are other internal unconscious pressures and symbolizations in operation.

Women can perceive their children as extensions of their own bodies, at times, like "part-objects" with a fetishist quality. They oscillate between seeing their children either as their healthy part or as undervalued mirror images of themselves. Early motherhood acts as a substitute for their own emotional growth. This is often associated with "compulsive caregiving" (Bowlby, 1980, p. 157). The caregiver attributes to the cared-for all the sadness and neediness she is unable to acknowledge in herself; instead, the cared-for person stands vicariously for the one who gives the care. This trait usually develops initially during childhood when children feel responsible for the welfare of their parents. These individuals are recognized as having what appears in the first instance to be a *prolonged absence of conscious grieving*, but they are actually suffering from unconscious *chronic mourning* (p. 138). This is inextricably linked to extreme traumas associated with loss during early childhood, which are responsible for producing insecure attachments. Obviously relationships between mothers and daughters are of fundamental importance in the function of motherhood. Bowlby adds that "should such a person become a parent there is danger of her becoming excessively possessive and protective, especially as a child grows older, and also of inverting the relationship" (p. 206). In my clinical experience, I have observed that these traits could also extend to intense ambivalence, resulting in periods of over-protectiveness followed by neglect and abuse.

The recognition of the cycle of abuse perpetuated across generations through women's bodies becomes even more painfully apparent when court reports are requested as evidence for life-making decisions regarding the future of the family, especially a mother and baby. In my long professional career and despite my own writings on clinical findings about perverted motherhood (Welldon, 1988), I had been rather skilful in avoiding writing court reports or appearing in court as an expert witness. This easy state of affairs ended a few years ago when I was giving a lecture on female abusers and was confronted by a professional colleague about my alleged cowardice in refusing to lend the weight of my clinical experience in assessing parenting abilities. At that point, I felt forced to "grow up" before retirement, so I reluctantly agreed to be more cooperative and active in preparing court reports and giving evidence. But it is an unbelievably painful and excruciatingly difficult process in view of the complexity of the decisions concerning the future of parents and babies.

I, myself, have felt completely immersed in an internal world of agonies and overwhelmed by a tremendous sense of responsibility, when confronted with a mother who really loves her baby and believes she is the one who should be the carer but simultaneously *knows* she is incapable of being so.

On one particular occasion I felt so very emotionally trapped in that particular situation that I decided to go to an art exhibition in an attempt to escape those painful professional duties and to liberate myself from my own emotional agonies, which were pervading my personal life in a massive way. The court report I was preparing then was of a mother who was deeply bonded to her child, but because of the difficult circumstances surrounding her baby's birth, adoption would be the likely recommendation.

Though I was not adverse to this initial way of thinking, I felt under extreme duress. It was then that I went to the Giacometti exhibition in London and in no time I found myself unexpectedly in a state of distress by closely observing a sculpture of a woman with hands ready to hold a baby who has become the "invisible object", not only metaphorically but in reality, like all those mothers we see whose babies have been or are about to be taken away. The woman's face in the sculpture appears superficially to be devoid of feelings, although when looked at in depth it appears like a frozen image conveying such an unbearable psychic pain that its experience has to be blocked off. I wondered why on earth, when so many sculptures were on show at the exhibition, my eyes, heart, senses took me to this particular piece which was so relevant to my then work. I realized the impossibility of escaping from the experience of breaking up the most profound bonding—that of mother and baby. I was just too emotionally involved with it to allow myself to have a break. And this is the nature of this type of work. It holds you permanently in its grip.

Evaluation of maternal abilities by placing so much attention on care puts considerable pressure on both mother and her "satellite" baby. The usual response is to bring forward the "best mothering". The baby represents the good part placed both inside and outside the mother's body; when all pressures disappear and the mother is left to her own devices and without professional help, the incentive to demonstrate the "best mothering" fades away. As soon as the pressure is over, the cycle of abuse is reinstated; an old and familiar sense of being neglected brings back the unbearable pain.

The knowledge of their previous emotional inability to bring up babies does not act as a deterrent for future pregnancies. The opposite is true: at times the quest for a new pregnancy becomes a most compulsive need. This repetition becomes not only in their minds, but also in their bodies, a triumph over the temporality of previous gestations, an omnipotent wish to overcome or actually deny the loss of a previous child with a renewed pregnancy. The mourning is intermittently forgotten, and a complete and multiple identification takes place—for example, the mother becomes not only both the lost baby and the new baby but also the maternal body, which simultaneously provides an illusory and concrete reality to be able to produce new pregnancies. The idea of the *forever* mother remains alive.

In 1923, Freud spoke of repetition as underlying the first great anxiety: the state of birth and infantile anxiety of longing—the anxiety due to separation from the protecting mother. Bronfen (1992) argues that "while the reality principle injures narcissism, it is also through repetition that narcissism asserts itself, tries to antidote the incision of the real by substituting it with images, with narrative, with objects" (p. 31). This becomes especially poignant when associated with repeated pregnancies in women with a very low sense of self-esteem. Bronfen, in using Freud's "*fort–da*" episode, makes a powerful argument in showing that the maternal body becomes the site of death because it is so uniquely connected to the stage prior to life. According to her, any attempt at mastering the maternal body could symbolize being in control of both the forbidden and the impossible, since the maternal body is inscribed by the death drive, the beginning of life, and the essence of loss and division. This theoretical approach might partly help to understand the clinical findings of the repeated and constant attacks that women inflict on their own bodies and on their own babies. Babies could be seen as fetishes that the mother uses as a denial of separation and death; hence, the repetition of pregnancies may be seen as an attempt to preserve the lost object, but this aim is doomed to fail since the lost object is her own internal mother, and further internal and external suffering is at stake.

Green (1972) links the pleasure principle and the reality principle in the dead-mother construct, where the subject is submitted to the repetition compulsion, remaining totally unconscious of the identification with the dead mother, returning to the trauma but, by repeating the old, bringing further disappointments. He talks of the identification with the dead mother as the only means to establish a reunion with the mother, but instead of a real reparation, a mimicry is created which becomes a melancholic reparation.

As discussed in chapter 1, a fitting term for my female patients' specific predicaments in relation to their bodies and babies could be "the body as the torturer", signalling the compulsive urges these women experience towards their bodies and their babies.

I shall try to demonstrate the existence of these theoretical speculations by presenting the case of a woman whose early life and pattern of relationships correspond to the descriptions made above. Ms B, 28 years old, who had had a most horrendous early life history, was the second child in a family of four—a sister 29 years old and two brothers aged 25 and 27—of the same mother and father. She also had two younger half-sisters of 7 and 8 years by her mother's later remarriage.

I was asked to assess Ms B's maternal abilities because of the impending birth of her fourth child. Her other three children had been taken away by Social Services at an early age because of domestic violence. This new baby was the product of a relationship with a 14-year-old boy, whose parents had taken Ms B to Court because of "indecent assault on a minor". The new baby, Cindy, was immediately placed with foster parents after being born, and Ms B was allowed three hours of supervised access three times a week.

Let me tell you some of Ms B's history. Her father began to sexually abuse her from the age of 12 years, involving masturbation, oral sex, and full sexual intercourse. She referred to these as being raped by her father, who apparently used much force while drunk, forcing her to have sex with him almost every day while her mother was away from home. She was extremely scared of him and frequently wished she were dead. Ms B always felt very different from the rest of the family and felt that her father picked on her at all times.

Her father secured a small flat from where he began to operate as a pimp using her as a prostitute to older men, with whom she had to perform all sorts of "kinky sex". Ms B believes her father made her have sex with other men not just because of money, but also because it gave him much sexual gratification to see her suffering at being abused sexually. According to her, her mother, although aware of all these events, did not intervene, either because she was unconcerned or because she feared her husband's violence. When she spoke to her mother about it, her mother's first reaction was to beat her up and later to join her husband in the sexual abuse. He advertised the services of his wife and his daughter in the local newspapers for pornographic and prostitution purposes; Ms B had kept cuttings of these adverts. Both parents were engaged in a sort of "malignant bonding" (see chapter 2), becoming united "parents" in this cruel and sadistic attack on their daughter.

Strong elements of oversexualization and erotization appear in both parents, which may have been used as a manic defence against the severe emotional deprivation they themselves had gone through in their own early childhood. A process of denial is being created to avoid "the black hole", the dread of emptiness, which is represented by its "absence" and becomes instead a chronic but masked depression, which is linked to experiences of deprivation, neglect, and abuse.

Ms B. had to struggle against deep wishes either to be dead or to kill herself. She also experienced murderous feelings towards her father. In the light of my own clinical work I often wonder at the resistance of some psychoanalytic authors to acknowledge the existence of the death instinct, first defined by Freud. For example, Stoller in his highly valued work on perversions makes only *one* passing reference to the death instinct: the "'death instinct' is too religious for my taste" (1975, p. 96fn). Freud (1923) states: "The emergence of life would thus be the cause of the continuation of life and also at the same time of the striving towards death; and life itself would be a conflict and compromise between these two trends" (p. 43). I have noticed that our patients experience the death instinct as destructive narcissism that is immensely erotized. It is an extreme enacted masochism where the individuals feel pushed from within to take risks that involve life-threatening situations to fight death itself in order to secure survival. The survival, despite and because of all risks involved, reassures and offers a guarantee to them that they are still alive. Risk-taking is being used as a "survival minikit".

Ms B told me that she spent most of her childhood "opening my legs for different men to make them and my father happy. . . . Whereas I was fighting it for years, in the end I just gave up fighting. Then I looked on rape as an everyday thing like housework."

While all this had been taking place, she continued to abuse alcohol, because, she said, the more drunk she got the less pain she felt. She had "always been very good at just blocking the worst bits" so that she didn't have to face any of this pain. This has been a long-established pattern. For example, at school she pretended that everything at home was all right: "I learnt to live in a world where nothing is as it seems. All I have around me is silent fear. I lived with more self-hate as the years of being raped went on. I felt there was something wrong with me." These events were obviously interfering with her progress in school, manifesting in her being out of control and difficult to handle.

As a teenager she was involved in violent actions, including attacks on herself, progressing to attacks on the outside world. She used to cut herself on her arms and her face, sometimes requiring many stitches, the scars of which are still visible.

At age 17 she left home together with her mother with hopes for a nurturing relationship with her. This failed bitterly, since after a few months and many quarrels, her mother left her. This disappointment led her to call her father in a compulsive need to continue the abuse. He told her how remorseful he felt about all he had done to her and was able to convince her that she should return home. But as soon as she came back, her father began again to rape her and beat her up. He was worse than ever because he was very angry, not only because she had dared to leave home, but also because he blamed her for her mother's leaving home. She still remembers vividly the last time her father raped her, because he became more violent than usual. She "saw everything red" and decided to leave home and to report him to the police.

She described bringing the case against her father in court as a big nightmare. "I didn't know what I was to be put through, it was like a knife going through your heart. My Dad looked at me and told me: 'I will kill you.' My Dad's solicitor was very nasty to me and said I was making it all up. I started shouting at him, telling him he was sick in the head."

As a result of the court appearance, and on the strength of the evidence the prosecution put forward of the newspaper cuttings she had carefully kept, her father was sentenced for rape, prostitution, and incest and sent to prison.

Ms B's violence turned for a while against authority, but soon after she began to be rather promiscuous, which is a frequent outcome for girls who have been victims of paternal incest. She started a relationship with Martin, a well-known offender and drug addict with a criminal record. They both used to indulge in heavy drinking and drug abuse. Martin became the father of her first three children. At the beginning he was considerate, but in no time he became very nasty and violent towards her. Soon after she first got pregnant, he was sent to prison. After his release a baby boy, Sean, was born, but Martin never helped her or shared any of the duties regarding the baby. The fights continued, and the violence at home escalated. She began to experience him as just like her own father, but felt very much in love with him. Revealingly she said: "Things have not changed a lot really because Martin hits me in front of the kids and does the things my Dad used to do to my Mum. When Martin starts beating me up, I feel as if it is my Dad beating me up again and that I am the child again. I get very scared because he behaves then like a madman. Every time I tell Martin that we are finished, he starts acting like a child about to lose his mum, then I feel sorry for him and stay with him."

Her relationship with Martin was deteriorating, and becoming even more violent, when she fell pregnant for the second time. She was against pursuing this pregnancy because she felt it was too soon after having had her first baby, when she had been extremely sick. However, she acquiesced to Martin's determination for her to have his second baby. On the many occasions she had tried to get rid of Martin, this proved to be ineffectual because of her own inconsistency and ambivalence. By this time, she had become "addicted" (her own word) to more violence and brutalization.

Martin was delighted at the birth of their second child, a boy called Martin after him. However, soon after that Sean and Martin junior were placed with foster parents because of domestic violence. She felt very upset about Social Services taking away the children, because, in her opinion, they had never been hurt. This response revealed her degree of dissociation, being utterly unaware of the long-term consequences the children would suffer from being constant witnesses to their parents' ferocious fights and of her own battering (see chapter 6).

She felt completely isolated and unable to rely on anybody including her brothers and sister, who were very angry with her because of her "sending" their father to prison.

Meanwhile, her own mother had remarried and now had two children of the same age as Ms B's children. Curiously enough, Ms B had been left on her own without any family resources and had further perpetuated herself in the victim role. However, as a direct consequence of her reporting her father, she had inadvertently liberated her mother from her own marriage to her father and had "allowed" her to find a "good" relationship, leading to "good" parenting of new babies. After the court appearance she received some counselling, but she interrupted it because she could not tolerate looking back at old areas of intense pain. She resorted to drinking in excess and to taking overdoses. In talking about her drinking she said that "without the drink I would most likely have gone mad. Drinking did save my life, in a funny sort of way". Dissociation was progressing even further. Betty Joseph (1981) describes the silencing of psychic pain that patients attempt as the only concrete way of dealing with it. She makes reference to Bion's conceptualization that people who are so intolerant of pain also fail to "suffer pleasure" Bion (1970, p. 9)

Quite unexpectedly, she got to know that her son Martin, aged 18 months, had died in an accident while living with foster parents. Surprisingly enough, she never expressed any angry feelings against the authorities on this account. Quite the contrary—she expressed guilty feelings for not having had her little boy living with her at that time. Instead, she felt in urgent need of an immediate replacement for Martin junior; a pathological mourning process was in full operation. I was amazed when she told me that, on reflection, her "serious" problems began when this new baby boy, John, was born, since she was bitterly disappointed because he did not resemble Martin junior at all. She felt completely detached from him and unable to create any bonding with him. Clearly she was chronically unable to mourn, and this new bereavement had brought alive all her old and apparently dormant episodes of grief. This mothering disturbance following the unmourned loss of a previous child with attempted resolution by a replacement child has been well described by Lewis (1979; Lewis & Page, 1978) and by Etchegoyen (1997).

Perhaps this sense of estrangement from her new baby and its detachment enabled her not only to give up the baby for adoption, but also to terminate her relationship with Martin. She began to live on her own. A few months later, Martin was found dead from an overdose.

A brief period of promiscuity was followed by her openly seducing Denis, a 14-year-old boy, whom she used to baby-sit. According to her, despite his age, Denis was very supportive, mature, and kind to her, and both were very happy about the pregnancy, which was a "planned" one. What appears to be a new scenario was actually the old one turned upside down. She was now cast as the abuser. She may have anticipated that for once she would be in complete control of a relationship by being involved with a teenage youngster who would only feel very proud at becoming a father at such an early age, with her being the responsible party. Instead, as soon as the pregnancy was announced she became again a victim, with Denis's parents taking her to court, on a charge of indecent assault on a minor. During the court case Denis denied being the father of the baby, and she was very much mocked by him and his parents. However, she kept insisting that he was a very nice person who treated her very kindly, and she never admitted feeling exposed and humiliated. She felt unable to acknowledge the degree of cruelty and sadistic behaviour from Denis towards her. She was sentenced to two years' probation, which she breached by approaching Denis with written letters.

She used denial and defensive self-deception when claiming she was able to have a good and equal relationship with Denis, whose views about becoming a father could not have been taken seriously in any realistic sense. Once more her self-deception, lack of emotional maturity, and inability to learn from past experiences were in evidence at her surprise that her new baby, Cindy, was taken away from her at birth. She had never imagined that this could happen.

Ms B was obviously unaware of the links between the early abuse and her "addiction" to form sadomasochistic relationships. In effect, the sadomasochistic relationship *is* the abuse—the abuse lives on encrypted in the present sadomasochistic relationship. This is what repetition compulsion means. The past is the present (Abraham & Torok, 1986).

The most striking feature that appeared almost throughout the six sessions with Ms B was her fixed smile, by which she tried very hard to convey the picture of a person who has resolved all her previous problems and is ready to lead a different kind of life. It seemed to me that her fixed smile and her continued readiness to laugh at any comments contained an intense denial of the pain and very deeply ingrained hurt feelings. I am reminded of Betty Joseph's conceptualization of the "growing pains", making the important point that only when people can take in the capacity for suffering are they able to experience the capacity for enjoyment (1981, p. 88).

The problem about this complete split and denial of her feelings of frustration, anger, hurt, and pain is that they all could emerge unexpectedly and suddenly, in acts either of self-destruction or of violence against the outside world. I felt it was impossible to predict if these could be directed against her new baby girl.

Even though she had been able in her late teens to disentangle herself in a most courageous way from the incest, her self-destructiveness then continued in a merciless way, which included repeated episodes of self-cutting, overdose-taking, and attempts at suicide. These were provoked by feelings of anger, despair, isolation, and an extreme inability to trust anybody with any of these feelings. She was acting out her sadomasochistic needs against her own body, protecting everyone else around her from her own rage, this being her only way of making herself feel better and at peace by acquiescing to her sadistic superego's demands. Later, in her relationship with Martin, she became a victim of violent attacks by him, and every attempt to terminate this relationship was doomed to fail since she tried to convince herself that he was a caring, loving person, and she consistently facilitated their being together. De Zulueta (1993) describes this pattern vividly and accurately when she talks of the aftermath of the violence that brings victim and abuser together in a state of calmness, in which the victim forgives and becomes reconciled with the brutal partner in the yearning for the fantasy that all sexually abused victims have of "being one again" (p. 186). Both become mirror images, with a deep unconscious awareness of the early sexual abuse and the compulsive need for revenge.

Person (Person & Klar, 1994, pp. 1075–1076) notes that the significance of the trauma seems to be cut off from any awareness in the person who has suffered the trauma.

With Ms B, the effect of the abuse was also extended to their children, but she was utterly unaware of this. When she was a victim of Martin's brutal attacks, she became severely dissociated—in other words, completely unavailable or unable to take proper care of herself or her children, so the children became the object of neglect as a continuation and expansion of her own abuse.

There are frequently clashes between legal requirements and psychodynamic evaluations. One of the most common disagreements revolves around the question put by the legal system to these young women and their assessors as to whether they are able to place their baby's needs before their own. A young woman with such a traumatized early-life history should be well advised to take care of her own needs before she can consider taking care of anybody else's, especially those of her own child.

Another area of contention is the question about a new pregnancy bringing a new disposition or a bettering of the maternal abilities due to "changes". The problem, as we know, is that repetition is in itself the evidence of the lack of internal changes. To repeat is an obstacle to change. The cycle cannot be broken by having another baby. Instead we should be offering professional help to these young women who are so badly emotionally and mentally damaged.

For example, exploring Ms B's ideas about what she would like to do in life, she expressed a wish to be either a nurse or to work in an old peoples' home. This is typical of the extraordinary claim made by most of these young women—many of whom protest "self-sufficiency" (Bowlby, 1980), which is precariously based and suffused by strong ambivalence—that the only thing they want to do in life is either to keep on having more children if the young ones have been taken away, or to have a job taking care of other children. They also often express a desire to be with handicapped people, since they like to teach. It is very difficult for them to see any link between their own areas of need, deprivation, and neglect as children and their wish to take care of children in the way that they themselves would ideally have liked to have been treated. This desire to work with children or handicapped people could lead to serious consequences. We should be more attentive to the psychodynamics involved in the choice that young women make to take on a caring role, especially of children.

The problem is, as Garland (1998) argues, that the nearer the re-enactment to the original trauma, the more this represents an inability to intersperse a thought process or to use any symbolism. This will certainly indicate a compulsion to repeat, which again brings us back to the original trauma. Perhaps we are able to look at this cycle of victim–perpetrator much more easily in histories of abuse other than in the repetition of getting pregnant. Maternity, or the capacity to be fecund, is viewed in a different light because the mother's body is actively involved in the delivery of both a perpetrator in action and a victim in the future.

It was painful to watch how all Ms B's efforts to fight against this terrible fate were doomed to fail due to the fixed belief she held of not being able to contain any good bits or not being deserving of some peace of mind. From first perpetuating her role as the abused child in her sadomasochistic relationship with Martin, she switched to becoming an abuser herself, albeit a more benign one with Denis. But although a 14-year-old boy may have appeared as the desired object, giving her the chance of being in complete control, this was not so. At the crucial time, she was reported to the police and, as a result, again became the abused party. Is the cycle of abuse completed? I do not believe so, since a new baby has been born whose father denies being the father and whose mother is left once more on her own with a highly self-denigratory image, since her expectations of her self-esteem being increased by becoming a mother has once more bitterly failed.

CHAPTER SIX

Children who witness domestic violence: what future?

Some familiar scenarios

In writing this originally as a lecture for a congress in Florence, I was literally paralysed and unable to think. This was rather intriguing considering my very extensive clinical experience of abuse in the family, and specifically with the perpetrators and victims of incest. I knew I had to look at my patients' histories from a different angle to understand the complexities and consequences attached to the witnessing of domestic violence, but I still felt unable to put down my new thoughts and was confused as to what was going on inside myself. In the midst of my anxiety I was struck by two then recent experiences abroad, which for once were not from my clinical work but from my own daily life.

The first involved having brunch with three friends, one of whom was a newly acquired friend, a prestigious feminist writer, famous, smart, chic, rich, whose writings I had always admired. The four of us exchanged views about our lives, and I was stunned as she described in an impassioned tone of voice the bitter, even venomous daily fights she had had twenty years ago with her husband over a very long period, and how this domestic scene had actually prevented her children, now aged 41 and 33, from achieving any committed and loving relationships. This was a shocking revelation in the sense that even after twenty years or so she was till keeping alive those terrible scenarios. Seemingly, the fighting had never reached the physical dimension, but the scenes were still vivid in her memory and she was painfully aware of the emotional damage they had produced in her children.

A few weeks later I went away for a weekend, and I met and had dinner with close friends of mine. It was a couple in their middle age, their teenage daughter, and the wife's aunt. Towards the end of dinner, the husband and wife began to have a dreadful bickering dialogue that seemed to go on forever and was tinted with much bitterness and sarcasm. The reason for their fight seemed irrelevant; actually, it seemed that anything would have served as a justification for this relentless, open, angry tirade. This was nothing new—I had already witnessed their constant and chronic fighting, but this time I felt extremely uneasy and unable to stop them. I became alarmed when the aunt shared with me her concern about this abusive behaviour and its possible future effect on their young daughter.

Suddenly an immense awareness that had previously been buried in my unconscious emerged from within. Of course—how was it that I had never before considered the serious possibility that her parents' constant fighting would affect this young girl's future emotional life? Something became clear. My own resistance to the idea of writing that lecture was closely related to the fact that I myself had been witness to much domestic violence in the form of verbal abuse between my parents when I was a young girl. Obviously conflicts, disagreements, differences of opinion about life easily provoke tension in people who feel and live close together. That is part of ordinary life, and we, as adults, get used to it—so much so that we can remain blissfully unaware of the emotional consequences on our offspring.

At times, family tensions are expressed in angry contests, which can easily escalate into verbal abuse; mocking and derisive remarks are experienced as deeply degrading experiences. Anger and humiliation set in and hungrily and immediately demand violent revenge. Humiliation is unquestionably always the precursor of violence. I shall come back to this theme in more detail later on in this chapter.

Some definitions

When we look at most recent definitions of domestic violence, they all include verbal abuse as one of the sorts of abuse that produces short- and long-term effects in children who are witnessing it. For example, the definition of domestic violence used by the Metropolitan Police Service (MPS) in the UK is: "Any incident of threatening behaviour, violence or abuse (psychological, physical, sexual, financial or emotional) between adults who are, or who have been, intimate partners or family members, regardless of gender."

They report that approximately 95% of domestic violence is committed against a partner, ex-partner, or immediate member of the family—such as father, mother, son, daughter—and the majority of domestic violence incidents reported to the MPS are by male perpetrators on female victims. At the same time, it is refreshing to notice that the MPS recognizes the fact that domestic violence occurs with male victims and female perpetrators and within same-sex relationships. The MPS Domestic Violence Strategy therefore seeks to identify and address the needs of all.

Here is another definition, from Barbara Hart, a Canadian expert: "Many victims suffer all forms of abuse. Verbal and emotional abuse may be subtler than physical harm, but this does not mean that it is less destructive to victims. Many have said that the emotional scars take much longer to heal than the broken bones" (quoted in Deb, 2006, p. 3). Hence, if we include verbal abuse between two partners, we shall have to admit that, far from considering domestic violence as a rarity, we should consider it to be an inevitable happening and part of our emotional development. One could even argue that what we need is to establish the delicate borderline between its necessity as a frequent occurrence and the point when it becomes damaging.

Effects on children

There are several important studies by child psychiatrists dealing with domestic violence and its effects on children, and there is much controversy about this subject. Edleson and Syers (1990) address some methodological problems, including the difficulties of definition—how to differentiate between being a witness to and being a victim of ill-treatment. They give a wide and comprehensive review of the literature, pointing out enormous differences in research findings. They are of the opinion that automatically defining witnessing as maltreatment is a mistake, since a large number of children in the studies showed no negative development problems and some showed evidence of strong coping abilities. Jaffe, Hurley, and Wolfe (1990), for example, show that there are children who suffered few negative symptoms, even showing higher social competence than comparison children.

Because most of the studies have been carried out in shelters or with battered women who (with their children) have been taken away from an abusive male partner, this has led to a tendency to over-reliance on measures of the mother–child relationship and the little data existing on the father–child relationship. Fantuzzo and Lindquist (1989) have also suggested that multiple stressors can be associated with them moving out of their homes and into a shelter. Wolak and Finkelhor (1988), in their important study on children exposed to partner violence, describe the wide implications that this can have for all family members, and they provide a very useful guide for clinicians dealing not only with the children but also with the adult family members.

I shall keep in mind not only clinical evidence from my own work with violent adult patients, but also discussions with colleagues and the sharing of our own biographical backgrounds, which include witnessing domestic violence. I hope to convey that there are many variables; among them, varying degrees of exposure to witnessing violence and different coping strategies with different outcomes. The possibility of the transformation of trauma into a positive feature will also be mentioned.

Humiliation as a precursor of violence

This takes me to James Gilligan's wonderful 1996 book *Violence* and its poignant opening paragraph. He describes vividly and beautifully a series of violent incidents that took place a long time ago in Nebraska. It reads like a parable of family destructiveness and violence, which extends to homicide, violent death, and the disappearance of various family members. He shares this account with us in neither a histrionic nor a sentimentalizing way. Actually he is very lyrical in describing the landscape, the uncertainties, and the tribulations that the family goes through. He then eventually discloses that these incidents are part of his own family life, two generations back. This admittance that violence was part of his own family vernacular took me by surprise, and my first reaction was that it was a very courageous thing to do.

Afterwards, I wondered: why should we think of it as an act of courage? My own memories took me to my family and my childhood experiences of being a witness to my parents' constant squabbling and struggles over the most trivial things. I felt ashamed, as if I could never have had the courage to be open about this part of my life and to talk about those awful experiences. But why the shame—unless I felt responsible, at least in part, for their behaviour?

Gilligan writes:

I have chosen to begin with a story I know—and know deeply—in part, because this family story raises so many of the issues I will be discussing in this book: the themes of family violence; of relations between different nations and races; women and men, young and old; questions about justice and morality, crime and punishment, guilt and innocence, shame and pride, victims and perpetrators, and overshadowing all these themes—the sheer human tragedy that violence always is.

He continues:

For a psychiatrist to begin a book on violence by telling a story of violence from his own family's history is to say, as plainly as I can, that violence, like charity, begins at home. The use of violence as a means of resolving conflict between persons, groups, and nations is a strategy we learn first at home. All of our basic problem-solving, problem-exacerbating, and problem-creating strategies, for living and dying, are learned first at home. . . . Human violence is much more complicated, ambiguous and, most of all, tragic, than is commonly realized or acknowledged. [p. 1]

Shame and remorse

So, things are not that simple. I have found it extremely useful to learn more about the important differentiations between shame and remorse and how they are consistently associated differently in victims and in perpetrators. Shame is usually associated with being a witness to domestic violence, whereas remorse is frequently experienced afterwards by the perpetrators. Shame is focused on the witness's feelings of powerlessness and impotence, and it has a powerful impact, especially on the children involved. Black and Newman (1996) have also recognized that victims experience a sense of shame and humiliation and a wish to keep the abuse a secret from others, reminding us of the feeling of entrapment described by Finkelhor (1983).

Once more I got caught in the vicissitudes and complexities of understanding this concept while watching Britten's opera *The Rape of Lucretia*, based on Livy's *The Early History of Rome*.

Lucretia is awoken by one of her husband's friends, who then, despite her pleas for him to stop, rapes her. She summons her father and her husband. When they arrive, accompanied by two trusted friends, she is overwhelmed by grief. She describes what happened to her and tells them of her devastating sense of guilt. The four men try to console her by turning the guilt away from the victim of the outrage onto the perpetrator, urging that it is the mind that sins, not the body, and where there has been no consent there can be no guilt. However, what Lucretia is really experiencing is not guilt, in the usual sense, but shame, and the only way she can redeem herself in her own eyes is to kill herself.

Shakespeare explored the same theme in his poem *The Rape of Lucrece*. The writers of that period saw rape in terms of lust, although there were also some insights about destroying the object of envy. Nowadays we are much more aware that rape, particularly male-on-female rape, has much more to do with power than with sex. From my own point of view, having written extensively about woman's violence against herself and against her babies (the objects of her own creation), it comes as a gloomy corroboration to read of Lucretia's self-destruction. It shows how a trauma strikes not only at the woman's sexuality but also at her sense of identity, how violence can lead to violence, directed not only outwards but also inwards, towards self-mutilation and death. This is also clearly demonstrated by Shakespeare's Lucrece: "with her nails her flesh doth tear".

Power and domestic violence

All clinicians and researchers agree that domestic violence involves the abuse of power, which is why it is perpetrated most often against women and children. However, what may appear to be acts by the strong against the weak are often carried out as attempts by the abusers to compensate for their "perceived lack or loss of power" (Black & Newman, 1996). For example, the rape of Lucretia was done by Sextus Tarquinius who was full of shame at his wife's unfaithfulness and envious of Collatinus, husband of Lucretia, who was not only beautiful but also virtuous and faithful.

According to Motz (2001), clinicians show reluctance to explore the role of the victim or her participation for fear that it will be seen as blaming her for the abuse: "the relationship between abuser and victim is one in which both play an active part". She states that the abuser tries to create an illusion of omnipotence to compensate for his own feelings of inadequacy and helplessness, which are unconsciously projected onto his victim. The victim then introjects or absorbs his feelings of inadequacy and contempt, becoming increasingly depressed. So, the abuser is totally dependent on his victim's devotion and dependency on him for the boosting and stability of his own self-esteem. The victim represents, unconsciously, other figures from his early history, such as a powerful, dominating, and contemptuous mother. Motz sensitively states that "The abuser projects his blueprint of uncaring and rejecting women onto his partner and is oversensitive to any issues of separation. . . . He will often have had an early experience of witnessing parental violence and have learnt that fathers beat mothers, [and that] concern and emotional involvement are all expressed through violence." Hence, the unconscious role taken by both partners, which frequently goes back to early witnessing of parental violence, facilitates a repeated pattern of being involved in an abusive relationship and makes it very difficult if not impossible, without professional help, to part from one another.

The cycle of violence becomes transgenerational. In discussing the dynamics of partner violence, Kaufman Kantor and Jasinski (1998) mention that many risk-markers in the partners' families of origin are interwoven into the current dynamics and then can be passed on to future generations. These include exposure to abuse, alcoholism, and hostile and/or depressed personality styles in the parents. They also describe an intense shame and humiliation in the victims and a wish to keep this abuse a secret from others—a feeling of being trapped in the system, since there is an unconscious awareness of being part of it.

Some biases and myths

The way that research has been done in this area may reveal more about our own prejudices than the realistic reporting of domestic violence. This may reflect in part our unconscious resistances to accepting painful facts that challenge our stereotypes and prejudices.

First, many questionnaires are designed almost apologetically, asking whether the subjects have ever had any experience of domestic violence, in a way that inhibits them from "disclosing" information. I think there is a need to reverse these ways of thinking, which tend to convey avoidance and resistance, so that we can discover more previously unreported cases. (Statistics make it clear that when domestic violence goes unchecked, it usually increases in frequency and severity.) We may have to design questions relating not to the presence but to the *absence* of domestic violence, since I believe that its absence is far more infrequent that its presence.

Second, it has generally been assumed that domestic violence exists only in the lower working classes, where it is triggered by unemployment and economic problems. However, there are internal factors—such as traumatic bonding and a history in which the woman has been undervalued—that are not linked to economics. Such women may be incapable of asserting themselves and, perhaps even because of their "better" social class, can feel unable to report because of pride, shame, and the fear that the outcome may harm her children. For example, there may be the possibility that the children will be ostracized at school by their peers, and perhaps the threat that they may no longer be able to continue in costly private education. In consequence, the apparent acquiescence of a woman to her male partner's demands, her acceptance of sarcastic remarks, and her constant denigration are reminiscent of the relationship between hostage and torturer. This phenomenon has been accurately and sensitively described from the legal viewpoint by the barrister Helena Kennedy (1992, p. 101) in her book *Eve Was Framed*, where she also asserts that "understanding domestic violence is a challenge to the courts".

The unequal power relationship between abused and abuser leads me to another myth—that it is always women who are the victims and men the perpetrators. Although this may be true in the majority of cases, it is by no means universal. Whereas men are, generally speaking, in charge of public power, women are usually in charge of domestic power. This split affects both individuals and society in general. Women, seen to be the victims, are treated with sedatives. Men, seen as perpetrators, are faced with "penalization" and punishment. In this connection, it was very stimulating to find a study entitled *Partner Violence: A Comprehensive Review of 20 Years of Research*, by Jasinski and Williams (1998), in which they describe the then current research on the dynamics and patterns of family violence, the types of abuse, and the major risk-markers:

> The cycle of violence associated with the battered woman syndrome may be typical only of the more severe form of intimate violence. . . . Aggression by women, though studied less than aggression by men, differs in regard to the greater incidence of physical and psychological injuries experienced by female victims compared with male victims. Women also appear at greater risk for a system of victimization that includes physical, sexual, emotional, and economic forms of abuse. [p. 41]

Female violence

Female violence exists, even if it appears in different forms from that by men. In both men and women, as already described by Gilligan, violence emerges as an outcome of shame and being subjected to humiliation. However, whereas men will usually attack an outside target, women tend to inflict harm onto themselves. This has been further researched and documented in Anna Motz's rich and comprehensive book, *The Psychology of Female Violence* (2001, 2008).

The onset of female violence will often be triggered by circumstances in which early and sometimes "forgotten" events have become re-enacted. The origins of these disturbances may be as far back as birth if, for example, the baby's gender was not welcomed by her family but was a source of disappointment. Obviously, this will seriously affect the relationship between mother and baby girl. On the other hand, if the baby born was a boy whereas a girl was expected, the disappointed mother may start cross-dressing the little boy as a girl, doing this unwittingly and unconsciously, a violent act perpetrated against the child with serious consequences for his future emotional development.

We must keep in mind that women can feel both powerful and powerless when confronted with their children. It is surely not difficult to envisage the scenario: the woman is left every morning by an angry male partner who goes off to work after a bitter argument. She feels humiliated, frustrated, and unable to face the growing demands from her children. She is now overtaken by the need to express those angry feelings towards those who are weaker and unable to defend themselves. So she takes it out on her children. This common scenario is usually unrecognized or ignored, and this makes it extremely difficult for the mother to obtain any professional help.

We need more resources devoted to providing appropriately for mothers and babies in order to prevent the abuses of domestic power that cause pain, suffering, and distress, both to the mothers and their babies and to society in general in the long term.

The family as a system: why is a child born?

We can no longer think of family members in isolated terms but as part of a system, a family system of many generations, responsible for its own dynamics and its own malfunctioning. It may be that mother and father have unconsciously met and got together through some sort of radar. They may, for example, have a shared experience of a family background in which domestic violence was the norm. Other families may act out because of some hidden circumstances that need understanding if we are ever to break the cycle of violence.

For example, it may never have occurred to clinicians to ask parents for their reasons for having that particular child. It tends to be rather casually assumed that all couples want to have more children, but there may in fact be all sorts of unrealistic and outlandish motives surrounding a baby's birth. The baby may, for example, be conceived as the future "marital therapist", expected to resuscitate a "dead" relationship or to erase conflict in the marital partnership. He or she may even be there to express revenge—especially by a woman who feels undermined by an arrogant and scornful male partner.

Of course, more often than not these expectations are not fulfilled. After an initial period of novelty and excitement about the new arrival, the couple first experience disillusionment and then in no time the child often becomes the target for their anger and frustration. After all, the "miracle" solution has not worked, and who is to blame for it? Whose failure is it?

Recriminations come to the fore, and whereas the child may appear to be a gratuitous bystander of the ensuing domestic violence, he is actually very much part of the dysfunctional system if understood from its unconscious roots. At times, the children unconsciously try to respond in a complementary way to parents' expectations, and they start a pattern of parenting their own parents. They may want consciously to save their parents' relationships and attempt to obtain help, which is not always available or taken seriously. This would leave an enormous sense of utter helplessness, which will come to the fore when facing similar situations, and violence will irrupt. At other times, they may unconsciously try to destroy the couple, in a rather oedipal fashion taking away one partner and almost "offering" themselves as sexual partners. This has devastating consequences, since these children can easily fall into becoming incest victims, with the added problems of unhealthy excitement, shame, and guilt. We have all been recipients of this variety of experiences. For example, while watching violent films we "witness violence" in different ways that may evoke different responses. We may become active and do something about the images on screen that are affecting us, such as covering our eyes or even leaving the cinema. However, at other times we react in very excited ways, identifying with different protagonists.

It may be useful not to see these children simply as passive victims; rather, we need to look at their unknown, unseen, and unconscious contribution to their own problems. In order to understand fully the future of the child who witnesses domestic violence, we must look at the roots of the problem, at the ways in which the family system was ready to create a matrix for the perpetuation of future family violence.

Precipitating factors in domestic violence

Apart from the sociological factors—employment, poverty, and so on—there are other factors that profoundly affect the family dynamics and are prone to produce violence. An analysis of life-course risk-markers found that rates of intimate violence are increased during courtship and early marriage, pregnancy, separation, and divorce (Jasinski & Williams, 1998). It is interesting to note that bereavement is not mentioned, when we know that it is another unexpected or unexplored area of life-altering events which may threaten the so far "good-enough holding environment". The unexpected death of a daughter or son has a profound effect in the lives of grieving parents, and the sense of violence and violation inherent in the experience of the child's death may alienate the most solid family dynamics. Parents surrender to a sense of impotence and emotional pain that either paralyses them or produces silence, mutual recriminations, shaming, and isolation, all despite their conscious efforts to behave in a "civilized" way.

At such times of transition, there is an increase in vulnerability and frequently a sense of being out of control, which can induce feelings of uselessness, impotence, and humiliation.

The consequences of being a witness to domestic violence

The consequences of being a witness to domestic violence may be short term and temporary, or there may be much longer term effects. Witnesses to violence may, either at the time or later in life, suffer intrusive memories and flashbacks, separation anxiety, aggressiveness and hyperactivity, emotional detachment, and other problems as well. Witnessing violence as a child is also a risk factor for becoming a child abuser; these "co-victim" exposures to violence are directly related to the acceptance and use of violence.

According to Wolak and Finkelhor (1988), children who are exposed to marital violence experience both direct and indirect influence. From the former effects, the authors include suffering from aggression, cruelty to animals, tantrums, acting-out, immaturity, truancy, delinquency, and attention deficit disorder. They also anticipate that children grow up fundamentally confused about the meanings of love, violence, and intimacy. The indirect effects include maternal stress, in that victimized mothers are unable to respond adequately to their children's concerns and fears.

From my clinical findings, I have become aware that some witnesses to domestic violence may eventually be drawn to act out sadomasochistic patterns. This was the case with a patient I saw many years ago, who used to involve himself in serious masochistic acts. This man exposed himself to much self-inflicted bodily suffering, concentrating on his genitals as the preferential area for the pain. He began to be aware of an added sense of excitement if this humiliation, a sort of symbolic castration, was performed in public. He became a member of an S&M club with the aim of entering weekly contests and, in this way, entertaining a captive and captivated audience.

I considered this man to be at high risk of further self-destructive actions, but as soon as he became aware of my concern, he strongly denied any suffering. This patient came to see me two or three times, and he eventually decided not to continue with his sessions. In a rather petulant manner, he told me that since he had got to know many of the people in this milieu, he had come to realize that this behaviour was just an "alternative" normal practice. By now he had access not only to clubs but also to the private homes of "professionals like you" where these acts of sexual sadism in groups and the continual change of partners were the usual practice. He also claimed that he was experiencing a great sense of elation and internal freedom for the first time in his life.

His early history was characterized by being a "watcher" of his parents' constant bickering and fighting, from which he had been incapable of defending himself. He was unable to look at the connection between the unbearable pain of the past and his present predicament. Instead, he had created for himself a belief in his own freedom by virtue of being an "active" participant in the inflicted pain. It was more manageable for him to go on repeating these experiences, over which he had a degree of control, than to go through the process of psychotherapy into an unknown picture of the extreme emotional suffering in his own life. The need to be watched or witnessed by others—the accompanying voyeuristic and exhibitionistic features—is often present in people who have themselves, as children, been witnesses of domestic violence. They become, now, the leading actors in an open arena, displaying their emotional pain in a systematic and organized way, and in a manic fashion.

On the possibility of the transformation of trauma

I would like to end with an optimistic touch. We know of the cycle of violence and the serious possibility that those affected will continue a similar pattern in their own lives, often becoming perpetrators. But, of course, there are unknown factors, such as resilience and coping strategies, that are variable in each case. So, not all of us who have been witnesses to domestic violence have become perpetrators. In fact, those experiences may have been specifically responsible for triggering off stimuli to act in other directions, such as trying to comprehend the mechanics of violence. This has obviously been the case with James Gilligan, whose professional life is devoted to the understanding of violence, perhaps in an attempt to understand his own ancestors. For myself, I have consciously or unconsciously done some distancing from my own witnessing experiences and have tried instead to understand other, more severe aspects of violence such as physical and sexual abuse in families and what makes a perpetrator become one.

It is obvious that for clinicians the choice of such a difficult profession as forensic psychotherapy reveals the presence of previous challenges in their personal lives. For example, I have often noticed rescue fantasies and wishes for reparation in people who embark on this sort of work. It is then that I ask myself, "Have they all experienced some kind of emotional trauma that consciously or unconsciously they feel the need to metabolize?" How many of us, who are driven into this profession, have experienced not only severe traumatic losses, but also a great sense of helplessness and impotence in dealing with family disturbances, which have created a desire for reparation? I mean by this a need to achieve an internal sense of justice for whatever was felt as an inflicted pain, from the inside or outside, over which we had no control.

In this particular field, where awareness of unconscious processes is crucial, we must be humble enough to acknowledge the importance of external factors and not just internal ones. At times we felt, just as our patients do almost all the time, too wounded to adjust to a "normative" development or too angry to compromise and to settle down into what would have been considered a safer or more amenable profession. I have also wondered whether these "safer" professions would have left us frustrated and irritated; we might have found them "futile" and "trivial". It may be our need to feel on the edge that makes it possible for us to believe that our lives are worthwhile.

This might sound like a rather pretentious assertion, but discussing this personal subject with friends, colleagues, and students has given me some evidence that this is a shared truth. It is also quite probable that we, as opposed to our patients, may have had some early "good-enough" experiences to "allow" us to make such a choice from within. So we organize ourselves to work in an environment considered by most to be risky and in which we can be exposed to sudden violent outbursts. Are our patients able to sense our own vulnerabilities and propensities for violence? At times, we are fortunate enough to make use of our own violent impulses in a creative way, and that is how we can communicate with our patients.

In contrast, forensic patients are driven by a lack of choices because of traumas that have been too numerous or too brutal, coupled with recurrent adverse circumstances, unmanageable emotional deprivation and neglect, and too little care. They feel "pushed" into a life of revenge and hate to create a sense of justice for themselves. In so doing, self-destructiveness is at the forefront of their identity, perpetuating the lack of care that was present early in their lives. This obvious feature is frequently overlooked, misunderstood, and even ignored, not only by those around them but also by themselves.

For example, trauma and violence are often associated with negative qualities thought to be destructive, but I believe there are also positive elements in both of them. Traumas can generate an enormous amount of creative energy, which could have remained forever underground if unchallenged. Also, learning how trauma and violence survive can facilitate opportunities for psychological growth at times of adversity. Outbursts of violence could also be seen as attempts to break new ground, opening up new possibilities. So both trauma and violence have the potential for destructiveness, but equally for emotional growth. The experience of self-recovery achieved in dealing successfully with helplessness and life threats may trigger a sense of mastery, the capacity to establish safety and containment. Our lives are enriched through the integration of traumas—when we have effectively survived serious threats to our identity and have come out whole and not in fragments, as previously feared.

An interview with Estela V. Welldon, July 1999

BRETT KAHR: *Estela, we've spent a great deal of time already talking about the development of your work as a consultant at the Portman Clinic, and now I'd like to focus on how you had a special responsibility for taking the work of the Portman Clinic out into the wider community. Can you tell me when you first began to establish links with other forensically like-minded people in the UK and also on the Continent? Who were the first people outside of the Portman who had an interest in working psychoanalytically with perverse and delinquent patients?*

ESTELA V. WELLDON: I remember very well going to a conference in 1980 in Oxford, sponsored by both Law and Psychiatry and Mind. I felt rather battered in this meeting because of the way other psychiatrists were being treated by those from America, who had a lawyer to accompany the patient to hospital in the fear that there'd be electric shock or some other therapy then believed to be extremely dangerous—and so the lawyer was the most important person. I felt really quite enraged by this, and I was able to pick out three or four psychoanalytically inclined people at the conference and invited them to liaise with one another in relation to some future meetings we could have regarding problems with forensic patients. They were delighted at the idea, and from then on annually we had what was called the European Symposium, held at the Portman, although attendance was limited to colleagues from the Continent and senior staff from the Portman (see chapter 10). At the beginning, it was extremely gratifying to be able to talk in dynamic terms about our difficulties with patients, most of whom were very complex to deal with and presented

98

many challenges that were not successfully met as often as we'd have wanted. When I became clinic tutor, I began doing ward rounds and taking students, and I found it very frustrating that these new students were not allowed to attend the meetings. I tried to break that mould. Many of these students are now well-established clinicians, having achieved academic distinctions and become professors in forensic psychiatry around the country. I tried to widen the circle and invite them in but got the response that the symposium was not for people from the "outside".

We had had very successful meetings for about ten years, and simultaneously I was going to the annual meetings of Law and Psychiatry in Canada, directed by David Weisstub. At these meetings we weren't facilitated or offered much time to do presentations about forensic psychotherapy or dynamic psychotherapy. So eventually I got very frustrated about both the European Symposium and these other meetings. Some of us were overlapping—those from the Continent were also going to Canada. At one point I was invited to a meeting in Montreal, as one expert among twenty or thirty, to address issues to do with forensic work. I felt very flattered, since not only had they invited me but they had also asked me choose a colleague to represent the field of forensic psychotherapy. Although there were extremely good clinicians I could have chosen from the Portman, I felt that someone like Murray Cox, working at Broadmoor—who should have been part of the European Symposium from its inception but couldn't because he didn't work at the Portman—would be ideal, and he came with me. It was extraordinary, because as soon as he met all the European colleagues they fell in love with him and he became the most popular member. I, of course, left centre-stage then, because he took the limelight! It was very nice, though.

Q: *So you had another colleague from the UK. Murray Cox is a very important figure in the development of forensic psychotherapy in the UK, alongside you. How did you and Murray Cox first come to know each other?*

A: A long way back—I think 1970—I remember going to Broadmoor as a visitor. He'd been working there for two or three years. We had a meeting, with lot of patients coming and going, acknowledging Murray and greeting him. We'd already met at a conference in Copenhagen where he was chairing one of my presentations about sex offenders. We always had a good, cordial working relationship. It was fortunate that he also used to go to the Law and Psychiatry meetings, and in the meeting in 1991 at Leuven in Belgium we felt very frustrated at being given so little time to present any papers there. At that point, since we now had many people representing the new discipline, we felt we needed an association of our own. Interestingly enough, when we got together—that is, people who are now key professionals in forensic psychotherapy here, like Chris Cordess, Gwen Adshead, Cleo van Velsen; Rob Ferris, Murray Cox, as well as others from the Continent—the people from Law and Psychiatry said they didn't want us to be a separate body, promising us all sorts of goodies to be part of their organization. But by then we were all serious about wanting our own organization. Some, like Frank Beyaert, a professor from Utrecht, a very good man who'd helped us all along, was not keen on our separating, so there were some problems, but we believed that on the whole it was better to start our own association (the IAFP). Of course, we'd already started the course in Forensic Psychotherapy the year before at the Portman Clinic in association with the British Postgraduate Medical Federation (BPMF).

Q: *So you really tried to carve out a separate identity for forensic psychotherapy, which would be distinct from the Law and Psychiatry colleagues. Was the term "forensic psychotherapy" your own creation?*

A: Well, in a way it was extraordinary. I remember my old colleagues—including Pat Gallwey, from whom I had a lot to learn in forensic matters—used to laugh and say it was impossible to make someone in the forensic world, where the work is hard and callous, believe in the use of such a treatment as psychotherapy. But, as I have said before and will say again, I'm very grateful to Professor Sir Michael Peckham (see chapter 10), who was the first person to listen to my idea and was surprised that this kind of thing hadn't been set up before. To him it made perfect sense.

Q: *And how did you first come to meet him?—because he played a very important part in getting the course established.*

A: He was Director of the BPMF. I'd just become the clinic tutor at the Portman, and he wrote a memo to all the clinic tutors, inviting them to submit any ideas. I took it very seriously; I didn't realize it was just a routine letter, so I waited three months to have an interview with him. Eventually when I told him my ideas about bridging the gap between forensic work and psychoanalytic psychotherapy, he was only too delighted! He said something about just listening to complaints all the time and was amazed when someone came up with a new idea, something to pursue.

Q: *Fantastic. And what do you think gave him the receptivity, because I imagine that, as an oncologist, he might have been quite resistant to psychological ideas?*

A: Not at all. The opposite. He knew how to mix things, how to combine arts and sciences, so it made a lot of sense to him. It was very lucky that he was the Director and an oncologist and not a psychiatrist.

Q: *That's fascinating. So these seminars that you'd been running for multidisciplinary professionals at the Portman Clinic then grew into the Diploma Course in Forensic Psychotherapy . . .*

A: That's right. And when the BPMF was dissolved, the course was taken over by UCL. This was very much the outcome of sterling work by Wendy Riley, then Head of the Education Department at the BPMF, who later moved to UCL and through her very efficient negotiations enabled the course to be placed in the curriculum there.

Q: *Tell me about the early days. The first intake for the forensic psychotherapy diploma was 1990. Tell me how that first year went. What kind of students did you have on the course?*

A: Funnily enough, the students have continued to come from the same core professions, more or less. They are people who are aware of their need for more understanding and knowledge of psychodynamic processes, in relation not only to their patients but also to their institutions. They feel they should know more and more in order to feel better. There's a tremendous feeling of inadequacy, that they have incredibly difficult jobs they don't know how to handle, and it's this awareness of not knowing that's very important. It's an incipient degree of insight that brings them to us. One of the strengths of this course is the multi-professional aspect that puts people together, and they start respecting one another and knowing what the others are doing, which is very important.

Q: *And you used your knowledge as a group practitioner to bring very disparate multidisciplinary professionals together on the same level?*

A: That's right. In a way the more heterogeneous, the better it becomes. If you remember, we had the Cleveland child-abuse case in 1987, which Elizabeth Butler-Sloss chaired the inquiry into, and the report resulted in a change to the DHSS *Working Together* guidelines. So I was able to talk about that to Professor Peckham to let him know how important it would be for disparate professionals to work together in a harmonious way. Most of my students over the last nine years have been able to establish professional links with one another from the same year and from different "vintages", too, through the Annual Alumni day, a network that operates to the benefit of forensic patients throughout the country. Many of these professionals are members of the IAFP and get together at international meetings, and every year the numbers grow and it's very rewarding to see them cooperating with one another.

Q: *Can you tell us about the nature of the training? I know it consists of a number of different components, teaching in large groups, supervision, but I think it would be very useful for colleagues around the world to know what you regard as the essential components of training in forensic psychotherapy.*

A: Well, first of all, the course now has the much more accurate title of the Diploma in Forensic Psychotherapeutic Studies, which doesn't give the impression that it's formal forensic psychotherapy training, although we might start this in the future. The course is to give a flavour of the psychodynamic factors underlying the problems of those who commit antisocial actions and of the difficulties and complexities of working with this patient population and the forensic settings available to them. (I give a detailed account of the course and the founding of the IAFP in chapter 10.)

The whole country is moving more and more towards forensic psychotherapy, so much so that it's now become a specialty for the Royal College of Psychiatrists, and seven new Specialist Registrar jobs have been created in forensic psychotherapy across the country. This is an extremely interesting and important movement, with more beds in hospitals and units and more and more jobs.

Q: *How did forensic psychotherapy come to be taken up officially by the Royal College of Psychiatrists?*

A: Well, it was a lot to do with our own efforts to get a Senior Registrar with dual accreditation in forensic psychotherapy and psychiatry, and the invaluable help of Dame Fiona Caldicott, who at the time was the President of the Royal College of Psychiatrists. The first person to have this dual accreditation was Carine Minne, who's now a fully-fledged consultant at both Broadmoor and the Portman Clinic. She was also a student on the diploma course. The first person to be appointed as a consultant in forensic psychotherapy was Gill McGauley, who holds appointments at St George's and Broadmoor. It's a very interesting movement, which I believe will become more and more sophisticated as time goes on. I believe very strongly that it can't just focus on doctors but has to extend to other professions also. Forensic psychotherapy is not the heroic work of a loner, but is very much teamwork.

Q: *What are your hopes for the future of forensic psychotherapy? Do you think we should have more training for forensic psychotherapists, or is this something that can only be practiced by a very tiny number of very highly trained people who come from a forensic psychiatric background?*

A: No, there are so many professions involved—art therapists, drama therapists, music therapists, nurses, psychologists, managers, probation officers. I feel this is the only answer to some of the tremendous problems we now have. We don't think we can cure all the problems, but helping a few people will be worthwhile.

Q: *In 1997 you received a great personal recognition, in that Oxford Brookes University awarded you an Honorary Doctor of Science degree for your contributions to forensic psychotherapy. How do you understand the awarding of that in terms of both the development and the recognition of the field?*

A: A landmark. Exactly that. I feel that in a way it was the recognition of what has already happened in this country, which is *the widening and acknowledgement of forensic psychotherapy.*

Q: *Do you think that people in the UK on the whole are becoming more compassionate and tolerant towards people who are criminals, seeing them more as mad than bad, or is there still a strong wish to punish rather than to treat?*

A: The normal response is for people to seek revenge against those who act against society, which is a very usual, normal response. The only problem, if you're a professional, is that you have to be far more sophisticated and far more precise and responsible in your response, in order to help people who believe the only hope they have is to create an antisocial solution to the neglect and abandonment they've experienced at their parents' hands.

Q: *In 1996 you delivered the annual Foulkes lecture to the Group Analytic Society and the Institute of Group Analysis, and you chose as your subject the question of punishment versus treatment. Do you feel the idea of treatment is gradually beginning to take root and gradually beginning to replace punishment as a more sophisticated response to the dangerous patient?*

A: Well, I hope so.

Q: *Or are we still caught in the grips of punishment?*

A: I think party politics are very important in this, too—when you consider that most people would vote for capital punishment, but that most left-wing people would vote against this. So we have a system that is polarized by political parties, and sometimes they overlap and sometimes there are clashes. But there are now people who can see ill society not just ill individuals. Mrs Thatcher believed there was no such thing as society, so therefore was reluctant to own up to any social problems, whereas now there is much more scope for that.

Q: *What are your hopes, dreams, visions for the development of forensic psychotherapy in the future? You have the international society, there is a training programme in England, and I don't know how many comparable training programmes there are in other European countries. What would be* *your personal wish list for the development of forensic psychotherapy as an international clinical profession?*

A: There are so many ideas floating in our minds that we need to discuss. There's still around 150 people in the IAFP, and for the first time we're going outside Europe to Boston for our meeting. The whole conceptualization of post-traumatic stress has a lot to do with wars and conflicts in different countries right now, keeping in mind countries that have had civil wars like, for example, Yugoslavia or Ireland.

I believe we shouldn't be arrogant about this movement—I was very pleasantly surprised to be invited this year to the third National Conference on Forensic Psychiatry in Sardinia. The delegates were all high achievers, professors in forensic psychiatry from Bologna, Rome, and many of the most important universities. I was most impressed by their way of working with extremely sophisticated psychoanalytic ideas—for example, in their understanding of hostages and kidnapping, using Kleinian conceptualizations about identification with the victims and talking about the envy of captors towards their victims. I thought "Oh my god! This is forensic psychotherapy—they don't use the name, but they use the working." They want to become part of a much wider circle but they speak only Italian.

I would like the awareness of, let's say, domestic violence to improve. We're all aware of it, but we have to be much more open about needing to understand the men who are being violent and not just the women and children as victims. I know that I had to be careful in talking about women being violent, even in the context of violence towards their own bodies or their children, because it produced political outrage. People who commit acts of violence are really extremely vulnerable men and women, and domestic violence is being taken much more seriously everywhere. In both Italy and Spain, rape within marriage is now considered a criminal offence. I feel we have to be able to understand the roles of victims and perpetrators much more, to see how we can effectively break the terrible continuum. We can become victimizers or victims too.

We have to be much better prepared to deal with all eventualities. I feel it's hypocritical to be up in arms when, say, it's discovered that people in charge of a children's home have been abusing children, while in the meantime they haven't been given any help, support, supervision, or monitoring. People doing very difficult jobs with very little pay are expected to produce wonders that not even parents are supposed to do, and these people come to the task with an enormous number of vicarious problems and unresolved needs. I really feel that we're all partners in society, and we have to take part of the responsibility and own up to these terrible predicaments. We have to be much more responsible, rather than critical and judgemental.

Q: *Estela, one of the features that characterizes your work has been, I think, tremendous bravery. You chose a field that, at its inception, was not a popular one, namely working with people that others wanted castrated, killed, or locked away for life. You showed great compassion for offender patients, but you also created a new modality for treating offender patients by pioneering group work in addition to individual work, and you also took on the whole problem of female perversions and female delinquency, whereas previously perversion had been seen as an exclusively male prerogative. So you've been a very great pioneer and you've worked in some very provocative areas. Tell me, because the work is hard and costly in terms of resources for the psychotherapist, what is your advice to young practitioners taking their first steps in the field about how forensic psychotherapeutic work fits in with one's own life? I know you have a particular viewpoint and philosophy on how to live a full life and how that is important for the work.*

A: Well, I believe that when we are confronted with crimes of violence—on a domestic, national, or international scale—that appear superficially to be senseless, we appeal to old clichés like "This is irrational, utterly mad, how does it happen?" This reflects our wanting to remain ignorant, and intellectually lazy—we don't really want to understand what's really going on—whereas I think the *understanding is extremely important*. And I don't mean condoning or sanctioning, I mean really understanding. It seems to me that understanding will only come when we start seeing in each person three generations of history, so we have a three-generational dimension of the patient. You have to be compassionate because you see the mother and the grandmother as well as the patient. I also think it's very important to look at society in terms of groups of poor and rich people; the greater the gap in between, the more violence is produced. I also believe that sometimes the so-called sophisticated classes could be those who are less understood because they're not supposed to have problems. Sometimes people aren't offered professional help because the providers don't think they have these kinds of problems; the "patients" don't want it either, for fear of stigmatizing themselves. I think we have to look beyond social classes, beyond the individual, and have a much more comprehensive look at family history. Some families have been involved with social services for many generations. We have to be

aware not only of psychological problems but also of societal problems, which interfere and create a rich source of injustice.

Q: *And what impact does this work have on the private life of the psychotherapist?*

A: I think we work very hard, so *I think it's very important to play hard*
and to enjoy life. This may appear as a duality of purposes but actually both work and pleasure are, or should be, in complete agreement
and deeply interrelated. Of course, at times we feel on edge: there is
so much and of such intensity that we are close to what could at times
become overwhelming. Knowledge of oneself is invaluable, as well
as are rewarding friendships in and out of the profession. You see,
I believe in life there are things such as vocation and passion, and
certainly in working with these patients we are certainly in touch at
least with the latter in whichever way passion has manifested itself. (I
know these are concepts English people don't feel too easy to explore,
but that doesn't mean they don't believe in them). Forensic psychiatrists do go to the opera and to concerts, and it's a very good way to
relax. I do notice a difference in the Royal College faculty meetings:
in the residential meeting of the psychotherapy faculty, people go to
bed early and usually won't indulge in excesses, whereas at forensic
faculty meetings people stay up till the small hours of the morning,
talking, drinking, and using the meetings to discuss, share, air difficult
predicaments they deal with daily and at times without much support
from their own settings. I don't know how they manage! Obviously
there are a lot of very difficult situations they have to cope with every
day and they have to use a lot of escape mechanisms, but one has to
respect them too.

Q: *What's your final advice for young psychotherapists entering the forensic
field? What wisdom would you like to impart to them?*

A: To be very open about feelings of inadequacy and uncertainty (we
all have them), a creeping sense of fear of failure, but not to yield to a
sense of defeat. It's often when you are near to giving it all up that a
change in the most difficult patient is on its way. I feel that most people who go into this work feel rather impatient as well as somewhat
omnipotent in the production of positive changes. After all, we enter
the field because of a wild and ambitious project—we want people
who have gone through much deprivation, neglect, and even abuse of
all sorts to be able to maximize their own abilities, to obtain a degree
of contentment as opposed to frustration and revenge, to abandon
violence for achievements that will result in better self-esteem and as a
whole to contribute to our patients' sense of well-being. So, as you can

see, this is an enormously ambitious project, especially in this patient population. I would say young colleagues should acknowledge their limits, lower their sights, and engage themselves with colleagues they can talk to, and then get out and switch off in the evening and get on with "the other part of life" that is ourselves. It seems to me this is the only way to deal with this situation. I know some of us go on looking for other rewards in family life, in the arts, in television, or in films, and others try to escape completely. I think opera's good!!

Q: *Thank you very much indeed, Estela. It's been a great privilege talking to you.*

CHAPTER SEVEN

The unique contribution of
group analytic psychotherapy
for victims and perpetrators of incest

Family dynamics, secrecy, acknowledgement, and disclosure

The importance of family dynamics in incest can hardly be over-stressed, but somehow this has not always been acknowledged, since it was overshadowed by a marked adherence to the seduction theory, with its emphasis on unconscious fantasies. McCarthy (1982) clearly and courageously stated: "I think it is a criticism of the contribution of Psychoanalysis to Psychiatry and allied professions that locating the theme of incest in the world of unconscious fantasy deflected attention away from the reality of incest and delayed the discovery of sexual abuse within the family."

The evolution of an incest situation goes through many stages. Typically it begins with a masked breakdown of the family structure, which perhaps is not consciously felt by any of its members. There may be, or may appear to be, some specific events that, when they come to light later on, are identified as "causes" of incest.

Incest operates on a number of different levels simultaneously in different family members, including a discharge of tension between both partners, as well as a degree of satisfaction and sexual gratification where the child is easily available and can be seduced, always in a secretive manner. There is also in the case of father–daughter or father–stepdaughter incest a discharge of intense hostility and revenge directed towards the female partner, in the person of her child. Incest provides, through some sort of emotional and physical "scaffolding", a re-establishment of some balance in the family dynamics. Later on, when disclosure makes its appearance, it heralds its ending, since incest is no longer necessary to the family dynamics (Welldon, 1988).

It is very important to notice the family circumstances when the facts are disclosed. Is the wife over her depression, or her mourning period? Is she able to be "present" now? Has she resumed sexual inter-course with her husband? Or has another daughter become aware that her sister is the "favourite one", and so she feels undermined? Is this the moment at which a sibling suffering from intense jealousy towards the incest victim denounces father and sister? In fact, the study of the timing of the "disclosure time" and its effects on all family members could act as an accurate indicator of the many layers and their contents that have been hidden away for a long time. This timing and its effects could also serve as criteria for prognosis and treatment.

The importance of these dynamics have not always been recognized. Professional workers, especially in the past, have often made incredu-lous or sceptical remarks about a mother's denial of any knowledge that paternal incest had occurred. Such attitudes are not conducive to accurate diagnosis of the family dynamics. The mother in these cases cannot acknowledge the incest, because temporarily she is emotionally and/or physically unable to respond to the demands placed on her as a mother, caretaker, wife, and partner. She is too depressed, detached, or exhausted to accept and fulfil her "duties". She can no longer cope. Bitter comments are made about mothers who knew but didn't know. Some disbelieve their daughters; others ill-treat them when confronted with the reality. At other times, when the mother is on the threshold between not knowing and knowing (something like a twilight zone), she is able to hear and acknowledge what is going on, and then she may call upon outside help, from GPs, social services, the law, the police. But there must be many cases that remain secret.

I have heard from many male patients who have committed incest how much they have felt rejected by their wives and have also been made to feel small, humiliated, and inadequate just as they did when they were young children with a very possessive, domineering, or neglectful mother. A period of impotence towards their wife can be a clinical indication that incest is about to begin. In quite a number of cases, this relates to the wife's new pregnancy and labour, or depres-sion. The patient usually talks about his wife's coolness, distancing, and frigidity, and he describes her as not wanting to have sex with him. He feels unable to pursue any extramarital affairs; indeed, he claims he has never dreamt of being unfaithful to his wife. He even talks about incest as "keeping sex in the family" (to him, this seems to be less of a betrayal of his wife than going outside the family), and there is no cynicism attached to this statement. The "solution" in these cases, especially for a couple in which there is some emotional deprivation and lack of communication, seems to be the seduction of a child.

Secrecy

Sometimes the "secret" of incest has been hidden away for years. When patients involved in incest situations are very cautious in making critical remarks about their parents or early life history ("everything was just normal, absolutely fine"), their statements should not necessarily be taken as true. If we listen carefully for what has been omitted, incidents usually emerge that point to an early traumatic event or events that occurred when they were small. In other cases, when there is an apparent lack of memory about early childhood events in people who have committed or been involved in sexual offences, it may be fruitful to investigate further to see whether they have blocked off episodes from early childhood that are too painful to recall. This could be particularly relevant for the incest victim's mother, who not infrequently turns out to have been an incest victim herself.

I repeat that secrecy, especially in paternal incest, is at the core of the situation: each member of the family is involved, whether "know-

---

Secrecy

Secrecy is pervasive and may be disguised as confidentiality, threatening the therapeutic process in individual psychotherapy, re-enacting a symbolic incest, and recreating an ineffectual locked-in stalemate position between two people.

Why is secrecy so important ?
Because it is deeply ingrained and gives rise to—

- Threatening behaviour

- Violence

- Inability to think

- Lack of trust

- Trespassing of the generational differences (stolen childhood)

- The victim feeling both abused and favoured

ing" or "unknowing", but nobody talks about it. Indeed, it is irrelevant when paternal incest has occurred whether mother acknowledges the possibility of incest or not: had she been able to acknowledge it in the first place, incest would never have happened. Incest is committed in an effort to create ties to "keep the family together". Secrecy is the new taboo that has emerged from the breakdown of the taboo against incest (Ciba Foundation, 1984, p. 13). Nobody "knows" about it, or, rather, nobody acknowledges it.

Long-term consequences of father–daughter incest

Sometimes the daughter unconsciously colludes in the incest, not only because of her father's demands but also because she is responding to her mother's inability to cope. That is why most girls report their fathers' sexual assaults on them only when the father takes another daughter for this "duty". The first girl then feels debased and betrayed, not so much because her position as her father's favourite is being usurped but because she is no longer the one chosen to fulfil this "duty" for her mother. Before the incest, she felt her mother did not understand her, and she longed to get closer to her. Sometimes, she has even become her own mother's mother in an effort to create some sense of intimacy with her. So incest, if this is required, seems inevitable.

Incest gives much and then takes everything away, all at once. The little girl is now supposed to have all that she could have dreamt of in her wildest unconscious fantasies, including her father as her lover. And what does this situation bring for her? She shares a secret with Daddy that nobody knows about. Her dreams have become true. Now she has Daddy's love, penis, the lot. And she is left in utter misery, with a complete lack of trust in anyone. Those who were supposed to look after her, and to keep firm boundaries between her worlds of fantasy and reality, have failed her, and all is now confusion. She has an enormous sense of loneliness. Such girls have difficulties in acknowledging any angry feelings because these feelings are extremely intense. They feel angry with their mother, whom they see as having failed to protect them, and angry with their father because he has abused them. As a patient of mine said: "I hate women and distrust men." They have been left with deep scars that will have a marked impact not only on their emotional lives, but also on all their physical relationships since they often feel that the only way to gain love is through sexualization.

I believe that girls who have been victims of incest see very few alternatives to prostitution upon reaching adulthood. In any event, their bodies will respond in a massive way, either with an exaggeration of the libido or with completely repressed sexuality. Their severe problems range from prostitution to chronic psychosomatic symptoms. In my work over thirty years I have observed acute psychopathology, but I have not encountered more positive outcomes such as the absence of sexual or emotional conflicts arising in adulthood in incest survivors.

The two damaging effects—promiscuity and sexual coldness—might seem to be complete opposites, but there are strong connections: I have often encountered women who are promiscuous, or have been involved in promiscuity, whose problems are related to sexual coldness. More often than not, promiscuity is accompanied by frigidity and prostitution by sexual coldness, which leads to promiscuous behaviour and perverse sexual fantasies.

Let us start with the "prostitution solution". The disparity in statistics reveals a confused picture, but one that corresponds to the nature of the problem—the secrecy surrounding incest. In the dynamic process of incest, girls have learnt how to keep to themselves important and intimate secrets. This knowledge is turned into primitive defence mechanisms such as splitting and denial. Their "knowing it all" and their tendency to self-sacrifice, flamboyancy, and self-destructiveness could be bitterly exploited in adulthood for the "excellence" of this "new trade". It is well known that most incest survivors "may attract later on in life sexually aggressive and demanding partners" (Ciba Foundation, 1984, p. 16). Are those early acquired "skills" determining their fate? This "solution" will be exemplified when referring later on to Fiona and her own incestuous activities involving her daughter.

At other times, they develop severe chronic psychosomatic pathology, which renders medical practitioners unable to make proper diagnostic recommendations and to effect proper treatment. Such was the case with Patricia, who for seventeen years had experienced much somatic pain for which she sought radical treatment. She was fortunate enough that her GP did not collude with her wish to damage her body even further with inadequate "treatments". Eventually the mystery was solved when after fifteen years she found the courage to tell him of her being the victim of paternal incest from the age of 11. She had tried successfully to erase this from her mind, but she had not succeeded to do the same with her body.

It has been recognized for some years that abuse is an intergenerational problem and that most abusers have been damaged in childhood by abusive action perpetrated on them, most usually by their parents but sometimes by other significant adults. At times, in becoming adults, the early emotional damage could manifest into psychopathological features, including perversions or paraphilias and perpetration of abuse against children.

Patients suffering from perversions present great difficulties for psychiatrists. One of the difficulties is based on these patients' inability to intersperse a thought process before they commit the perverse action. Treatment has often been considered at best unrewarding, at worst impossible. Treatment programmes for abusers are rarely available within the NHS. Many sufferers encounter forensic psychiatrists in the course of brushes with the law, and many spend much of their lives in prison. When such patients present a dangerous threat to the community, custodial care may be the only realistic option. However, punishment and incarceration are unlikely to have any effect upon the perversion.

One of the aims of forensic psychotherapy is to enable both victims and perpetrators of abuse to more fully understand the antecedents of their behaviour and to take responsibility for their actions. Without so doing, there is no possibility of change and healthy maturation, nor is there any possibility of remorse and reparation. According to Yakeley (2010), the cycle of victim–perpetrator "can only be halted with the recognition that within each group and individual reside both victim and perpetrator, which is of course a central tenet of the psychoanalytic understanding of violence and perversion".

In recent years, recognition of incest and sexual abuse has led to the development of services for survivors (Ashurst & Hall, 1989) and to the acknowledgement that such traumas are implicated in much psychiatric illness.

Many people, including medical and legal professionals, assume that these patients only go for treatment after their conduct has been discovered and a court has ordered treatment. This conclusion is partly based on the notion that sexual deviants have no insight and experience no shame. In fact, this is seldom true. Most of these patients refer themselves, seeking treatment because of their tremendous loneliness, despair, and desolation. They want to understand why they experience the compulsion to commit inexplicable acts, and they initiate contact by writing. They are usually insecure, inadequate, and profoundly ashamed.

Another relevant stereotype is that in which women are victims and men perpetrators. When men are sexual abusers, all sorts of different agencies—social and medical—intervene, and very soon the police are called in. In contrast, the female "offender" finds it very difficult to get a hearing. Nobody wants to hear about her predicament, and nobody takes her too seriously. This happens even in group therapy, where she finds that other patients minimize her problems.

On countless occasions, agencies and establishments have expressed alarm, sometimes verging on panic, when referring male patients to me as sexual abusers. This contrasts strongly with the difficulty my female patients have often had in being taken seriously by some agencies. The few women who eventually refer themselves to me for treatment do so because all their previous attempts to get caring attention for their feelings of being too close, emotionally and physically, to their child, whether boy or girl, were not really taken seriously. I have noticed that mothers are more ready too report incestuous feelings and actions towards their daughters than towards their sons. In the latter case, one does not hear until much later, and then usually from the son's history.

Acknowledgement of maternal incest: is it Oedipus or Jocasta?

Do mothers commit incest more frequently than we think and more at the mother's initiative than we imagine?

Are we blocked from perceiving this by our idealization of motherhood? Surely we are, and this is why even in the original oedipal situation we fail to notice Jocasta's responsibility. Hers is the most important case of incest (Welldon, 1988). Typically, we have always blamed Oedipus and not his mother. Here we are once more attaching the sole responsibility to the male child and consequently developing a whole new concept of a complex, taking it for granted that Oedipus unconsciously "knew" his mother and was behaving perversely by marrying her. In fact, Jocasta was far better equipped, even consciously, to recognize Oedipus as her son than vice versa. She was the only one to know that Oedipus could be alive, as opposed to Laius who believed him dead. Why do we not charge her with, if not all, at least a large share of the responsibility for enacting her own incestuous desires? It is clear that, if not perverse herself, she had associated with a most perverse individual, her husband Laius, who was a paedophile, his most important reason for not wanting children. She not only married him, already giving signs of being the willing victim of a perverse partnership (the clinical analogy still applies), but contrived to get him drunk in order to get herself impregnated. In other words, she already knew her own power as the master of her own offspring, even to the extent of giving him away at birth. She might unconsciously know that she—or indeed he, the offspring—could pursue the lost relationship, the power of motherhood later being replaced by that of incest, which would be more rewarding for her.

It seems unnecessary for researchers to develop an Electra complex parallel to the oedipal one, when Jocasta already fulfils that role. Is this again an obstinate tendency to see women as the weak sex, always the victims and never the perpetrators of sexual assault? It has always been made to appear that women are incapable of effecting their own perverse sexual designs in a skilful and masterly way, with young boys reckoned to be the only ones to enact sexual fantasies. I believe that many theories concerning female sexual development are misguided. This might have been born partly of a need to see an "earth mother" operating at all times, a woman who has been so idealized or perhaps even idolized that her faults are overlooked. She is portrayed as power-less in the penis-envy dilemma or, according to the new feminists, the victim of social attitudes, even perhaps contemptible because of her seeming less importance than the male. It looks as though we have all become silent conspirators in a system that women, from whatever angle we look at them, are either dispossessed of all power or made the sexual objects and victims of their male counterparts. We do not attribute to them any sense of responsibility for their own unique functions, deeply related to fecundity and motherhood, and liable at times to manifest themselves perversely. Why is it that Jocasta, when both she and Oedipus learn the facts of their incestuous relationship, promptly commits suicide? Apparently Oedipus cannot at first grasp the situation. The truth must therefore have been much closer to Jocasta's consciousness.

In this context, a patient of mine, Fiona, was originally referred from a child guidance clinic where her daughter, aged 6 years, had been sent because of behavioural problems mainly related to school refusal. Following diagnostic assessment there, it was decided that the little girl's problems were the result of a very disturbed and difficult family situation, particularly in her relationship with her mother.

My patient was described as an inadequate mother who showed intense exhibitionistic behaviour, such as exaggerating her physical demonstrations of affection towards her daughter. However, when she previously tried to make a consultation because of these preoc-cupations, she was told not to worry: "It is just natural for a mother to feel very fond of her children, especially if they are single parents." She had so closely identified with her daughter that she had come to act like a little girl, expecting her daughter to take complete care of her needs, including being cuddled and bathed by her. The little girl defended herself against these excessive demands by a most primitive and infantile acting-out.

Mother and daughter had created a symbiotic relationship to the extent of sharing the same bed. The mother had initiated the girl into active sexual incest, which involved caressing of breasts and eventually masturbation of her daughter's genitals. The mother had not allowed the girl to attend school because she could not bear the idea of her being away. Nor would the mother let her have her own friends, or life, or allow her to grow up. My patient explained:

> "I want to be the mother I never had, someone who could be all the time with me and whose attentions could be entirely devoted to me as her daughter instead of being like my mother, hating me so much for being a girl and so involved with the other children and her husband that she never had a minute for me alone. She never forgave me either, that I was born a girl, being the first child. She had so much longed for a boy. I was always the victim of humiliation, and it became much worse when the other five children were born, all girls. Then my mother turned to me with even more hatred than ever and my father began to approach me sexually. As soon as I could, I emigrated to this country with the purpose of making my own life as a 'woman'."

From the moment of arrival, she pursued prostitution as a profession that could leave her free all day long to be with her daughter. I saw her for a diagnostic appraisal when she was still a practicing prostitute.

There are many possible outcomes surfacing from being incest victims, from either maternal or paternal incest to boys or girls, but a frequent one is to suffer from a sexual perversion. In this context, there are female patients who have suffered from sexual perversions as a result of a perverse/incestuous relationship with their mothers.

Such is the case of 34-year-old Miss E, who was sent to me for consultation because of her compulsion to expose herself sexually to figures of authority, particularly women. This had led her to be expelled from everywhere—schools, training centres, jobs, counselling groups, and even mental hospitals—such was the havoc, puzzlement, and sense of impotence she had created in everyone.

When I first saw her, she appeared to be eager to please, though very scared. She gave me this impression despite the fact that I had been previously warned of her "dangerousness", meaning her tendency to develop crushes on women in authority and to make an absolute nuisance of herself to the point of pestering previous doctors with letters and phone calls and even unexpectedly showing up at their home addresses and pursuing them with her exhibitionistic behaviour.

She told me that her compulsion to "flash" occurred when she became attached to a person whom she invested with idealized "maternal" qualities. She wanted to get closer, to be noticed, and to be taken care of by that particular person but she also wanted a shocked response from her "victim". She carefully planned the "appropriate" gear to wear; usually she wore an overcoat covering only a little vest in order to respond readily to her urges. She knew this was wrong and that she would be rejected, but could not stop herself. She had had this urge since she was very small. At school she had a crush on one of her female teachers, but she limited her actions to undressing in her presence. This gave her much sexual pleasure. At the age of 17 while being trained in an institution, she developed a crush on the head person and succumbed to her compulsion for the first time. Since then she had been unable to bear the tension and had repeated the same action over and over again, She was expelled from everywhere because of her "antisocial" behaviour, even by psychiatrists and psychotherapists, who could not tolerate it.

On one occasion a victim of hers got furious and slapped her. Miss E was surprised at her own reaction of intense enjoyment and sexual frenzy. She then instantly "learnt" that what she most wanted from these "mother figures" was to be either masturbated or slapped on the bottom. The referral letter stated that her actions seemed to be responding to masochistic needs rather than sexual relationships. She had never had a close relationship, emotionally or physically, with either sex. She had lived in institutions from the age of 8 years as pupil, trainee, employee, or inpatient.

It was not difficult to believe her own account of being masturbated by her mother from a very early age every time she felt sad or upset or to make her go to sleep, and her account was confirmed when the mother was interviewed. Not only had she masturbated this little girl but also the other four children. In the mother's own words, "it was easier than to use a dummy". She said that at the time she felt depressed and had an unhappy marriage to a man who used to get drunk and beat her up constantly. She also admitted that these actions with her children gave her an enormous sense of comfort and elation. It was also her only way to make herself go to sleep.

My patient, like all perverse patients, had used splitting, projective identification, and sexualization as a survival kit in dealing with the outside world. She was employing manic defences in an attempt to deal with her intense, chronic, masked depression, which resulted from a very deprived childhood in which she was made to feel a part or continuation of her mother's body, only existing to provide her mother with narcissistic and sexual gratification. She was literally "something" located between her thighs that mother could touch, caress, or rub; whenever the patient felt like crying, that was the only way to pacify her. She responded to this repetitive, incessant, and restless motion. She was nothing else, that was all. And in this she was not alone; she had siblings who simultaneously had the same experience. She learnt that her way of survival was communal living, where the law lay with the head person and independence or self-assertion were not permitted. The next move in her strategy was to develop a crush on the female head person who, like her mother, would then use her. She was giving herself as a sacrificial victim in order to keep all of them together in harmony.

Her expectations for a shocked response in her victims had to do with a hopeful outcome in which women in authority—symbolic mothers—would not respond like her own mother, using and exploiting her as a part-object, but she had to test them to the extreme. By her pestering them through letters, phone calls, and visits to their "private" homes, she was in deep projective identification with her own mother's intrusiveness into her own "private" parts. She felt justified in so doing, since this had been done to her. She had now become the aggressor; she even saw herself as such through her own admission that what she was doing was wrong, though she could not help doing it.

So, as usual, behind her perverse actions lay the hope of a magic hopeful outcome. She hoped to escape from her traumatic experiences as a child, yet her actions were imbued with such perverse psychopathology borrowed from her mother that she also sought total revenge. No emotional relationships had ever populated her inner world.

Sibling incest

Mariam Alizade (2005) accurately differentiates between asymmetrical plus intergenerational incest and symmetrical (sibling) incest. She acknowledges the possibility that sibling incest may become asymmetrical, when not consensual.

I have observed cases of sibling incest presenting within a wide range of severity, but all related to a degree of neglect and emotional deprivation in the family. Sometimes sibling incest appears to be a "solution" to the neglect suffered by the children in that they try to provide one another with nurture and support, which culminates in sexual activity. At other times, the sibling incest appears as vertical incest in the sense that it is between a much older child and a younger, defenceless one. I recall the history of a patient in a group that I facilitated who was devastated not that he had been sexually abused by his own sister since the age of 6, but that at the age of 13 his sister suddenly stopped, without any explanation. All their interactions had taken place in complete silence. Juliet Mitchell (2000, 2003) emphasizes the importance of the sibling relationships, which, until recently have been absent from traditional psychoanalytic theory. In her words, "looking at siblings is looking anew at sex and violence . . . bringing in siblings changes the picture we are looking at".

Luisa Brunori (1997) was one of the first in the field of group analytic therapy to emphasize the importance of sibling relationships.

Assessments:
differences between incest perpetrators and paedophiles

It is important to make a differential diagnosis between incest perpetrators and paedophiles in order to make accurate risk assessments and treatment recommendations. At times they appear in the same category because of inaccurate research. The classification of sexual abuse in the DSM-IV (APA, 1994, 995.5) relates only to children victims and not to incest perpetrators. The distinction I have drawn, therefore, is based on my clinical experience.

While incestuous parents as well as paedophiles involve themselves in child abuse and frequently have had a traumatic early childhood, their presenting problems and surrounding circumstances are quite different. Incestuous parents have been able to achieve a fully developed relationship with another adult and to have a family. In contrast, paedophiles target primarily under-age children, male or female, and they are not engaged in adult relationships.

Incest may be the outcome of a dysfunctional family dynamics, often including an external event such as a pathological bereavement. Paedophiles, on the other hand, do not present significant changes in their behaviour towards children related to external circumstances. Incestuous fathers shift from wife to offspring, whereas paedophiles may target women for their offspring. Furthermore, paedophiles have intense fears of relating to their peer group—men and women. Their attitude towards the children involved is marked by intense externalization, rationalization, and justification of their actions, making themselves believe that initiation into sexuality by adults is a healthy process. Paedophiles also claim to be completely unaware of the serious long- and short-term consequences involved for the children they have abused, whereas incestuous parents are usually more aware of the long-term consequences produced by their actions, especially when they are taken into therapy.

Attitude towards treatment is also different. Incestuous parents are often more motivated, and frequently we see couples who come for treatment because of their incipient awareness of their need for understanding and professional help. In contrast, paedophiles rarely seek treatment voluntarily. In practical terms, risk assessment and dangerousness are quite different for both groups (so far as the two categories do not overlap, as sometimes could happen). Incestuous fathers, on the whole, do not present future danger to other children, whereas often paedophiles could, regardless of treatment and management, still offer future danger to children in general. Incest perpetrators have, if properly assessed and treated, a better prognosis than paedophiles.

I want to alert professionals to a particular pathology found during my clinical work with both victims and perpetrators of both sexes. This pathology at times links both categories of mothers alone with male paedophiles. Many single mothers who have children from either one or more partners find themselves on their own. It is not unusual for some men to leave the particular household after parenting one or more children because of the responsibilities associated with parenthood, and they go off to find another partner. The pattern may repeat itself many times. These women have been victims of sexual abuse themselves, are lacking in self-assertiveness, are depressed, have a low sense of self-esteem, feel despondent and valueless, and have very poor quality relationships or none.

Some of these women consider the children responsible for the absence of a man. They feel sexually abused by their partners, ostracized, unable to socialize, despondent, and depressed. Facing such predicaments, they fall into despair and start abusing their children, trying to obtain some comfort for their frustrated lives. I do not agree, however, that the motivation for these women in initiating the sexual abuse with their children is just to "achieve non-threatening emotional intimacy", as stated by Mathews, Matthews, and Speltz (1989). I believe that this abuse contains a hidden and unconscious revenge since they apportion blame to the children for their being left alone.

Other women continue their search for male companionship and, unable to meet them in the usual venues because of being housebound, advertise in lonely hearts columns. They place adverts giving detailed and rich descriptions of their children, since they want to be open about what they consider to be handicaps in their domestic lives. In fact, these "handicaps" will be quite a bait for male paedophiles, who readily answer such adverts and in no time make their way inside the domestic scene. Women in this position are taken by surprise. They can't believe their "luck", because this man for the first time is so nice to the children. Women do not even mind whether they have sex or not, because they had lots of it before and it was very, very unsatisfactory. But they are delighted that he is so caring and nice to the children. A new relationship starts, and marriage follows. Eventually the incest or sexual assault or sexual abuse comes into the open, and often these men appear in reports as incest perpetrators because it happened inside the family, whereas they have been paedophiles from the beginning. A confusion has been created, and as a result records may show inaccurate statistics.

Differences between types of sexual abuse

According to Argentieri (1988, p. 23), there are different cases of incest such as "dramatic cases of explicit and consummate incest over a long period of time, undergone by someone who has then come into analysis", other "cases of 'soft' incest, masked as ambiguous bodily contacts (the most frequent) reported by those who have committed them and also by those who have been the victims", and finally "cases of pathological defensive solutions against inhibited incestuous drives and fantasies".

I tended to agree with this classification until later on during the group sessions when to my surprise I learnt from patients who had suffered from sexual abuse a rather coarse and unexpected classification of the abuse:

- A "sadistic" one, in which the abuse took place after much seduction and grooming.

- A "benign" one, when the abuse was clearly violent, sadistic, and unexpected.

This surprising classification, which reached general consensus among group members, had its own reasoning. In their own experiences, under the appearance of being rather soft and "benign", the first one had created ambiguity, bewilderment, and a tremendous sense of confusion, which left them unable to disentangle from the abuser.

The second one, instead, created a clear and raw sense of being *really* abused, and it was relatively easy to express alarm and anger and to rapidly push the perpetrator out forever.

Countertransference

Assessments of victim and victimizer patients can easily trigger off emotional responses in the professionals that may interfere with clear and unbiased treatment recommendations and are at times a re-enactment of early family situations. Sinason (1991) has described how the therapist's most painful interpretations were connected with trauma of an abusive nature and with difficulties in linking internal and external worlds.

The victims may succeed in making the therapist feel not only protective but also possessive about them, which could lead to patients feeling favoured and unique in individual treatment. There is a generation gap in their real and emotional lives in which role reversal has occurred, and the group interaction offers a completely different experience.

Patricia was a victim of incest that had taken place between the ages of 11 and 21. She joined the group at the age of 36 after referral from her GP when, for the first time in her life, she admitted first to herself and then to him her repressed or "forgotten" history of incest. Though her GP was an experienced doctor, he had for fifteen years felt puzzled at not being able to understand the causes for her extensive and serious psychosomatic complaints. During the assessment, I felt protective of Patricia and had the idea that the only person capable of fully understanding her was myself. At that point, I became aware of alarm bells ringing, which indicated that my initial response was in itself a contra-indication for offering individual therapy. When I offered her group therapy, she was terrified at the prospect of having to confront and be confronted by so many strangers about her secret, but she was able to understand the reasons for this recommendation.

When dealing with perpetrators, the therapist may feel cornered or blackmailed by confidentiality issues, which may provoke feelings of collusion. Alternatively, the therapist might feel like either the consenting child or the seductive parent in the incest situation. Either way, dynamic therapy—meaning internal change—is in real jeopardy.

Keith was referred for treatment after the disclosure of his incestuous relationship with his stepdaughter. Several agencies and establishments had been involved in his referral, and this inquisitive attitude tended to obstruct the possibility for an accurate diagnostic assessment and treatment recommendations. I saw him for several diagnostic interviews. These were beset with complications as all the different agencies involved demanded information about his activities. At that time, it was very clearly stated by the Medical Defence Union that the confidentiality rule regarding these cases was always on the side of the patient. In this particular case, Keith had threatened the consultant psychiatrist who first saw him with breach of confidentiality after the consultant had denounced him to the Social Services on account of his incest. The patient had written letters to, among others, his local MP, the British Medical Association, and the Medical Defence Union complaining about the consultant's action. At this point, the consultant decided to refer Keith for treatment to the Portman Clinic. During the long assessment period, one of my senior colleagues took care of all calls regarding this patient and handled them in a positive way while not giving information that might be detrimental to the patient's future treatment at the Portman.

His demands for immediate treatment and his request for complete confidentiality produced a double-bind situation. I began to feel cornered and blackmailed into giving him treatment in the utmost confidentiality, which actually in this particular case meant secrecy. I became deeply aware of the transference–countertransference issues involved in "incest with a consenting child". These were very powerful feelings. At times I would feel like the child keeping quiet about it all; at other times, I would feel like the controlling and exploitative parental figure. After a great deal of careful thought, I decided to offer him group therapy, a suggestion that first surprised and then enraged him. I gave him time to think about it, and I tried to explain to him clearly why this would be the most suitable therapy for him: secrecy between parent and child is a key pathological trait in incest, which in group therapy becomes no longer available. Everything is open to everyone. A few weeks later it was my turn to be surprised, when he accepted my recommendation.

Workers of all disciplines involved in cases of incest frequently find it difficult to maintain a detached professional stance. They tend to take sides, usually becoming emotionally bound to the victims. For example, a social worker dealing with a mother became so involved in supporting her that she lost sight of the mother's parenting inadequacies (Trowell, 1996). Additionally, or alternatively, they feel punitive towards the perpetrators. In their distress, they lose their understanding of the dynamics of what is happening.

At other times, professionals become so indignant that they fail to see that victims who become perpetrators experience a conscious or unconscious desire to take revenge for the pain inflicted upon them. These victims-perpetrators believe they are creating a situation in which justice is satisfied. Actually, however, they are identifying with their aggressors. In somewhat similar ways, the professional workers often identify with the victims.

In the course of group analytic psychotherapy of a group composed of women and men, both genders containing perpetrators and victims of incest, the patients' psychopathology involves shame, manic defences, and primitive defensive mechanisms such as denial, projection, and splitting. This tends to divide the helping professions, taking sides for either child or perpetrator and making them forget the neutral stance necessary to understand the whole family dynamics.

Supervision has an important role in clarifying these issues, thus enabling therapists to avoid such pitfalls. Otherwise, the result would be the splitting off from society not only of this type of patient but also of their therapists, both through fear and as means of punishment. The following incident is most relevant to this assertion.

One of the most powerful experiences of being a victim of prejudice on the grounds of treating incest perpetrators took place a few years ago in New York at an annual meeting of the American Group Psychotherapy Association. I attended a pre-conference professional workshop dedicated to incest. This had not been my first choice, but since that was full up I reluctantly agreed to attend the incest one, with some foreboding that it may not be a useful experience for me. I warned the group therapist who was the leader of this particular workshop that I might have to leave the two-day workshop before its planned ending because of an urgent phone call I was expecting.

During the introduction, the convenor asked the fifteen or so participants to talk about themselves and their own field of work. This was a group dealing with incest in a professional capacity, all of whom began to announce their own place of work and, in so doing, also offered some personal information about themselves. Not completely surprised, I was still stunned nevertheless as I listened to the "con-

Countertransference

Therapists' feelings towards—

Victims	Perpetrators
Protective	Judgemental, non-therapeutic
Patronizing	Angry and sadistic
In empathy and in identification	Trapped as a consenting child
Uniqueness in understanding	Immobilized because of confidentiality

fessions" from these colleagues—both female and male—of having been recipients of sexual abuse by some family members. This was greeted with enormous enthusiasm by the leader, who very warmly congratulated them on being so open and honest about these recollections and in sharing them with the group. This was, according to her, an indication of an enormous amount of acceptance and tolerance and understanding of one another. Some tension began to grow inside me. How could I make an admission or rather a "confession" now of not having been a victim of sexual abuse? I began to feel like the odd-one-out in the group. In so doing, I overlooked the response that my chosen work in groups would have in the others. I clearly stated that I was the conductor of groups with both perpetrators and victims of sexual molestation and abuse. Frozen silence surrounded me; followed by some cries of horror and disbelief: "You mean, you treat perpetrators? How could you do that? How could you stomach that? Those people don't deserve any understanding, only punishment!" In a fraction of a second, all tolerance, goodwill, and sympathetic response had faded away and been replaced by judgemental, critical, hostile reactions, so much so that in our first coffee break, I found myself in complete isolation, everyone fleeing away from me, forming into little groups talking in whispers and looking at me. How much I felt in empathy with my patients! Whatever I had tried to explain about perpetrators often being victims of sexual abuse themselves was completely cut off and eliminated. This insight could not reach their minds, so much was their over-identification with the victim group and, as such, never wanting to change. It was fortunate that in experiencing some foreboding, I had earlier given myself a justification to leave, which I promptly did.

Group therapy for victims and perpetrators of incest together

In treating both abusers and sexually abused patients, group analytic psychotherapy is frequently the best form of treatment not only for severely disturbed sexual and social deviancy, but also for sexual abuse. Victims and perpetrators of incest share, by the nature of their predicament, a history of an engulfing, intense, inappropriate, distorted, physical and sexual relationship of a highly secretive type within the family situation. Patients' psychopathologies are the product of severe traumas and early learnt survival mechanisms. Group analytic therapy breaks through the patterns of self-deception, fraud, secrecy, and collusion that are invariably present in these cases. The amount of fear, rejection, and humiliation that such patients experience when confronted in a group therapy session with their secrets and shame is difficult to convey.

A group treatment approach allows a new transferential–countertransferential process to take place for patients who present problems related to violence and secrecy in the family. Trust towards peer members (sibling figures) is facilitated, and exclusive reliance on the therapist (parental figure) is discouraged. Group members open up and overcome the taboo of secrecy.

Example

"I am writing to you in desperation. I need help. I am an adult, 30-year-old woman, with three children presently in care and one due within the next few weeks, which it also looks as though I am going to lose.

"I desperately want my children back, but also recognized that because of my own abuse as a child and in many other ways throughout my adult life, I could not avoid leaving my child in a potentially abusive situation. Hence my daughter being sexually abused by one of my abusers when she was younger.

"I have attended some treatment but have not found it useful—everyone seems to be so judgemental.

"I am now at the stage where I am experiencing flashbacks, nightmares, awful depression. I can't bear to be touched by my partner. I also recognize that my relationship cannot continue as it is—I don't even know if I want it anymore, but I seem to be addicted to it somehow . . .

"I know that somewhere I have to find the help I need and see it through, not only for my children, but also for myself so that I can feel like a person, a human being, and not one of society's rejects.

"I hope and pray that you can help me.

"PS: I was sexually abused by three different people from the age of 2½ years, then raped at the age of 17 years. My mother was physically abusing me at this time too."

This is a self-referral letter from a patient who was charged with aiding and abetting sexual abuse. She had taken her daughter to be babysat by her own stepfather, who had previously abused her as a child. A high degree of unconscious identification with her own daughter is present. There is also a sense of self-loathing, which is confirmed by her sadomasochistic relations and her brutal treatment of her own body. This constitutes yet another category in which the abuse is simultaneously active and unconscious. In other words, she is quite unaware of her own participation in the process, because the original trauma—her own abuse— had been buried away and only emerged into consciousness when she became aware of her daughter's abuse. She was placed in a therapeutic group, and only there, when supported by others with similar histories, was she able to look into her own "abusing" behaviour. There was no chance for her to feel judged by others. On the contrary, she experienced this constant confrontation of "taking in" her own sense of responsibility as enlightening and extremely helpful. Her own capacity for internal and constant change provided the others with reassurance about their own capacity to give positive things. Much cohesiveness, connection, and mutuality emerged in the group affiliation.

Group treatment of both victims and perpetrators of incest together, but who are not related, offers unexpected qualities of containment and insight that are virtually impossible in a one-to-one situation (20th Foulkes Memorial Lecture; Welldon, 1997). Perpetrators become deeply aware of the extensive long-term consequences of their actions. When confronted by the other members mirroring their victims' predicaments, it provides an opportunity for reflection, so that they can see how they experience themselves only as parts of their parental figures and lack the ability to see themselves as separate human beings. Every member experiences a powerful sense of belonging to the group. Throughout treatment, patients gain a capacity for self-assertion, emotional growth, independence, and individuation. They see themselves and others developing into respected individuals possessing self-esteem, which is acknowledged by others and by themselves. They are not only allowed but encouraged openly to express the anger and frustration that has been kept hidden for lengthy periods. This encouragement comes especially from "old" members who have gone through similar predicaments and who are now ready to leave the group.

Whereas group treatment of both victims and perpetrators of incest together can be successful, the combination of incest perpetrators and paedophiles in the same therapy group is thought not to be clinically appropriate. It was originally practiced for a number of years and provided us with a rich source of learning, one conclusion of which was that such a combination can easily lead to serious confusion and disruption of the group dynamics, and that it should therefore be avoided. For example, other group members immediately noticed the consistent difference in attitude of the two categories of patients and often expressed a wish to get rid of the paedophiles, who were experienced as the cause of a stalemate in their own treatment.

The inclusion of children or young people in these groups is also not recommended, since this could easily produce emotional disturbances that could be repetitive of the early traumas to youngsters who are not yet emotionally equipped to deal with the strong confrontations that happen in these groups.

Mirroring processes

Female perpetrators joining groups experience first a sense of bewilderment to have fellow patients with similar problems. They feel a tremendous sense of relief in being able to talk to others about those "horrid" urges. Newcomers may attempt, on arrival, to blame Social Services and other outside agencies for "interfering", having taken away their children, and they feel empty, dispossessed. Initially, the other women—their "seniors" in the group—listen to them with much empathy but, soon afterwards, when they sense that the newcomers are ready to face realities, confront them with much sensitivity. Actually, they help them to admit their own sense of responsibility for the situation they find themselves in. They are also able to interact regarding their relationships with the cruel men they completely submit themselves to. They also bring out nasty habits they may have that affect their personal appearances. They see themselves constantly changing and make generous remarks about one another. They obviously obtain a great deal of satisfaction of helping one another in a womanly comradeship.

The interaction between males and females is of a very intriguing nature since the group contains perpetrators and victims, of both genders. Female perpetrators observe how different their attitude about their victims is as opposed to that of their male counterparts. They are able to help male perpetrators to become deeply aware of the vast consequences of their actions when confronted by other members analogous to their victims.

When Keith was admitted to the group two years after its inception, Fiona reacted with the most anger to Keith's admission of incest. Fiona had been referred by the Tavistock's child department due to an incestuous relationship with her daughter. She had many rows with him because she saw a mirror image of herself in Keith, in her own engulfing relationship with her daughter and previously with her father. Keith confronted her with the inconsistency between her alleged wish to change jobs and her feeble attempts to do so; by now it was obvious that she was still a practicing prostitute. Keith himself was a conscientious worker and had kept his job and been promoted several times. Fiona, on the other hand, confronted Keith with his erotic feelings towards his stepdaughter, which he admitted with much pain.

Eventually, Fiona started a series of clerical jobs, in which she usually got into conflict with women in authority. All this had to do with her idealization–denigration of me. Group members were confronted with great expectations of and dependency on the mother figure but, simultaneously, with fears that I would be inadequate in dealing with all their demands, as had happened with their real mothers. This was interpreted in transferential terms that involved the whole group, since this experience was shared by all. In one session, Fiona caused much alarm when she mentioned how much she had regressed in her relationship with her daughter, to such an extent indeed that in accordance with the group members' suggestion I took the unprecedented action of suggesting a referral of her daughter for treatment to a child guidance clinic. The draft of this referral letter was left on the table, in the centre of the group, where all communications about patients and outside agents are shown (see chapter 9). Fiona was at first distressed by this, but quite soon she was able to come to terms with it as being the best solution. The other patients appeared to be contained and held by this action, with which they had all agreed. From then on, Fiona began to appear more reassured, far less resistant, and more insightful. She had experienced me and the group as caring and supportive in her feelings of inadequacy in dealing with her functioning as a mother. In so doing, she had used projective identification with me as an omnipotent mother, who was supposed to deal with all problems within the group, even the outside ones.

Everyone in the group had some lesson to learn from my lack of resources to deal with everyone's problems solely by treatment within the group. This was acknowledged by my requesting help from the outside, which was promptly implemented. I was not aware that this experience had been so deeply felt until we eventually learnt that Keith had followed suit and had himself referred his stepdaughter to the same place for treatment. We got to know about this two years later when Keith confronted Fiona at her folly in wanting to stop her daughter's therapy. He told her that he knew all the processes, since he had thought it such a good idea that he had taken his stepdaughter for treatment. Obviously there was a degree of identification and role modelling in operation that could never have occurred in individual treatment.

"The ideal assistant to the group analyst"

It is not uncommon that soon after entry to the group, female patients with a history of early incest may behave as pseudo-ideal assistants to the therapist. Even those who have never been familiar with unconscious processes seem immediately to discover pseudo-appropriate ways to "help" the therapist-mother-father keep the group-family together. This is exactly what happened when Patricia joined the group: she started behaving as the "ideal" assistant to the therapist, even though she had never previously been in any kind of psychotherapeutic treatment. She fulfilled perfectly the role of the incest victim who tries to keep the family together. Fellow patients often react with surprise and bewilderment at this show of false maturity. Later on this is replaced with competitiveness. When interpretations are made to the effect that the newcomer is only repeating a pathological pattern learnt early in life, other fellow patients seem relieved by this understanding, but it is then the turn of the patient pseudo-helper to be filled with rage. After all, she is "doing her best"—why is she being so "harshly criticized"?

Our group therapy programme treatment has provided new understanding of the complexities of abuse, though we are still far from understanding everything. In such mixed groups, male perpetrators become aware that their actions are not just limited to temporary or transient physical effects but also inflict deep psychological wounds on their victims. Months after Patricia was admitted to the group, many members still clung to the belief that she was the most assured member and quite healthy, such was their wish for a "healthy incest" that could have no damaging effects on the victims. She fulfilled perfectly the role of the incest victim who tries to "keep the family together". This produced much aggravation among most members but especially in Fiona, who in her adult life, as a victim of incest by her father, had "chosen" the "prostitution solution", as opposed to the psychosomatic one "chosen" by Patricia. In a subsequent session, there was a very active confrontation between the two of them in which both were "assessed" by other members, who thought Patricia to be by far the more mature of the two, despite her recent admission. All sorts of interpretations on my part about Patricia's re-enactment of her early behaviour seemed to be to no avail. Fiona felt hurt and humiliated by the others "misunderstanding" her maternal role; she failed to attend the group and wrote several letters threatening to leave it. Eventually, and on subsequent occasions, she returned to the group.

The other side of the coin

However, at a later session Patricia appeared distraught. She told us how the evening before she had been "prevented" from watching a TV programme on incest, due to a telephone call from her father at exactly the start of this programme, which ended after it was over. Now it was Keith's turn to become aware of the deep implications that incest had for Patricia when he confronted her with her inability to stop her father and with her lack of assertiveness in not being able even to ask him to phone her an hour later.

A few months later, Patricia was in tears telling us of her extreme humiliation on her recent visit to her parents, who, despite knowing that she was a vegetarian, confronted her on Saturday morning with an enormous breakfast of sausages and bacon, specially cooked by her father, which she reluctantly but acquiescently ate.

These two incidents gave a strong indication of her "consenting" attitude. However, it looked as if father had "read" some inner changes on her part, because later on he angrily "questioned her about being in some sort of nonsense or therapy".

Whereas previously Keith and Patricia had been unable to make any connection with each other, even refusing eye contact, they were now in open confrontation with one another. Keith suddenly became aware of the long-term consequences of the incest when he repeated his indignant questioning of her inability to assert herself and her compulsion to give in to her father's requests. Suddenly and quite unexpectedly, a complete understanding of their own respective roles and of the implications was available to us all. No one was able to resist the realization of Patricia's suffering despite her maturity, helpfulness, and "insight". Fiona now learnt about Patricia's real predicament, and indeed she became caring and helpful to her in a realistic manner and was able to see the chronic disabilities that incest had inflicted on Patricia. We all became aware that incest is much larger than life, that its power is not only physical, sexual, or erotic. This secret union provides both partners with a "uniqueness" that it is almost impossible to describe. It gives as much as it takes away.

It is also clear that victims, who may at the start be quiet and compliant, have much anger to express that they have never felt free to display before. This is fundamental for them in being able to achieve any real change. It is essential to make an important difference between *anger* expressed in a straightforward manner leading to self-assertion, and the harbouring of *revenge* revealing the passion still existent in the victim intertwined with the original victimizer. At times, the victim claims she can now express anger against the perpetrator, but when this is in a twisted and vengeful way, it is clear that she is still a partner in the old incestuous process.

In the group treatment, Patricia began to assert herself slowly and in a determined fashion, but only after an initial period of being extremely compliant to the therapist in order to keep the "family" together. Eventually, she began to express anger, when she was able to scream at another group member and tell him to "sod off". She and everyone else was extremely surprised at this, and we all experienced a sense of achievement at her newly gained ability to express anger.

However, our reaction was completely different when a few months later we saw her looking extremely elated, radiating a sense of triumph. Although everyone was aware of her mood as soon as she entered the room, nobody felt at ease with this feeling, and somebody asked the reason for her feeling so triumphant. Her answer was: "The bastard got what he deserved." Then she said, "The bloody bastard just got to know that his testicles will be removed because of cancer. Isn't that wonderful?"

A few members attempted a smile, but most people felt extremely worried about her. I offered her an interpretation dealing with her inability to separate herself from her father in her strong need for revenge. We all know that the expression of anger is therapeutic and a healthy sign, but the wish for revenge is an unhealthy trait that poisons the person who suffers from it and everybody around her too.

This situation revealed how much the victims cling to the perpetrators like a necessary enemy.

Termination issues to do with the incest group

Many incidents took place in the seven years that Keith remained in the group for treatment, and they offered many unexpected insights. For example, the crucial unconscious link between acting-out and denial of mourning became vital when Keith could remember some of his repressed feelings when his first-born son died of cot death. This occurred after a violent fight he had had with his wife when he suddenly left home, only to return a few days later when his wife contacted him to tell him about this death. He failed to react in any way apart from apathy and lethargy. In contrast, his wife was over-whelmed by grief, to the point of becoming emotionally unavailable. A few months later he approached his stepdaughter sexually, and the incest began.

This issue is sensitively approached by Mitchell (1997), who was aware that in certain cases of paedophilia and of incest by male adults on their children of both sexes, it was not a real sexual drive that came into play, but a primitive problem of envious attack against the female wife/mother. In Keith's case, his abuse of the girl was a desolate but also furious attack on his emotionally "absent" wife.

I would like to concentrate here on some of the powerful dynamic changes that it is possible to achieve through group analysis and that are elicited and evidenced in our powerful countertransference responses to equally strong transference processes in our patients.

When Keith announced that the following week would be his last session, which had been decided within the group a long time before, I felt a need to work through my own countertransference, including a deep sense of bereavement about his departure from the group. By then, he was the most senior and most experienced member. The others found it very difficult to express any feelings about his departure since his input was of such great importance; in a way, he had taken up the "co-therapist" role most effectively. This is a very important feature in the life of the patients, one that only emerges in a single-therapist group as opposed to a co-therapist group. I questioned myself: shall I need to perform the co-therapist duties? On reflection, I considered that what I should miss the most about him was the element of hope he provided us all with, especially myself. After all, the first time I met him eight years earlier I disliked him immensely and thought he had no chances for improvement. (This is rather unusual, since I am known to be naïvely optimistic about the most intractable cases.) I offered him a place in a group, with a near conviction of his refusal to accept it. He was resistant in so many ways: pedantic, pompous, superior, arrogant, full of complaints about other colleagues. But now I experienced him as one of the most rewarding patients. I also realized that I must facilitate his exit, to let him go, and to acknowledge in this way the important degree of his changes. I am also aware that, with our patient population, envy runs high and sometimes fellow patients make it difficult for others to depart, especially because of their difficulties in acknowledging someone else's improvement.

In the next session, the other members did not want to know about his leaving; there was much denial, and they were unable to deal with any idea of being faced with mourning processes. Keith talked of his enormous changes and that, on the whole, he felt grown-up enough now to stand on his own two feet and to leave. It is a duty he has to perform. He confronted the group and told us how he came here for one problem, the incest, but by now he has learnt so much more about everything in his life. He has got an awareness and wisdom he never envisaged before. Eventually he was also able to say how much and how deeply he has got to know himself. Reluctantly, then, he admitted to being grateful to me for having "shaking him up a few times". While saying this he looked at me with Labrador dog's eyes.

I felt very moved and quite unable to make an interpretation that would accurately convey all those years of seeing him interacting very little with others to start with and, later on, challenging others with their "consenting" behaviour and his own way of interacting and making others aware of their collusiveness and lack of insight. These also included his own reactions of initial rage and his later response to confrontations, admitting consequences of his own actions and his increasing development into maturity.

How to convey all this? I just said, "This is a time for loss, mourning, and hope; he has learnt so much, and his changes are so apparent that everyone is experiencing great difficulty in letting him go, because they fear they are letting the hope go."

The group went on for a long time after his departure. There was much grieving for him after he left, but later on we became ready, with trepidation and anticipation, to welcome a new batch of members who were to join us four months later. Such is the magnitude of the learning processes we go through in group therapy and its intricacies, which involve most feelings but especially those to do with hope and the inner changes inherent to it.

Sometimes nonverbal communications take us by surprise. Such was the case with the admission of a new member into the victims–perpetrators group. This man was much older than the rest—62 years of age—whose daughters had recently disclosed his sexual abuse of them some twenty years before. He was quite frail and very willing to take on treatment. During the assessment period, he demonstrated he could absorb new insight and take on board this new—but old—situation. I thought him to be a suitable patient for group therapy. I have already expressed how difficult it is for people to come into a therapy group for the first time. So I was very surprised to see this man, after tentatively finding a place to sit, moving to another place, this time next to Patricia, who, as we may remember, had been the victim of her father's incest some twenty years before. Not only did he sit next to her, but he also told her, "I can sense that you have a very soft voice, which will be very hard for me to hear, as I am having hearing problems. And I can also sense that you will have important things to say, so I would like to sit next to you." A sort of "radar" was in operation in which he had already allocated his seat next to the victim.

I would like to emphasize how rewarding my experiences with such patients has been. Although they offer a great challenge, they cherish their opportunity for therapy, and it is gratifying to see how much they can change.

Perpetrators initially display defensive mechanisms such as denial and avoidance. However, later on, with the tolerance and acceptance

---

Group analytic psychotherapy

Why group analytic psychotherapy for both victims and perpetrators of incest ?

Because—

- Secrecy is at the root of the problem; groups inhibit secrecy
- The group offers a family–social microcosm where every member knows about the secret
- Trust towards siblings is facilitated
- Exclusive reliance on the parental figure (therapist) is discouraged
- Expression of anger and revenge is facilitated

Transference

Patients' feelings towards therapist (vertical) and other group members (horizontal)—

Victims may appear:	Perpetrators may present:
Acquiescent	Anti-authority feelings
Victim-like	Rebelliousness
Passive	Denial
Sexualized and eroticized	Lack of insight
Afraid/fantasies of being seduced and abused	Poor motivation for treatment
Feeling guilty	Inability to mourn
Unable to express anger/ revenge	Unawareness of consequences

of other fellow members, they are able, perhaps for the first time, to look at themselves as abusers in a different light. This can only happen when understanding and not blame is the aim. In his identification with the impotent and helpless victim, the perpetrator gets angry on her behalf and demands that she be self-assertive and able to sever herself from her own abusers. In this way, incest victims gain recognition of their own "erotization of cruelty" (Milton, 1996) and are able to look at problems they are most ashamed of and in need of help with, including the addiction to the abuse and the abuser (van der Kolk, 1989). Artificial idealization of the victim status is no longer necessary.

The advantages of group therapy for both victims and perpetrators of incest

In a one-to-one situation, patients are fearful that the therapist will lose control and will fall prey to the patient's seduction, the outcome of which is both hoped for and dreaded. Their underlying anxiety is associated with tremendous fears of separation and being discarded by parental figures if they do not comply with their inappropriate demands. In group therapy they are confronted with reality testing from their co-equals, in which the power of being so favoured and unique (Ganzarain & Buchele, 1993) has to be worked through in the group situation, a bit like the family, though it operates on very different dynamics. Bentovim (1976, 1991, 1995) has produced extensive and invaluable studies that have highlighted the importance of the family dysfunction in the understanding, treatment, and management of families with histories of incest.

Group analysis offers a strict sense of boundaries with awareness of links between acts and unconscious motivations. The interpretation of the vertical transference of the group in relation to the therapist-parental figures—usually with regressive elements—facilitates independence. Horizontal interpretations to do with mixed feelings about peer groups (sibling figures) provide the needed capacity to empathize with others, who actually represent parts of themselves. These are multiple transference processes, which are effectively used for the working through. They are not to be thought of as diluted, since they lead to heightened degrees of awareness.

Patients become aware in confrontations with their opposites of the important dynamic processes involved, especially those related to their inability to think and to their identification with the aggressor who was actually present in their early lives. Patients become aware of the reasons for their lack of trust and their intense need to be in control of all situations.

These patients benefit from being in a slow-open group. The advantages of such a group, which offers different developmental stages, are discussed in chapter 9.

I hope I have been able to convey that group psychotherapy offers particular advantages as a treatment option for victims of sexual abuse, since secrecy and isolation are replaced by disclosure within the containing atmosphere of the group, which resembles a family in which secrets are not kept. The threat of intimacy and the fantasized risks of seduction/exploitation are reduced for both patient and therapist. The power of the group as a whole acts both as an auxiliary ego in strengthening individuals as they confront past pain and abuse, and as a moderator of the sadistic need for revenge that fuels their innate capacity for perpetrating abuse in their turn, thus making it possible to break the cycle.

Conclusion

Group analysis has considerable potential in the field of forensic psychotherapy. Small groups reflect the disordered early family experiences of forensic patients, but they can also offer not only containment but also enlightenment to both victims and perpetrators of abuse. The group also functions as a microcosm of society and thus provides an opportunity for group members to constantly renegotiate and develop further a sense of social responsibility, and to understand the consequences of antisocial actions. Argentieri (1988), in a most comprehensive study of incest, produces a succinct, tough, and most illuminating insight regarding the effects of incest: "The most illustrious victim is the thought process", adding that "In Bionian terms (1961), the impact of the cognitive interrogative on one's origins and one's own identity becomes fragmented and weakened."

As mentioned, the most important endeavour of forensic psychotherapy is the achievement of the capacity to interpose *thought* between impulse and action. Achievement of such insight and understanding of the unconscious motivations can free the forensic patient from the tyranny of having no choice. The application of group psychotherapy in forensic patients may contribute to freeing society from the damage that results from forensic psychopathology.

CHAPTER EIGHT

Introduction to forensic psychotherapy

SOCIETY AND THE OFFENDER

Forensic psychotherapy is a relatively new discipline. It is the offspring of forensic psychiatry and psychoanalytic psychotherapy. Its aim is the psychodynamic understanding of the offender and his—or her—consequent treatment, regardless of the seriousness of the offence. It involves the understanding of the unconscious as well as the conscious motivations of the criminal mind, and of particular offence behaviour. It does not seek to condone the crime or to excuse the criminal. On the contrary, the object is to help the offender to acknowledge his responsibility for his acts and thereby to save the offender and society from the perpetration of further crimes. Gill McGauley (McGauley & Bartlett, 2010, p. 134) adds that in helping forensic patients to understand their minds, it is central to make them aware that they are "inadvertently" contributing to their own difficulties. So, a person's unconscious mind and its tendency to repeat actions against the person himself and society are being acknowledged.

A discipline such as this needs explanation. Only through the understanding of the dynamic relationship between the offender and society is it possible to make progress in research into the causes and prevention of crime. The more is understood about the criminal mind, the more it is possible to take positive preventive action. This, in turn, can lead to better management and the implementation of more cost-effective treatment of patients.

Psychodynamic and legal considerations

The form of psychotherapy involved in forensic psychotherapy is different from other forms precisely because society is, willy-nilly, involved. Forensic psychotherapy has gone beyond the special relationship between patient and psychotherapist. It is a triangular situation: patient, psychotherapist, society. As Robert Bluglass points out, "The role of the forensic psychiatrist in confronting and trying to reconcile the differences between the interests of the law and those of psychiatry is a crucial and important one" (1990, p. 7).

If forensic psychotherapy is the handling of three interacting positions—the therapist's, the patient's, and society's criminal justice system (de Smit, 1992)—it follows that treatment of the forensic patient population should ideally be carried out within the NHS, and not within the private sector. Forensic psychotherapy has to be considered in the overall context of health care for people involved in the criminal justice process. Its aims, however, are not identical to those of the criminal justice system. There is an inevitable, and indeed necessary, conflict of values (Harding, 1992). Evaluations should ideally be conducted independently, according to criteria that correspond to health-based values (Reed Report, 1992).

Annie Bartlett (2010, pp. 325–326) acutely points out the confusion regarding the language of both health and criminal justice and the "bald dichotomies" of them, since social policies often combine both elements of treatment and punishment. The political focus is centred not on the therapeutic efficacy of working with mentally disordered offenders but on the societal understanding of risk and moral responsibility.

Karl Menninger (1967) clearly delineated the fundamental differences between the law and the psychodynamic understanding of the criminal mind. According to Menninger, science, represented by psychiatry, looks at all such instances of lawbreaking as pieces in a total pattern of behaviour and focuses our interests on the internal pressures and external events that lead up to the criminal act as a logical link in a continuing chain of behaviour and adaptation. This is neither a legal question nor a legal concern since the law is only concerned with the fact that its stipulations are *broken*, and the one who breached them—provided he can be convicted—must pay the penalty and, as such, must be officially and socially hurt—"punished". "Justice" will have been done.

In our terms, forensic psychotherapists when confronted with a criminal action will be asking: "Why? What was behind the discovered act which brought the matter to our attention? What pain would drive a man to such a reaction, such a desperate outbreak, or such a deliberate gamble?" At around the same time in the UK, Winnicott was thinking along the same lines with his insightful axiom: "The antisocial tendency is characterized by an *element in it which compels the environment to be important. . . . The antisocial tendency implies hope*" (1956, p. 309). This apparently paradoxical concept will become clear later on when describing the changes that the previously careerist criminal goes through in becoming a neurotic delinquent since his actions become so clumsy as opposed to the cold, calculated performances he used much earlier on. When the action becomes clumsy, the person is easily detected and his intense need for help is quickly recognized by a society that, in his own internal world, was previously so completely blind.

Hopper (1998) reminds us that Winnicott made us aware of the importance of interpersonal relationships and the expectation of unconscious hope for containment and benign authority in the understanding of antisocial and criminal actions. Winnicott also created a most important change from the previous Kleinian assumption that the antisocial tendency was likely to be based on an unconscious search for punishment for actual and imagined crimes.

Winnicott added that "The treatment of the antisocial tendency is not psycho-analysis but management" (1956, p. 309), and he defines the "setting" as "the summation of all the details of management" (1955–6, p. 297). This setting is of prime importance in the treatment of the acting-out behaviour since it provides these individuals with safety and containment. Both he (1955–6, 1956) and Glover (1949) have wonderful descriptions of successes with delinquent children who were treated through management, care, and love. They saw their transient delinquent behaviour as symbolizations of their need for love.

The understanding of our patients would require giving up orthodoxy in favour of "paradoxy". To say it provocatively and in a nutshell, let's abandon our position of "normopath" therapists (McDougall, 1980) to understand our patients' ethics of life and death. We have to adopt what I call "the upside-down" position. It seems to me that Jaime Szpilka (2002) supports this view when talking about an ethical paradox that only human beings are called upon to deal with being Good in Evil and Evil in Good. Chasseguet-Smirgel (1983), in trying to understand the pervert in general and the Marquis de Sade in particular, writes: "They make a mockery of the law by turning it upside down." Incidentally, it was none other than Freud, in his work "Criminals from a Sense of Guilt" (1916, Chapter III), who first postulated the "paradoxy" that guilt precedes some criminal acts rather than follows them, as is usually assumed. In other words, individuals break the law as a means to alleviate already existent guilty feelings. Later, in 1944, Glover links this with the crucial acknowledgement of the unconscious: "Crime and common sense are refractory bed fellows. So long as the existence of unconscious motives is disregarded, we cannot learn anymore about crime than an apparent common sense dictates."

There is a tendency to simplify all acting-out problems as an outcome of unresolved mourning. This is part of the process, but it does not provide the whole answer. The repetitive, compulsive acting-out behaviour, be it a perversion or a criminal offence or both, has to be understood as a minikit survival used as a manic defence against the dreaded black hole of depression. We have to understand that this turning death into "life", even if in a manic way, leads to mourning and hope. I believe that hope and creativity are closely linked and are associated with the work of mourning. In Hopper's words: "the golden rule of forensic psychotherapy is that the traumatized do unto others as they have been done by, because this is the only way that they can obtain a degree of relief from their own suffering, and in the desperate hope that they will be understood" (2001, p. 219).

Educating the general public

Crimes are directed against society—at any rate, that is what society believes. It is unfortunate that the focus of attention is most often placed exclusively on the offence and on the punishment of the offender. Any attempt at psychodynamic understanding of the offender and of his delinquent actions as a result of his own self-destructive internal and compulsive needs is automatically equated by society with his acquittal. This is an understandable but serious error.

Society presents our field with at least three different "cultures": of learning, of concern, and of blaming. As a "caring" society we should be regulated by a culture of learning, although this is generally absent when dealing with offenders who blatantly break the law. Unfortunately the culture of concern is almost exclusively left to clinicians, health workers, and the judiciary. The culture of blaming is left to the lay public and society at large. The titillating front pages of tabloid newspapers make it very difficult if not impossible to understand the inner world of the offender or the motivations for their crimes.

In the words of Baroness Helena Kennedy (2009),

> In the early 1990s John Major as Prime Minister called for a little more condemning and a little less understanding. His wish was granted. Understanding why people commit crime or involve themselves in aberrant behaviour is the only way to create adequate responses, the only way to drive down the prison population. But it means having a grown-up conversation with the general public about what it means to be human.

Prejudicial and judgemental expectations in society are responsible for splitting between the hard option of punishment, which is often met by failure, and the soft option of "false understanding", which is met by scepticism and disdain. In the meantime, our forensic patients appeal to similar mechanisms to conceal their "real selves", resulting in encapsulation of their offending behaviour. An effective collusion between society and offenders is at work.

A major cross-disciplinary effort should be made to understand and eradicate at least some of the more correctable reasons for crime in our society. This involves action by political scientists, sociologists, and community leaders, as well as forensic workers. An imaginative effort is required to promote discussion and to educate the general public. Forensic psychotherapists can and must play a crucial role in this, but the main burden must fall on those in the media and in politics who have special skills of communication.

Society itself is often trapped in its own prejudices. Whereas the treatment of victims is encouraged and everyone is concerned about their welfare, the same does not apply to the perpetrators. They are believed to be the products of "evil forces", and thus punishment is the only response available. Of course, lip service is paid to the recognition that victims can easily become perpetrators. Victims and perpetrators are left without the benefit of a full understanding, since it is generally assumed that the first group is devoid of any negative, hostile feelings and the second group is filled only with hatred. This is a very primitive response. It has been used from time immemorial and especially at times of shock.

The sudden and unexpected "disclosure" of the encapsulation in what appears superficially to be a normal person is so shocking that our first reaction is to dissociate ourselves from those who have committed the terrible deeds. This is followed by a suspension in our ability to think. This inability to think is analogous to the criminal behaviour in that it is impossible to intersperse thought before action; it requires action that is impulsive, immediate, and without further considerations or consequences to anybody, including oneself.

Society's automatic retaliatory responses to violence are characterized by massive projective mechanisms, with a wish to split people into "good" and "bad". This makes our own work extremely difficult. Not only do we have to cope with the added burden of these projections; so, too, do our patients. With respect to deception, these massive projections are the product of self-deception by "good people", who need to reassure themselves of their own "goodness" by throwing stones at the "so-called bad people".

Adshead (2009) offers a most insightful concept when she writes: "Monsters and villains are fixed and inflexible; *it is their lack of interest in transformation that identifies them as evil.* Another way to see this is as lack of repentance or regret. Heroes know that changing the heart and mind is part of psychological growth and maturity." I find her assertion of the lack of interest in transformation so useful, since we know that our interest in works of art has to do with the inner journey the hero takes on to transform himself.

The talented actor, director, and playwright Steven Berkoff (2001) reveals an unusual insight into the dynamics of violence. He shows us that Shakespeare's villains are intended to make us feel good about ourselves by strengthening our values and commitment to justice and humanity. However, Berkoff sensitively adds that although the villain enables us vicariously to enjoy his lust, greed, power, and hunger, he inexorably ends up by being condemned.

Society is consistently reacting in a retaliatory way similar to the no-thinking, acting-out way used by those who break the law. Villains are far less conspicuous in modern times because we use stigmatization of "badness" and "madness" as scapegoats. For example, in the wake of the appalling tragedy brought about by the disappearance and death of 8-year-old Sarah Payne in 2000, the first reaction was one of a systematic, careless revenge of "naming and shaming", which was responsible for even more miscarriages of justice, including suicides of innocent people. The mob escalated to witch-hunt proportions, where irrationality, mindlessness and extreme violence were the rule. And why was this so? Simply because it was more convenient than looking at our own homes, where domestic violence and physical and sexual abuse to children are common occurrences. Once more, splits in the public domain took place, characterized by the need to manufacture a "monster" population viciously attacking a "pure uncontaminated" passive counterpart.

One of the main problems dealing with educating the public through the media such as daily newspapers is the fact that their proprietors know what the readership requires or wants—and this is always sensational news. The answer is given in a most candid and insightful way by Harold Evans in his autobiography *My Paper Chase* (2009): "Amnesia is a characteristic of all newspapers." A major example comes to mind: the furore in 2008 caused by the horrific situation surrounding Baby P's death and torture at the hands of his mother and her boyfriend. Of course, in the psychoanalytic world this phenomenon—of blind spots—was recognized very early on by Freud.

All newspapers covered the extreme situation regarding Baby P. Even a responsible broadsheet like *The Guardian* could not resist reporting the news as a surprising, uniquely horrific event. Interestingly enough, when *Mother, Madonna, Whore* denounced the fact that society was surprised that some women who, in becoming mothers, were left in situations of despair and isolation and adopted sometimes bizarre and abusive behaviour towards their children, *The Guardian* responded immediately in a responsible way by sending Michele Hanson to do a comprehensive interview. This appeared on 15 November 1988 and propagated news of this serious problem to the public.

For such a responsible and aware newspaper as *The Guardian* to fall into this situation of "surprise" or "naivety" is a repetition of a cycle of surprise that mirrors the cycle of abuse.

Exactly twenty years to the day after the interview with Michele Hanson was published, a comprehensive and insightful article by Anna Karpf following the case of Baby P appeared in *The Guardian on Saturday*, on 15 November 2008. Among many other professionals she interviewed was Anna Motz, an expert colleague in this field. It started with the revealing and insightful sentence: "Our first step towards understanding the death of this child should be not to blame social workers but to face the mother's experience of childhood" and it followed with: "Rather than dwelling on the horror, we should try to learn from the killing of Baby P."

Abuse flourishes because we choose to ignore it, not to see what is happening until a tragedy or a scandal makes the headlines. Was *The Guardian* ignorant of the evidence within its own history starting with Michele Hanson's article in 1988? Neglect and denial are the attitudes that permit abuse to thrive unnoticed. All newspapers in their zeal to provide us with sensationalist news contribute to this sorry situation.

A process of thinking and learning is essential for the integration of the "good" and "bad" bits, which should be sought after in a "caring" society.

"Falling from grace"

The general public daily experience feeling "assaulted" by the clever wording in newspapers of unexpected, bizarre, odd situations that have occurred within the confines of "ordinary" human beings. Our almost automatic response is one of shock, disbelief, and condemnation, with most of our intellectual capacities being cancelled out. In other words, we become a bit stupid, ignorant, judgemental, and devoid of any sense of discernment. Our capacity to think has become unavailable. Furthermore, we may even inappropriately laugh at and ridicule people caught in those actions. I believe it is vital that we look at ourselves and at our own reactions to enable us to understand the true nature of the antisocial actions, even more so when they include an unexpected sexual component.

In 2007 an American Republican senator, Larry Craig, a bastion of the community, extremely supportive of family values, highly judgemental in his ideas about homosexuality, and utterly against "gay" rights and marriages, said he "overreacted and made a poor decision" in pleading guilty to disorderly conduct after an incident in an airport bathroom. In his first public statement he said: "Let me be clear: I am not gay and never have been." With his wife by his side, he said he was the victim of a "witch hunt" conducted by the local newspaper. The lying continued, until he was convicted of lewd sexual behaviour, to his utter shame and disgrace. His ferocious attacks against homosexuality were the expression of his own self-hatred because of his rejection of his own feelings projected onto the outside world with much deception. The fact that he occupied an important office with his own constituency trusting and relying on him and his values made them feel cheated and humiliated by these revelations. Now, it was their turn to subject him to humiliation and utter contempt.

In January 2004 in the *British Medical Journal*, Dr Harold Shipman's obituary appeared under the heading of: "A General Practitioner and Murderer":

Few doctors have had as great an impact on British medicine as Harold Shipman. When he and his colleagues qualified from Leeds Medical School in 1970, none of them would ever have imagined that his obituary in the BMJ would have opened with such a sentence. But his impact, and his legacy, is incalculable. Few lives can have raised so many questions about how we practise and regulate medicine.

Britain's general practitioners are frequently the cornerstone of their community, offering care, compassion, and continuity. In return they are trusted—quite remarkably trusted. Shipman betrayed that trust in the most appalling and distressing way, killing at least 215, and possibly 260, of his patients. . . .

This well-measured obituary contains many important features that provide us with much food for thought. Both the obituary and the readers' responses to it offer us a plethora of awareness and insights. The readership, as usual, divided into two: some were in a state of shock, indignant at the space provided for such a "monster". Others had a more philosophical view and were able to change their views while reading it and accepted the need to acknowledge "this horrible story instead of sweeping it under the carpet, and to try to learn from it".

In 1993, news of the serial killer Beverly Allitt, dubbed the "Angel of Death", took the world by surprise. Allitt, a nurse at Grantham and Kesteven Hospital in Lincolnshire, was given thirteen life sentences for murdering four children, attempting to murder another three, and causing grievous bodily harm with intent to a further six. She was diagnosed as suffering from Munchausen Syndrome by Proxy when she carried out the attacks between 1991 and 1993.

Is there anything of any significance for us to observe?

Both Shipman and Allitt were *apparently* living "normal" lives as educated, middle-class members of the caring professions, and their actions had been completely unnoticed by those around them, despite the extreme and repeated violence inflicted towards those under their care. This non-detection is even more puzzling in the Allitt case because she was in daily contact with many other professionals, first in a training position and later working as a nurse.

Reflecting on these cases, it is possible to infer that the most noticeable feature is that of "encapsulation" or "split" of the "other side" or the "dark side" of themselves. We know of the temptation and propensity to demonize all those involved in horrific acts, but the Shipman case makes it obviously clear that, to the outside world, they appear to be people like you and me who have efficiently kept at bay the "other side".

We will never get to know Shipman's motivations, conscious or unconscious, for his behaviour since the real understanding of such individuals and their actions is achieved rarely and only through years of using psychoanalytic techniques of a consistent and laborious kind. This "working through" requires the unlayering of all the different and varied unconscious mechanisms that have been used by such individuals to protect themselves from very primitive, internal, terrifying objects that are populating their minds from within. So, as the *BMJ* obituary states, any explanations or speculations as to why Dr Shipman murdered all those vulnerable elderly women are all too glib and superficial, except perhaps that his clumsy forgery may provide us with an explanation that, unconsciously, he may have wanted to be caught. Perhaps because he was then no longer able to project his murderousness outside in the figures of his extremely vulnerable patients, he was left with his own vulnerability, remaining in control until his very last minute when his self-hatred emerged, powerfully ending his own life.

Apart from *encapsulation* (see chapter 1), we find in the accounts of both Allitt and Shipman a *compulsive need to repeat the action* and *deception*, as well as extreme *violence*. In Shipman's case we learn eventually of his history of violent mood swings, responsible for him not being tolerated by colleagues in his GP practice and leading him to being a single-handed practitioner. In Allitt's case, she had a severe history of self-harm, including eating disorders, self-cutting, and self-burning. In both killers, these features escalated to murderous violence directed at those under their care.

Social class, external power, and risk-taking

The forensic patient refuses to recognize social boundaries: they are too superficial for him. He is really playing Russian roulette with himself, and just as the gambler goes from abject poverty to great wealth and high social position, he belongs everywhere and nowhere.

I would stress that deception, especially in this class-oriented country, actually becomes an effective way of trespassing and attacking the boundaries. Of course, it is ironic that, if members of a "lower" social class are caught, they are likely to obtain a more sympathetic response from the public than if they are from a "higher" "educated" class, whose offences elicit scorn.

These three phenomena can be seen in the case of Lord Archer, whose life reads as a catalogue of deception, from being deceived to deceiving. On 19 July 2001, Archer was found guilty of perjury and perverting the course of justice in a libel case in 1987. He was sentenced to four years' imprisonment.

In 1991 Sir Alan Green, then Director of Public General Prosecutions, was apprehended for alleged kerb-crawling in a well-known area for prostitution. He was later charged with this offence. This was met with the most unsympathetic response from the media, leading to humiliation, disgrace, shame, and the utter destruction of his personal life and career. His estranged wife committed suicide two years later.

There are many contemporary examples of media personalities involved in petty criminal acts that are punishable by the law and could cost their careers.

In deception and risk-taking, the presence of an audience or public is essential. The infantile wish for a captivated public or an audience requires at times an admiring response or, in the case of "flashers", one of shock and fear. In any case, the performance is created as a protection against the dreaded black hole of depression and the possibility of a psychotic breakdown. At times, higher and higher positions of public power are achieved by those with encapsulated "terrible secrets", which adds to the excitement. This addictive feature gives a thrilling sensation, which appears every time he is near to being found out. At times, it could even trigger a life-or-death situation. These individuals may "choose" these positions as a result of a very sadistic superego, which has taken total control. The experience of "near death" actually works as a reassurance of being alive. Individuals in public positions feel trapped not only from inside but also from the outside. They develop a sense of double standards and duplicity, which may precipitate further excitement at the service of the superego. The fear of being caught, along with the fantasized ensuing humiliation, gets them into an unparalleled and overlapping position of excitement, which adds to the erotization of death as the final sentence. When caught, despite enormous losses, these individuals experience a great sense of relief at not being able any longer "to get away with it". The true nature of whatever brings them much agony, pain, and suffering is now in the open, and they are "seen" as they really are.

Creativity, art, and crime

There is a plethora of artistic skills, combined with a great deal of creativity, in forensic patients. I am not referring here to the artistic abilities that they can display when they have the opportunity, although this is an important subject in its own right; the work of delinquents or ex-delinquents has been displayed at a number of important art exhibitions. What I would like to call attention to are the creative resources that are utilized during our patients' pursuit of their misdemeanours. For example, in order to avoid paying for domestic services such as the telephone, some find at their disposal internal resources for creating complicated mechanisms—at times comparable only to those of great inventors. In other words, almost certainly, we have people like Alexander Graham Bell and Alan Turing within the criminal world.

It is also curious to observe how well such patients can perform in the dramatic arts. Of course, while artists use their talents to enhance society and themselves, our forensic patients direct their talents against society and ultimately against themselves.

The forensic patient's ability to deceive is of such high quality that it is comparable to fine acting. Their capacity to deceive is born out of the creative impulse and has to be treated as such. A capacity to produce the best performances out of their worst living circumstances has not only to be understood as an act of creation, but also recognized as a strong element of hope, although not in its usually prescribed form.

Thus, it is not surprising that people from the arts are better equipped to understand these extremely complex personalities. Art demands from them that they depict and reveal all the different layers of the characters they have to impersonate. The usual formula of "Them" and "Us" no longer applies.

Philip Roth shows us many insights into deception in his book *The Human Stain* (2000). I do not want to give away the plot, but I was fascinated to read: "You involve them in a mutual transgression, and you have a mutual corruption." The late John Cassavetes, a very talented and somewhat self-destructive film-maker of the 1950s, said in an interview: "I'm sort of my own Mafia, you know, breaking my own knees." This is such an apt description of how our patients act and feel. Cassavetes added: "I'm interested in how people fool themselves, not how they fool others."

Herbert Rosenfeld (1971) alerted clinicians to the dangers of an internal process of corruption in patients in connection with what he called the "mafia gang". In this, the individual's good parts are obliged by the demands of the bad parts to pay emotional protection money, thus idealizing destructiveness and devaluing love, law, and order.

The ability to reverse an unbearable feeling of despair and emptiness into a comic performance, such as the "crying" clown, is a familiar image. This is the manic defence against the masked chronic depression. It is a usual personality component of most successful comedians. In the biography of comedian Billy Connolly, the most appalling early background is disclosed, with his mother leaving home and later his being sexually abused by his father. In an interview, he describes his emotional survival and says that "comedy is a dark place, it's inspired by survival. The vast majority of the comics I know are kind of wounded in some way. They're kind of damaged somewhere along the line. And they've made it by laughing."

Public safety or personal rights?

Politicians, when aware of these complexities, are caught in the dilemma between public safety and individual rights. In fact, they usually choose to address the public safety because it is more popular with the electorate. Of course, it has to be acknowledged that clinicians are not without their own prejudices, insofar as they tend "to side" with the individual rights of the offenders.

Forensic psychotherapy implies challenge. In fact, it could be regarded as *the* challenge for our patient population, as well as for clinicians and society in general. Actually, all three are deeply interrelated, sometimes through conflict.

All words designated to classify these particular predicaments acquire a pejorative quality rapidly and are deleted from our diagnostic category, to be replaced by others. We can attempt to understand why this is so.

First, because these people are likely to be unpopular and to get into trouble. Second, because, according to popular, cynical, opinion, they never seek treatment, and when they do it is because they are trying to avoid punishment such as custodial sentences. Third, they are not always treatable, and even when they are, we are bound to confuse the terms treatability with curability, which is not appropriate since the delinquent acts are a form of adjustment, a way of managing otherwise unmanageable emotional conflict. Fourth, because unfairly it is always expected that they will develop into chronic recidivists. But motivation for treatment, changes, and remissions, even if they are few, can also be expected, but they may not present themselves as expected with other patient populations.

The scenarios have to constantly repeat where the existence of duplicity and double moral standards may precipitate further excitement at the service of the superego. The fear of being caught, with the fantasized ensuing humiliation, gets them into an unparalleled and overlapping position of both risk-taking and excitement, which adds to the erotization of death as the final sentence. In fact, when caught, despite enormous losses of all sorts, these individuals experience a great sense of relief at not being able any longer "to get away with it". The true nature of whatever brings them much agony, pain, and suffering is now in the open, and they have the possibility of being "judged" as they really are. This is itself an admission of guilt and a readiness to start therapy.

Many examples come to mind from my casuistic of thirty years' work. For example, Steven, a policeman, himself a flasher, who during the course of his work took enormous risks, concurrently with increasing sexual tension, going to open places such as parks, with the hidden desire to uncover, penalize, humiliate, and bully other flashers and cruisers. When eventually and after many years of being undetected he is apprehended, it is automatically assumed by others that he was "taking advantage of his job" to indulge in his perversion. But again, things are not that simple: inside what appears to be a conscientious and law-abiding citizen there is a frightened, driven man who could feel better off by not experiencing those terrible urges which have to be kept well concealed from his family and work colleagues. He obviously knows he is doing is wrong and needs punishment from his strong and tyrannical superego, which places him in such a ridiculous and apparently absurd situation. And when he is eventually found out it will be accompanied by the most humiliating circumstances. In this particular case, he was apprehended after twenty-five years of work, just the day before his financial stipend would be available to him! This constitutes his owning up to his criminal activity and his need for punishment.

The forensic population knows no social boundaries, affecting the highest and the lowest strata of society. Their internal lives are "upside down". For example, Mrs P was referred because of an unexpected episode of "meaningless" shoplifting after an earlier criminal lifestyle. She told me she was feeling depressed and that the *shoplifting had functioned as a "therapy"*. She felt low because her child needed her less than when he was a baby. At age 16 she had decided to have a baby to secure herself "love and company". With this aim in mind, she became pregnant by a bank robber. She had felt humiliated and shamed because not only did he not want to marry her, but he had also decided to marry another woman. Soon afterwards, he was sent to prison for robbery. She now with great skill chose a "father" for her unborn baby. He proved to be a caring and responsible father to her child, who firmly believed him to be his real father. When asked about any fear she might have had about the real father asserting his paternity, she thought this a joke: "Well, Doctor, this could never happen since I'm a very caring mother. The real father would never dare to come along—my husband, you see, is a much better bank robber than he is." Her main priority in her newly created family was the welfare of her son, providing him with good, psychological, and sound emotional surroundings, even though these did not correspond with our own set of ethics. And this example clearly demonstrates that ethics do not count—survival does.

FORENSIC PSYCHOTHERAPY IN PRACTICE

Referral procedures

I shall be dealing exclusively with the basic facts of forensic psychotherapy as it is practiced in a particular NHS outpatient clinic—the Portman Clinic. Other settings, such as special hospitals, medium-secure units, and therapeutic communities, though of great and increasing importance and relevance, are not directly addressed here, although the principles obtain in these institutions too.

Prospective forensic patients are referred for assessment of suitability for psychodynamic psychotherapy, either individual or group, via two main sources: external and self-referral. External sources include general psychiatric hospitals, GPs, probation officers, courts, and other institutions. In some cases, public knowledge of a patient's sexual and/or criminal offence is very wide, following a court appearance reported in the press. Usually self-referrals are by patients whose "bizarre" unlawful sexual behaviour is unknown to anyone except themselves and their victims. They come or refer themselves of their own free will.

An important characteristic in determining the prognosis and motivation for treatment is an intense sense of shame and despondency that some of them express about the activities in which they are involved. This is reciprocated by society's response in judging and condemning them when their behaviour is detected, regardless of their own feelings about their criminal actions. Both offender and society feel bewildered and unable to comprehend the motivations or symbolism attached to their deviant actions. According to Adshead (2009): "The presence of shame tends to make us less inclined to call an act or intention evil: because the presence of shame means that the person is aware of the social group to which he belongs; understand that his identity is connected to a social one."

NHS vs private practice

Therapists' inner knowledge that the State is paying for their professional services becomes invaluable while working with this patient population, since they too are aware of this basic fact. It reinforces both parties in the contractual agreement on which the therapy is based. The therapists are debarred from blackmail, and the patients feel neither exploited nor able to exploit anybody about money matters.

For example, it is a common occurrence that colleagues in the private sector treating women because of relationship problems eventually discover they are also involved in prostitution. One of my male colleagues got to know this when a patient indignantly shouted at him after a few months that he was "forcing" her to get involved in paid sex because of the exorbitant bills she had to pay him. It was obviously linked to transferential issues, and this disclosure made him feel not only confused but also like a pimp. It took him quite a while of interpreting her negative transference, which until then had been covered with a sweet but clear condescension on her part.

Clinical findings in NHS outpatients' clinics, especially in relation to perversion, are very different from those found in private practice (see chapter 1).

The importance of the team

A crucial point about the discipline of forensic psychotherapy is that it is a team effort. The full meaning of this phrase will emerge from the discussion that follows, but at the outset it needs to be stated that this is not a heroic action by the psychotherapist alone. The action begins with the referral agencies, which include the courts of justice. But court or no court, there is no getting away from the fact that the offender's actions are blatantly carried out against society or those principles that society values, and which we all share. Accordingly, a wide range of people are inescapably involved.

It is crucial to recognize that successful treatment rests not only with the professional psychotherapist but also with a team of helpers, including psychologists, social workers, and administration and clerical staff. Anne Aiyegbusi eloquently argues that the teamwork must be both intra- and interdisciplinary, aimed at understanding the "impact of the patients' psychopathology on the team and the individual prac-titioner" (Aiyegbusi & Clarke-Moore, 2009, p. 26). As a nurse herself, she also reminds us of the important work of forensic mental health nurses, which has to be located within a team approach to patient care and treatment. John Gordon and Gabriel Kirtchuk (2008) use a sensi-tive axiom enlightening us about the dangerous impact the forensic population poses to those treating them: "The more patients empty their minds of painful memories, the more staff members' minds and case notes are filled with them. Ultimately, the combined burden of remembering and the unrelenting pressure from patients to forget affects staff members and teams" (pp. 127–128).

For the general public, it is no doubt society that matters most, but for the professional forensic psychotherapist the prime consideration must be the patient. If forensic psychotherapy is concerned above all with the patient, it should be scarcely less concerned with the "treater" and his or her training. Why? Because, if the treater is not properly trained, the members of the team are bound to feel confused and overwhelmed by all the dimensions involved, many of which are unpleasant and stressful. The importance of the development of this discipline in the UK as an "evolving species" (Adshead, 1991) is our main concern. If the treater is not trained and equipped with insight into his own internal world and his own motivations, he may unwit-tingly react to a situation as if he were a normal member of the public. This is a very natural reaction, but unfortunately it is an abdication of responsibility: it is unprofessional.

Edward Glover, a pioneer of forensic psychotherapy and former medical director of the Portman Clinic, was one of the first—if not the first—psychoanalyst who went beyond the confines of the psycho-analytic consulting room to explore the unconscious origins of social problems such as criminality and war. It is amazing to see how the clinical work of Edward Glover overlaps with that of Donald Win-nicott, another forensic pioneer. In the National Sound Archives of the BBC, one can listen to broadcasts by Glover on psychoanalysis and politics in which he dared to suggest that politicians should undergo psychoanalytic treatment. One wonders what sense he would make of recent political situations. Glover was open enough and trusting enough with his own psychoanalytic ideas to share them with other colleagues who were initially hostile to psychoanalysis. I feel confident that he would be proud of our achievements, especially the applica-tion of psychoanalysis by multidisciplinary teams through the inter-national forensic psychotherapeutic network.

Importance of the setting

Setting and surroundings are important—especially since the forensic patient has usually had previous experience of the judicial system, having been caught, detected, and judged. In his dealing with the psychotherapist, he is prone to feel judged, charged, persecuted, and subject to prejudice. If the diagnostician is not well trained, a new confrontation could easily be experienced by the prospective patient as a further condemnation of his or her illegal action.

Because of their intense reluctance to engage in a close relationship, especially in a one-to-one situation, these patients form a strong transference to the clinic as an institution. It is important to keep this in mind in making treatment recommendations, when group analytic therapy may be rated as the best therapeutic option.

As a result of the strong transference to the treating place as an institution, the institution treating these patients can become as, or more, important than the therapist herself. A safe and containing atmosphere in which the patients feel secure and acknowledged from the moment of their arrival is essential. In short, the assessment is to be carried out like any other assessment, but, if anything, with even more care and sensitivity. It is worthwhile repeating that the forensic patient should be assessed within a formal institutional setting rather than a private setting.

The institution includes the administration and the clerical staff, who have to be trained to deal with day-to-day management and containment of difficult situations, which if not properly handled could give rise to dangerous and violent outcomes. The gamut runs from answering phone calls and greeting patients properly to helping with difficult and distressing incidents. All senior staff are involved in this "informal" training. When distress and crisis occur, such training proves its worth for everyone, including the senior staff themselves.

Forensic patients are very much in need of three structures—fellow patients, therapist, and institution. All are deeply related in their mental representations, which constitute a process of triangulation. There is also a fourth structure, which is often absent: the family.

An important function provided by the institution is that of containment. It reinforces a sense of boundaries and so acts as a container for all tensions involved and allows the emergence of trust and a collective awareness of, and sensitivity to, the recrudescence of violence, reducing its likelihood. At times of crisis, when for many reasons staff members are unable to fulfil these tasks properly, a breakdown of

---

Summary of general approach in the psychodynamic assessment

• Patient should be clear about the purpose of the meeting

• This should be obtained in one to three sessions, at irregular intervals

• Keep to the exact times for meetings

• Never engage in jocular response to the patient's "jokes"

• Keep a straightforward approach, neither too cold nor too friendly

• Make it clear that information is needed for accuracy of the evaluation process

• Listen to the patient's predicaments but, if the patient feels "stuck", ask direct questions

---

the system is likely—with serious consequences for all, including the patients.

At times the action is symptomatic, in which the person knows it is wrong but finds he is unable to resist it. At other times the action is an enactment that the person is not willing to admit is odd or wrong. This action has sometimes been unconsciously committed in an attempt to obtain a response from society to the predicament of the individual offender; the action takes over, and society focuses its attention on the action and not on the person who has committed it—until, of course, it comes to condemnation.

Therefore, it is of basic importance to "see" and to "acknowledge" the person in his or her totality. For example, it is important that letters regarding all appointments are properly and formally addressed to "Mr", "Ms", or "Mrs". The same attitude should prevail when the patient arrives at the clinic where he or she is to be seen. The building should be accessible, the atmosphere warm, and the attitude welcoming from the moment the patient faces the receptionist. Patients should be treated with dignity—surnames only, for example—and everything reasonable done to give them enough self-respect to face the complexities of their first diagnostic consultation with an unknown consultant. It is worth remembering that someone who has been referred for a psychiatric court report, fresh from involvement with police enquiries concerning offences, is frightened about having to face yet another figure of authority expected to be ready to judge and condemn.

Even the requirement to see NHS patients only once a week, which might appear on the surface to be limiting and restricting, has actually proved to be a most suitable "dose" for those patients who find it extremely difficult to take in more frequent sessions.

The topic of forensic psychotherapy and its contribution to forensic psychiatry in an institutional setting has been described by Cox (1983). As Iacuzzi (2009) perceptively states:

> in keeping with the Freudian style, I believe that at the present time the psychoanalytic movement is fulfilling an important task—to find new foundations and, from them, open trends in work areas which were alien before. One of them would be to emerge from lethargy and open new trails for research, training, communication, and integration, aiming to develop an eventual "prison psychology" with a psychoanalytic orientation. [p. 2, translated by E.W.]

The psychodynamic assessment

The psychodynamic assessment requires a wider understanding of all other factors concerning that particular person, his psychological growth, his family (taking it back at least three generations), his own sub-culture, and other circumstances. The psychotherapist needs to investigate the "crimes" in detail, especially the sequence of events leading up to the action as well as the offender's reaction to it. This can give clues to early traumatic experiences, and to the unconscious ways through which an individual tries to resolve conflicts resulting from these experiences. In this way, even during the evaluation itself, the psychotherapist is able slowly to uncover layers of primitive defences and the motivations behind them—enabling us to learn about the offender's capacity or incapacity for psychodynamic treatment, as well as initiating a process whereby the offender might acquire insight into the nature of his crimes.

Minne (1997) describes the assessment process in an extremely lucid and illuminating way. According to her: "The therapist's task is a delicate and complicated one: firstly, helping to cultivate awareness in the person's mind without seeming to commit a violent assault to that mind; secondly, to clinically judge that such awareness is developing and, thirdly, to continually gauge in what way that person is using his/her new awareness. These are the shifts that we look for in the monitoring of our work".

It is important to record how the patient interacts with the clinician and the changes observed during the series of meetings. At times it is useful to make a "trial" interpretation to elicit the patient's capacity to make use of it and his capacity for insight. In order to assess treatability for psychotherapy accurately in these patients, it is invaluable to modify terms and concepts from those used in assessing neurotic patients. For example, when the criminal action is committed clumsily, the person is especially susceptible to detection; the criminal action has become the equivalent of the neurotic symptom. The offender may also express fears of a custodial sentence, which may denote, in his own terms, motivation for treatment. This could signal that it is the appropriate time to start treatment, since the patient is susceptible, however much under implied duress. He is now ready to own his psychopathology, and this may denote an incipient sense of capacity for insight. From this therapeutic standpoint, it is not unfortunate that a patient has to face prosecution, but what is unfortunate is that just when he is ready for treatment he may instead have to face punishment. The patient may actually acquire a criminal record for the first time while in treatment or on the waiting list. Ironically, the very success of our treatment may produce this result. It is when the patient who has hitherto escaped detection starts to acquire some insight into himself that he becomes clumsy and is detected. So, in a way, it may be said that psychotherapy results in a higher rate of official, statistical criminality!

The relapse in delinquent and criminal behaviour is frequently found during the first long holidays in psychotherapy. This is associated with feelings of having been abandoned by their therapists at times of need. Gallwey (1991) points out that "The uncovering of areas of deprivation and unfulfilled dependency can produce enormous pressure on both therapist and patient, with a speedy move into delinquent acting-out, or even violence, when the patient feels let down or abandoned within the therapy. The least hazardous tactic is to contain the individual in a way which minimizes the reinforcement of delinquent strategies."

In short, the assessment is to be carried out like any other assessment but, if anything, with even more care and sensitivity. These conditions are far more easily available within the confines of an institutional setting as opposed to a private one, which can seriously complicate matters, including those of confidentiality and ethics. Cleo van Velsen (2010, p. 173) remarks that there is little acknowledgement of the paradoxical situation of the forensic patient during assessment for a psychiatric court report since he is encouraged to speak his mind even though aware that this could be used "against" him and could eventually determine the possibility of a future detention.

The patient should be clear from the outset about the reasons for the assessment interviews, particularly because the procedure could easily be taken as yet another legalistic encounter. If the purpose is the writing of a psychiatric court report, this should be made clear from the start. All interviews should embody the utmost honesty. If treatment is recommended, the patient should be told the length of the waiting list—especially if it is a long one—and be informed that the assessment process may involve three or four meetings. Forensic patients usually complain and are sarcastic about the fact that an "assessment" or psychiatric court report has been made within a mere twenty minutes of meeting a psychiatrist. They (patients and diagnosticians) should not be allowed to get away with this caricature of a professional assessment by making sure that the allocated time is adequate for the purposes of a psychiatric report. The "structuring of time", as coined by Murray Cox (1992a, p. 338), is a vital frame in forensic psychotherapy and is quite different as practiced by forensic psychiatrists, who should be ready to be summoned at any time. Instead, forensic psychotherapists are aware that patients can only rely on those therapists who keep a strict timing for their sessions. In the initial period of treatment, beginning with the first interview, it is especially important to follow firm guidelines. Always see the patient at the time agreed for the appointment, neither earlier nor later: earlier will be felt as seduction; later as a sense of neglect, repeating the experience of "nobody caring". These diagnostic meetings should be conducted at irregular intervals in order to avoid the intensity of the emergence of transference. The meetings are not as structured as psychotherapy sessions; there is some flexibility, but the timing is always to be preserved rigorously. The approach needs judiciously to combine silence and direct questioning so that the patient can feel allowed to talk freely about difficult and, at times, painful predicaments while also being expected to give, in answers to questions, more details for further clarification.

The clinician must not let the patient involve him in anti-therapeutic manoeuvring, such as laughing at a patient's joke. Frequently, such jokes are made at the expense of the patient's own self-esteem, with overtones of self-contempt and denigration: "Nobody takes me seriously." Patients often try to engage the clinician in a jocular response. It is a serious mistake, into which inexperienced therapist's fall, to appear friendly and non-judgemental. No sooner has the therapist laughed than a sudden realization emerges that he or she is laughing *at* the patient and not *with* the patient.

During the assessment sessions, there are often attempts to re-create the original injurious, traumatic situation as experienced by the patient. Frequently this will have been experienced as being treated as a "part-object" and becomes vividly alive in the transference.

A sense of boundaries is crucial, among many other layers of need, to establish a sense of differentiation, in which "them" and "us" create a sense of order and justice that can be rightly acknowledged. This is one reason why patients powerfully resent the "do-gooders". In their eyes, the "do-gooders" try to proselytize, to infantilize, to make them believe "we are all the same".

Specific characteristics of female dangerousness

The assessment of dangerousness, or risk assessment, is another area in which forensic psychotherapists have an important role. A significant percentage of the patients we see—and this refers to both men and to women—are themselves the victims of sexual abuse as children. Furthermore, the histories of women who are perpetrators of physical and sexual abuse of children contain a psychopathology of self-abuse and/or sadomasochistic relationships. For example, the history of Beverly Allitt included horrific self-mutilation while she was a student nurse. She was suffering from anorexia at the time of her trial. This self-destructive trait was never acknowledged. The reason that she was not found out by anybody may be explained by Susie Orbach (2005) when she talks about how the anorectic emanates a kind of coldness, a sort of frigid chill, that operates as an almost physical boundary that people do not dare to penetrate (p. 99).

Had this new concept of female perversion previously being taken into account, a job involving "mothering" duties would have been at least discouraged and might not have been pursued. It is this mis-assessment that has led some very "damaged ladies" being so misunderstood as to be denied the treatment they need and for which they sometimes plead. Such attitudes are among the reasons why it is taking so long for the profession, let alone the public, to accept that women as mothers or in mothering professions can inflict irreparable and permanent damage on the children they are suppose to care for.

The actual dangerousness in the Beverley Allitt case is devastatingly obvious, but what are the determinants for these horrific killings; what has been overlooked and even neglected? Could this violent behaviour have been predicted earlier on? Were there circumstances that establish a higher tendency to risk, which would increase the chances for this dangerousness? Furthermore, is this dangerousness intrinsically female? And if so why? How can we use this awful experience to learn how to improve our ways of detecting and assessing dangerousness accurately and to prevent further criminal behaviour in the future?

I believe that the important differences between males and females could help us in the prediction, assessment, and management of female dangerousness. These could be used in a positive way to promote further understanding and prevention of these particular conditions. But it is extremely difficult to conceive of predictability when society is totally unprepared to deal with the emergency of mothers inflicting harm on children, including their own, such is the glorification of motherhood.

I found it of extreme relevance to notice the link between the female abuser and dangerousness. For example, according to Scott's (1977) definition, "Dangerousness is an unpredictable and untreatable tendency to inflict or risk serious, irreversible injury or destruction, or to induce others to do so. Dangerousness can, of course, be directed against the self." This is a well-known definition, considered both practical and useful. Beneath the deceptive simplicity there lies a hidden wisdom and complexity. Incidentally and to prove this point, it is worthwhile noting that authors who quote the definition usually omit the final sentence of it. This omission is, in my view, unacceptable because it denotes a lack of understanding of a developmental process that may prove to be essential in the assessment of predictability of female dangerousness. Predictability and risk are frequently and relevantly associated with dangerousness. According to Scott (1977), "Prediction studies should aim not to replace but to complement the clinical approach, and vice versa".

We could actually suspect that future female dangerousness to others could occur in view of earlier clinical findings, including self-harm. This is not to say or even to predict that self-abuse will be superseded by child abuse. However, the knowledge that these two conditions could be associated might facilitate a better anamnesis, with proper care of all involved.

Scott (1977) already dispelled the myth that women are less dangerous than men because of being physically weaker, and he mentions the fact that mothers are as likely to batter their babies as are men. However, I strongly disagree with his contention that "women more rarely cross the threshold into dangerousness, but when they do, perhaps by substituting stealth for strength, they offer the same difficulties of prediction and treatment as do men".

It is worth noting that through unconscious motivations, many young and psychologically damaged women seek working positions in the caring professions with direct access to children. At times, they are oblivious to the dangers they are exposing themselves and the children to, with the possibility of serious consequences to all involved. As a society we should be more attentive to monitoring processes during selection procedures and be more caring and responsible in providing consistent supervision to untrained and poorly paid personnel whose difficult task it is to take care of children and disabled people.

It seems important to develop a personality profile that could lead to the prevention, accurate diagnosis, and better treatment of these conditions. Evaluations should include the number and gender in the family tree; the value of femininity in the family, noting educational achievements in both girls and boys; the mother's and grandmother's previous pregnancies and family; and known incestuous activities, with short- and long-term consequences. Some of the most common findings include an early history of abandonment and neglect in their psychoetiology, and being victims of either physical or sexual abuse or of both.

As discussed in chapter 2, prior to being perpetrators of child abuse, most women have a history of self-abuse, often manifest during adolescence in the form of eating disorders and self-harm. Pregnancy as an outcome of a sense of inadequacy, hatred, or revenge (conscious or unconscious), or as a "quick replacement" can also lead to child abuse. Lack of emotional and practical resources during pregnancy and early mothering is often the case, as well as associations with uncaring and violent men leading to sadomasochistic relationships. These could also involve other women. Describing the after-effects of childhood sexual abuse for a woman, Ashurst and Hall (1989) noted that "she is unable to assert herself because she feels that, since her boundaries have already been breached, she must satisfy any man's sexual needs" (p. 77).

In the diagnostic approach, we should be aware of some crucial factors that may be linked to the present psychopathology:

- Was the particular abused child singled out from birth?
- Did the gender of the child create a disappointment at birth?
- Did the child represent or re-enact another child, such as the product of a quick replacement pregnancy following the death or miscarriage of a previous child? or a brother/sister that the patient felt resembled herself as a child?
- Did the woman consider abusing that child for a long time prior to the actual abuse, or was it sudden and unexpected?
- Was the abuse taking place when the woman was feeling unable to convey to anyone her own sense of despair and desperation, or when she was in distress or feeling extremely isolated, helpless, or moody?
- Did the acting-out bring a temporary sense of relief and elation?
- Was this a chronic condition, or was it aggravated by superimposed conditions?

Another important characteristic to be elicited is the degree of emotional attachment that mothers feel towards the children involved in the abuse. The question should also be asked whether they are able to stop themselves from acting out these sadistic fantasies and, if so, how.

The inability to obtain professional help may be due to (1) the patient's enormous difficulties due to shame or (2) professionals' difficulties in listening due to both a marked response of disbelief and helplessness, and a tendency in the profession to call "problem" women hysterics, manipulators, inadequate, attention-seekers. This response is further reinforced by society's value of glorified motherhood and the all-too-frequent equating of motherhood with good mental health.

Transference and countertransference in forensic psychotherapy

Transference

It is necessary to understand the personality traits of forensic patients since they lead directly into an understanding of the transference and countertransference phenomena that appear from the beginning of the assessment and throughout the psychodynamic treatment.

An early and severe emotional deprivation is usually found in the psychogenesis of both sexes, which may include a history of neglect, abandonment, symbiotic relationship with mother, humiliation of gender identity, physical abuse, sexual abuse, wrong gender assignment at birth, and cross-dressing during infancy. All the above may occur, either singly or in any combination. However, the commonest case is being the victim of both seduction and neglect. There has frequently been an absence of acknowledgement of generational differences, especially in cases of incest, with children being "forced" to fulfil parental roles and victims becoming perpetrators, leading to a three-generational process.

These adult patients have experienced—as infants—a sense of having been messed about in crucial circumstances in which both psychological and biological survival was at stake. In other words they were *actually*—in reality, not only in fantasy—at the mercy of others. These traumatic, continuous, and inconsistent attitudes towards them have effectively interfered with the process of individuation and separation. There is a basic lack of trust towards the significant carer, which accompanies them all throughout their lives. This corresponds to a true traumatic condition. From this early ill-treatment it is possible to deduce some psychopathological features that will be understood in the light of that background:

1. A need to be in control, which is apparent from the moment they are first seen and also during treatment.

2. A vulnerability to anything that is in any way reminiscent of the original early experiences of deprivation and subjection to seductiveness.

3. A desire for revenge, expressed in sadomasochism as an unconscious need to inflict harm.

4. Erotization or sexualization of the action.

5. Manic defence against depression.

There are very elaborate and sophisticated unconscious mechanisms these patients have built-up for and in themselves. They operate as a "self-survival kit": this is automatically "turned on" in situations of extreme vulnerability when they experience being psychically naked or "stripped". They use oversexualization in the same way, as a means to deal with an enormous sense of inadequacy and of inner insecurity.

They themselves become the part-objects to be readily available and easily exploited, abused, seduced. Of course, this is no longer a unilateral, one-way system as happened when they were infants at the mercy of their parents or carers. Now, to the whole world, they appear to be adults, but actually much of their internal world belongs to far earlier phases of their emotional development in which an enormous sense of helplessness was acquired and much revenge has been harboured for a long time. The one-way system has become a two-way system in their own unconscious minds, which is in constant dynamic activity. This "survival" mechanism could reach such proportions that persons who are in extreme need of psychological help recoil in horror when offered psychotherapy; an immediate refusal is the automatic answer, claiming that they have conquered a complete freedom, such is the fear of examining their own terrible sufferings they were subjected to as helpless babies.

Here is where the work and aims of psychotherapy have to be defined, since there are turning points during therapy when they are likely to experience fears of dependency, with its associated rage at being either abandoned or seduced. It is obvious that all these different survival mechanisms and ways of functioning will appear intermittently when the defences are down. Then alarm and the old feelings re-emerge and put the person concerned on the alert. Defence mechanisms go in waves, and when a situation of closeness is about to be achieved, the person withdraws in horror. Such people loathe any new scenario that might involve or develop into trust. Thus, in their minds, the therapist can turn into a tyrannical and despotic parental figure, only there to satisfy his or her own whims, or into an uncaring, unreliable, and egotistic person devoid of any concern and prone to abandon and dispose of them as they wish.

Acknowledgement and understanding of the transferential and countertransferential problems is crucial to deal with the implicit difficulties therapists will be facing from the very start of evaluation proceedings and the subsequent psychotherapy. The many subtleties involving transferential and countertransferential processes include the patients' need for control; an apparently jocular attitude, which effectively covers distress and isolation; and attempts to seduce the therapist into collusion and unconscious participation in their delinquent behaviour.

For example, in the course of treatment, a female patient of 27, charged with soliciting, started to develop a "sense of trust" towards me. This was in open contrast with the initial phase when she had been

very reluctant to engage in treatment and had mocked the hypocritical, moral middle-class standards. Her husband was a notorious bank
robber who had managed never to be detected. In the sessions she told
me of her anxieties regarding his activities. One day she surprised me
by saying: "Doctor, I trust you so much that you're going to be the only
person to know of my husband's next job. But if the information leaks
to the police, I'll know that you're not trustworthy." With this provocative statement she was challenging me with undisclosed information:
as opposed to indicating a "sense of trust", she was placing me in a
double-bind position. I could easily feel threatened and ready to be
blackmailed, or I could become a partner in crime.

Countertransference

The forensic psychotherapist should feel safe and securely contained
in caring and unobtrusive surroundings. Institutions should provide
such structures, to protect the therapists from the inherent anxiety
produced by working with forensic patients.

Money matters are important, both in concrete and in symbolic
terms. This is obvious with patients whose day-to-day living is provided by their own or close associates' delinquent or perverse actions.
A frequent problem is the offer or "pushing" of a gift, which could at
times render the therapist a receiver of stolen goods.

In private practice, there is a real risk that the therapist feels or
realizes that she is being trapped in a corrupt and fraudulent interaction, where the patient has the upper hand in an unethical position
and both patient and therapist have failed in obtaining a process of
transformation; the patient is now in a "triumphant" position, having
effectively tricked the therapist and, as such, left himself without the
hope of being understood in his totality.

In my early days I almost fell into this when a male patient of 28,
whom for two years I had been treating in individual therapy due to
crimes of breaking and entering and of violence, came to his last session before the Christmas break. This was preceded by a relapse into
a stealing episode, for which he was almost caught; this constituted
an acting-out related to his early life when he had been abandoned by
his parents. At the beginning of the session he told me of this stealing, which I interpreted as a consequence of my impending Christmas
holidays. He was dismissive about this in a manic way: "Who cares
about your going away, I'll be lucky to have a rest." Then, at the last
minute of the session, he took out a package, which he explained was

his Christmas present for me. When I reminded him of the rule of not accepting presents under any circumstances, he was initially very upset and insisted I take it, despite knowing this was not acceptable. He got furious and in a flood of tears said: "You bloody bitch! You're insulting me; after all this time in treatment I have been saving money from my own work. It has not been stolen. This gift has been bought with decently earned money." I became suddenly and unexpectedly aware that, had I accepted the present, I would have unwittingly become the "receiver of stolen goods"! This had never occurred to me before. It was quite a memorable learning. That was his real gift to me.

It is never banal to emphasize the fact that these patients are quick in trying to destroy the effectiveness of psychoanalytic interpretations made at the right time and with the precise elements of understanding the destructive acting-out behaviour. This is the "acting-in" that is directed to attack the therapists, leaving them feeling de-skilled and utterly confused. It is another instance where the presence of other patients with similar predicaments but in different stages of their emotional transformation could offer the best help by sharing their own hard-learnt insights with patients who are ferociously fighting against any new process of learning that involves much suffering.

The psychotherapist must listen to the patient carefully, without interrupting, however difficult or painful the material may be. "The forensic psychotherapist spends much of his time and energy waiting and witnessing, while his patients try to unravel that vitally important nodal point of experience 'between the acting of a dreadful thing/And the first motion'" (Cox, 1992b, p. 255).

This is especially so since some of their disclosures are extremely difficult to listen to because they include cruel and sadistic behaviour towards themselves and others. Some supposedly "unusual" or "rare" predicaments are not that unusual: the so-called rarity is often due to the clinician's inability to listen because of the psychic pain involved. This is frequently the case with incestuous relationships. It is important to be aware of how our own feelings of disbelief may be the origin of, for example, the under-recording of female perversions such as female paedophilia and maternal incest. Patients may be ready to talk about these urges, but diagnosticians generally are not ready to listen to them. Even in groups (see chapter 7) not only the therapist but even other fellow members would not believe a mother talking about her awful, destructive, even hating feelings towards her child(ren), to the chagrin of the woman who perhaps for the first time has attempted to ventilate those inexplicable, "horrid" feelings. That other patients are resistant and reluctant to listen may be not so difficult to understand since there is an immediate identification, especially with this patient population, with the not-wanted or, better termed, unwelcome or even hated child—after all, all of them share the same predicament, but for a therapist not to be able to acknowledge this disclosure has grave consequences for all involved. I have often heard of health professionals making ignorant comments in an attempt to "calm down" the patient, such as "But of course you don't mean that, you love your child, this is just a whim thing that in no time will disappear", or, often, "Don't worry about it." By saying this they are trying to calm themselves down and to cancel any concern that may be too disturbing for the therapist. The requirement of personal therapy for future treaters is of basic importance, in order to be able to discern what belongs to the treater's internal world and what to the patient. The material from most of these patients can disturb profoundly because at times it feels like dealing with "dynamite". Sometimes, if unprepared, the therapist could easily become irate, as if he or she is being "taken for a ride", and indeed the patient often tries to be in total control of the situation. In other instances, patients succeed in making their therapists become their true partners in their specific perversions.

Here is a brief clinical vignette to illustrate the point. A patient came for a diagnostic interview because of his compulsive masochistic needs. These involved the hiring of a dominatrix to physically abuse him in a way that sexually excited him. In the course of the interview, the therapist found to her horror that she had become actively engaged in a dialogue in which, quite unawares, by the end she was almost screaming at the top of her voice every time she talked to him. This was in response to the patient asking or even "begging" her to repeat her sentences "just a bit louder, because I'm hard of hearing". In so doing she was sort of "beating him up" with her screaming. One of the reasons the therapist became aware of her own collusive response to his perversion was that at the time the patient was relating how he had secured the services of a nurse to function as a sadistic prostitute. The nurse, just as the assessor, symbolized the caring profession, which had been corrupted.

Alternatively, the inexperienced therapist may feel flattered by the fact that whatever positive change may have been achieved, the patient may ascribe this "success" to the practitioner's own professional efforts. However, the flattery won't last for long—it will soon be replaced by complaints and dissatisfaction about relapses or re-offending behaviour. If the therapist falls into the countertransferen-tial trap of being the one responsible for the patient's "improvement", it will now be assumed that any relapse is due to the practitioner's inefficiency and lack of "skills", just as, before, the "cure" of the prob-lem had to do with his or her excellence.

In other words, there is a constant switch between idealization and denigration. This happens because psycho-pathological predica-ments and offending behaviour are the result of a deep, chronic, hid-den depression. This turns into a manic and at times bizarrely funny acting-out. There is so much pain underneath that at times patients barely manage to confront it. They try at all costs to avoid their real feelings. The therapist could easily be caught in the countertransfer-ence process, assuming an omnipotent role in the patient's actions, regardless of whether these are law-abiding or not.

Main features of forensic patients

Most forensic patients have deeply disturbed backgrounds. Some have criminal records and very low self-esteem which is often covered by a façade of cockiness and arrogance; their impulse control is mini-mal, and they are suspicious and filled with hate towards people in authority. Some rebellious and violent ex-convicts have long histories of crime against property and persons. Others may refer themselves, and in these cases they are often insecure, inadequate, and ashamed. They enact their pathological sexual deviancy, such as exhibitionism, paedophilia, or voyeurism, in a very secretive manner so that only their victims know about their behaviour. Some patients have a great capacity for expressing anger, yet seem shy and awkward in showing tenderness or love to anybody.

Forensic patients are often deviant both sexually and socially. For example, some sexual deviations present themselves as criminal activities by definition, although some patients who indulge in these actions may never have been caught. This is a secret or secretive popu-lation who apparently lead completely normal lives. However, the links between criminal actions such as "breaking and entering" and sexual deviations are not always obvious, at least not until the uncon-scious motivation is revealed (see chapter 1). This connection has been noticed by many psychoanalytic authors (e.g., Glover, 1944; Zilboorg, 1933, 1955) and notably in young persons by Limentani (1984)

It is essential to realize that sexual deviance differs from sexual perversion. As Stoller (1975) has argued, "The term . . . 'perversion' is necessary—not withstanding its traditional pejorative meaning and dictionary definition—for certain character disorders in which the dynamics of hostility force a person to aberrant sexual acts." In other words, perversion implies an obligatory inclusion in the sexual act of defensive, alternative, or partial gratifications that allow genital release but usually not emotional intimacy. In contrast, "deviation" implies a statistical abnormality: it describes an act not usually performed in certain circumstances within a given cultural milieu.

Who is the forensic patient?

This patient population constitutes what is presently termed the "forensic patient", and the science or discipline applied to their understanding is, as already mentioned, forensic psychotherapy. It seems to me that no other patient population could obtain more benefits from group psychotherapy than this one. It becomes the treatment of choice provided that certain conditions apply, such as diverse modifications of technique and policies, plus awareness of some limitations that are bound to be encountered during both assessment and therapy.

I describe throughout this chapter, and also in chapter 9, how I work with such patients in groups, but several important aspects of these very difficult patients should be mentioned. The most severe, although not apparently obvious, is that the forensic patient is unable to think before the action occurs because he is not mentally equipped to make the necessary links (Bion, 1959). This is because as a child he was left to his own inadequate devices; the child then develops a substitute fantasy that is unable to contain or detoxify his fears of dying, and there is no chance left for him to develop a capacity to think or to tolerate frustrations. According to Bonner (2006), this could become a compulsive "fix" that the child will attempt to recreate in each subsequent relationship. This may be linked to the compulsive nature of perversion, where the pervert feels a prisoner of his own need to survive by repeating the action. Furthermore, his thinking process is not functioning in his particular area of perversity, which is often encapsulated from the rest of his personality. The essential work of therapy is therefore to make thinking possible, but at times the patient's tendency to make sadistic attacks on his own capacity for thought and reflection is projected and directed against the therapist's capacity to think and reflect; it is then that the therapist feels confused, numbed, and unable to make any useful interpretations. Such patients fear transformation, since it is felt to endanger their lives.

Acting-out behaviour, which is a constant trait in their personalities, is a substitute for verbal expression. Patients react, but these actions are devoid of any reflection. After all, that acting-out has a meaning, just like a dream, and instead of feeling hurt or annoyed at being "got at", it needs the right interpretation. That alone, though, is not enough; even if it hits the spot and makes a strong impact, the impact will be short-lived because the compulsion to repeat is stronger than a quick insight into unconscious motivations. It requires "working through" with more interpretations at different times; eventually no further act-ings-out of that sort will appear. Obviously, persistent acting-out indi-cates a deeper unresolved conflict that needs to be worked through from different angles. Acting-out is also a challenge to the system of boundaries, which has to be rigorous and strict with these patients. It is essential to take care of the analytic frame and to keep boundaries in respecting rules and regulations. The analytic frame is there to give a sense of safety and containment. Only when patients experience the setting as adequate will they feel (Winnicott) "allowed" a process of playing and thinking. In their early childhoods, they were deprived of the elements of safety and containment, since their mothers failed to provide the holding that would later have allowed both safety and playing. That is why they are prone to act out trying to break the ana-lytic frame, such is the dread of feeling betrayed yet again by the sig-nificant other. This is a stagnant position where playing does not exist. It is here that transferential interpretations make a unique contribution since they will lead to a process of thinking. We should keep in mind Winnicott's axiom that playing is the precursor to thinking.

These patients are involved in actions against society and against themselves in extremely destructive ways, usually of either a sexual or a social character, involving perversions or serious antisocial behav-iour. Sometimes this is well concealed; at other times, violence is openly expressed. Their actions towards others are characterized by a strong element of dehumanization; they are unable to consider others as full, separate/individuated human beings but just as a part of themselves, without much consideration about using or abusing them. There is a strong element of sexualization but without the habitual quality of care and love. These individuals as babies were treated as fetishes by their carers and, as such, experienced a total lack of control; they were at the mercy of the adults around them who were responsible for their maturity during their developmental process. This, obviously, was carried out in severely faulty ways, which as adults they tend to repeat in a compulsive way, unaware of why they are doing what they are doing. They have to keep a most tyrannical control of all circumstances and situations. At times they are drawn to most odd, bizarre scenarios, which they feel compelled to design and fulfil.

Furthermore, though, the pervert knows that his action is wrong, he is unable to interpolate a thought about the consequences of his action for himself or others. He proceeds to act on the impulse because of some basic aspects attached to the "bizarre", perverse action, which I shall attempt to underline. First, he acts impulsively because that particular action is the only one that provides him with immediate sexual gratification and release from unbearable anxiety. Second, in carrying out his "bizarre" perverse action he is completely unaware of the associated symbolism; in other words, he is as baffled by his actions as are all other witnesses. Some perversions are filled with abstract symbolism, but others operate in a rather concrete manner (see chapter 1).

Shame, remorse, and guilt

There are specific feelings that are expressed by these patients in different ways from those expected with other patient populations. For example, *shame* is usually associated with being a witness to domestic violence, whereas *remorse* is frequently experienced afterwards by the perpetrators.

This different set of feelings encountered in victims and perpetrators is of enormous significance, since shame appears in children in an almost automatic way. At times we experience a sense of inexplicability about children feeling shame, but its manifestation becomes obvious when we think how powerless and weak children felt in stopping their parents fighting or inflicting harm on each other and on others, including their own children. Shame is derived from the witness's feelings of powerlessness and impotence, and it can have a powerful impact, especially on the children involved. (A full discussion of such feelings can be found in McGee, 2000.)

Although shame and remorse share a sense of impotence, remorse is forever associated with a sense of irrevocability, even if associated with the need to reparation; what has been destroyed is something very valuable, and the act of destruction can never be reversed or remedied. Remorse only appears after a period of reflection and is usually associated with the capacity to think, previously cancelled out or obliterated. How often have I heard perpetrators, especially women whose children have been taken into care because of their own violence, saying with unbearable psychic pain: "If only could I turn back the clock."

Remorse is therefore comparable to grief, in that it is focused on the past and on the fact that something has been destroyed and lost. It relies on care and concern for what we value and necessarily involves an internal authority who is judging from within. The attitude of mind called up by the experience of remorse is focused not on action but on reflection, on contemplation of the damage done.

The remorseful individual gains release from his or her emotion by reliving a structurally analogous scene to that of the initial trauma. In Freudian terms, this is exactly a repetition of the compulsion currently used in the definition of post-traumatic stress disorder. The word "trauma" comes from the Greek "to wound" or "to pierce". Freud referred to trauma as a process that involves the breaching of a protective shield, which normally functions as a protection of the mind (ego) from internal and external stimuli.

In remorse, the guilty feelings occur after the acting-out; in other words, after the hostile impulses have been performed, the person will feel remorse. Actually, guilty feelings may prevent the acting-out of hostile tendencies and may become preventative because they have a sort of premonitory quality. The important thing, though, is that the unconscious makes no distinction between feelings of guilt that appeared before the event, and remorse that is experienced after the event.

The criminal action

The criminal action is the central fact. Sometimes it has the capacity to become explosive, violent, and uncontrollable, with attendant profound consequences for society. At times, it is the equivalent of a neurotic symptom. Pfäfflin (1992) describes the symptom as a constructive and healthy reaction. He adds that it is "conservative", meaning that the patient needs it and keeps it until it can be properly understood and then he can give it up. At other times, it is the expression of more severe psychopathology; it is secretive, completely encapsulated and split from the rest of the patient's personality, which acts as a defence against a psychotic illness (Hopper, 1991); at still other times, it is calculated and is associated with professional, careerist criminality. The criminal action always appears understandable as an action against society, and yet at the same time it is a self-destructive act, with harmful effects for the offender. This aspect of criminality associated with unconscious guilt has been examined by Freud (1916), Glover (1960), and Tuovinen (1973), among others.

The action may be characterized by a manic defence, created against the acknowledgement or recognition of a masked chronic depression. Alternatively, it may include compulsion, impulsivity, inability to intersperse thought before action and, as mentioned earlier, a total failure to understand it.

There are many different kinds of criminal acts, and to make an accurate diagnostic assessment it is necessary to look at the whole human being—including his or her present and past circumstances of living and ways of relating to others and especially to fantasy and reality. Sadly, and frequently, all attention is exclusively concentrated and focused on the action. Some criminal actions are devoid of any profit except, perhaps, some longed-for sense of superiority or a momentary sense of fame or a transient experience of celebrity.

The view is that however irrational the assault may initially seem, there is a meaning to the criminal act from the standpoint of the patient that might be discovered. According to Jessica Yakeley (2010, p. 23) "Analysis of the external crime scene or index offence, and in particular the characteristics of the victim, can shed light on the internal pathological world of the offender, who may be unconsciously re-enacting past conflicts in his violent acts. Here the victim and other situational factors may hold an unconscious representational role for the offender, mirroring an internal unconscious phantasy that is enacted in the external crime scene."

The law requires somebody to have a guilty mind [*mens rea*] before he or she can be found guilty of a crime. Similarly, in forensic psychotherapy and forensic psychiatry, the interest should be focused on the state of the mind of the person who committed the act, not just the act in itself. Doctor (2008, p. 2) states that "even the most apparently insane violence has a meaning in the mind of the person who commits it. There is a need to be aware of this meaning and to learn from it in an attempt to prevent further violence".

This use of the act to gain understanding of the patient's internal world is one of the features that makes forensic psychotherapy different from other branches of psychoanalysis and psychotherapy, where actual behaviours are viewed more metaphorically. The point about forensic patients is that internal scenarios are acted out concretely—fantasies, nightmares, or dreams become concrete reality.

This consideration of the action is an important part of the assessment, since it will be of decisive importance in the diagnosis and ultimate prognosis.

THE PSYCHODYNAMIC MEANING OF THE OFFENCE

Category 1:
The offence is the equivalent of a neurotic symptom,
committed clumsily without financial gain and easily detectable.

This is typical of a woman reaching her later years in life who has never had a criminal record—on the contrary, most times she has lead a life with some successes and satisfactions—but then is suddenly caught in some "inexplicable" shoplifting. She may have been suffering from a melancholic depression, being rather isolated and aloof, not socializing at all. It is a very sad state of affairs, especially if in the past she had been rather prudish and judgemental about others, because, when detected, she is faced with shame and mockery. And if the sensationalist press is nasty and even vicious about the case, she may end up committing suicide.

A similar pattern is a woman charged with "soliciting" for prostitution purposes; when suddenly feeling depressed, she obtains a "high" out of her self-hated body being wanted by somebody, not caring at all for any financial gains.

Category 2:
The offence is "careerist" oriented, committed for financial gain
and with care to avoid detection

Some individuals have learnt to live by dishonest actions that are repeated with much skill and professional expertise. They are easily recognizable because they have even anticipated the length of sentence they will be facing if detected. The criminal's pattern of thinking is similar to that of a scholar who takes a further educational course to improve his chances of obtaining a better professional position, thinking: I am aware that this course will take two years for me to complete, but by the end of it I shall be in position to apply for this better paid position. A criminal might similarly think that stealing a large amount of money is worth the risk of spending time in prison if detected and sentenced.

In the case of female prostitution where the clear aim is that of making a living, prostitution is also considered a careerist option.

Categories 1 and 2, though seemingly different, do at times overlap or succeed one another, and changes in patterns have to be recognized and diagnosed properly in order to make an adequate recommendation. A person should not be put into the careerist category just because of a long history of petty crimes or other sorts of delinquent activities. An open mind is needed to notice any dynamic changes that may have taken place inside this person's mind. At times, it is an easily recognizable sign of "hope" when the individual is detected while involved in some "silly" misdemeanour when in his or her mid-thirties. This may signal that this particular person is by now fed up with having to use a "false self". She may even become aware of the tremendous burden of a life of lies and deceptions as a cover-up for sadness and frustrations. She may now be contemplating looking at the real basis of her existence instead of prolonging the scaffolding erected around her as a cover for what she fears she really is. It is also of vital importance to advise the magistrate or judge of this eventuality, since the offender may well be in the right frame of mind to face psychotherapy. This change in behaviour may denote an incipient sense for insight, which is so necessary for a positive outcome in therapy. The following clinical vignette is of a patient who went from being a careerist offender to being a neurotic.

When I first saw Mrs D she impressed me as being a lively, attractive, intelligent, but not educated woman. She seemed candid and open in talking about herself, displaying constant changes of mood. To start with, she was very low and tearful but later this changed into bursts of laughter and being rather happy-go-lucky. However, her despondency, sense of worthlessness, and depression were always present. I was aware of her underlying depressive features, which had never been acknowledged by her, since she had been using delinquent/perverse behaviour in a manic way to avoid her chronic depression.

She appeared to be unduly upset about the nature of the offence—it was so uncharacteristic of her previous flamboyant criminal offences, committed some years ago, that she felt great shame and embarrassment. After those years in which she had resisted all temptations, what had happened for her to relapse in the way she did? By now her relationship with her husband was precarious; he had just been arrested again, and she felt let down, deserted, and lonely and had resorted to antidepressants and overeating. Her sad story was of being caught for stealing some cosmetics and underwear amounting to £8.50. She felt terrible about the fact that it was so insignificant and petty, something she had always sworn never to do. At the beginning I was taken by the face value of this statement, but afterwards I believed that *unconsciously* the offence had been designed with great care. Had she relapsed into her previous style of theft, it is probable that she would have been automatically sent to prison without the opportunity of seeking professional help. The offence, committed in such a clumsy way and with little financial gain, seemed to be expressing a new move, a change in her inner life (i.e., from careerist delinquency to a symptom revealing her motivation for a psychological change). I think that this woman, at the age of 38, felt the time was ripe for her to get help and to make the most of it. In other words, she was ready to give up her false self and to explore who she really was. She was by now experiencing an incipient awareness of a sense of futility and began to see herself as a pathetic and hopeless middle-aged woman, instead of the glamorous little princess she had been brought up to believe she was. This was assessed as evidence for the potential for dynamic change and her development into psychological maturity.

Mrs D was the first child of a young mother of 17, who felt extremely guilty at leaving her own mother, who in turn felt sad at "losing" her daughter. At the moment of my patient's birth, it was decided that she should be brought up by her recently widowed maternal aunt, who had shown great enthusiasm and willingness to do so after a long period of bereavement. This seemed to all involved to provide the "ideal" solution. The aunt now had a new psychological investment in the new baby, and the very young mother not only felt relieved of her responsibilities, but also elated about giving her own daughter to her aunt as a means to give her a relief for her grief. All guilty feelings were easily dismissed. The new life had been envisaged as responsible for bringing about a new situation and a hopeful outcome.

Throughout Mrs D's early infancy and adolescence she was considered her aunt's pet. As a direct consequence of this, she felt "*as if she was somebody else*". This particular concept was coined by Helene Deutsch (1942) in describing how a woman's need "for a mother substitute increases in the period immediately following childbirth, even if she has rejected her own mother". According to Deutsch, women try to imitate attitudes of a loving mother to make others believe that their motherliness is genuine. In our patient population, the "as if" is a key feature in delinquency and perversion, which are deeply interlinked with deception. Often these deceptive delinquent acts are carried out in order to deal with a low sense of self-esteem and are used to bolster fantasies of being someone else, usually more important and wealthier.

Though her family was not well off, my patient was indulged in having anything material she could wish for. However, from very early on she felt rejected by both parents but especially by her mother, whose subsequent children remained with their mother and father. My patient had been left in a state of utter confusion, not able to understand why she had been the rejected "chosen one". Her lifestyle continued until she was 16, when her aunt suddenly died.

At the time of her aunt's death, she was distraught. She was unable to get any emotional support from her own parents, partly because of her own rejection of them. It looks as if she was unable work through her mourning and feelings of grief. Instead, she isolated herself in a world of fantasy, imagining that she was of royal ancestry. The second step was escapism and denial. Suddenly, in a very manic fashion, she left home and came to London with fantasies of becoming a very "extra-ordinary" person and being reunited with her "own kind". Very soon, partly due to her attractiveness, liveliness, cleverness, and wit and to being "uninhibited", she became mixed up in the higher echelons of the criminal underworld. She had now become once more what she had left behind (but not inside): she was the little princess of the underworld, their pet, completely accepted and adored. She was the only one allowed to enter different criminal territories and was used as a go-between for different gangs in their negotiations. She felt unique—never before had anyone been able to transcend and trespass those worlds. Her elation prevented her from seeing how she was actually accustomed to being manipulated and abused from a very early age. She was involved in "hostessing" in famous night-clubs where champagne and amphetamines were always available in large quantities. From the description of this stage in her life it was obvious that she was "on the game", but since this always included "prestigious" or famous people it did not bother her too much.

Oversexualization and erotization are constant features in perversion, as a means to deny unresolved grief and mourning.

Eventually, she wanted to "assert" herself and to become "independent", so she now began to steal. She stole only the most beautiful garments and only from the most exclusive department stores. After two years of daily and persistent robbery she was caught and sent to prison for nine months. She told me that she had not minded this sentencing since she had been living so well for so long (a characteristic of the "professional" or careerist criminal).

Once in prison, she again became the pet, despite some pretty hard competition from other "toughies", and was surrounded by goodies sent by her associates on the outside and a lot of attention from the inside. After prison, she began a passionate relationship with a big-time crook, married him, and became pregnant. Once the baby was born, a girl, she relinquished all her criminal activities, but her husband did not. (This "going straight" is not an unusual occurrence, but the opposite—getting into further problems with the law—could also happen.) She felt extremely proud of becoming a mother. Her libidinal narcissism, previously placed in perverse-delinquent activities, was then channelled through motherhood into increased self-esteem. When the baby was a few months old, her husband was imprisoned for armed robbery. When she heard this news, she made her first suicidal attempt, for which she was in hospital for two weeks. This was the first time in her life that her depression and sense of worthlessness had come to the fore. She was shaken by her own action, since she claimed she cared a great deal for her daughter.

She was ready to start therapy, and I thought her ideal for group analytic therapy, especially considering the "as-if" quality she had, which is deeply linked to deception and very well understood in groups, and her good capacity for insight. It was unfortunate that her present living circumstances precluded this choice: she was still married to a "functioning" thief, and this would eliminate her from the group choice since the confidentiality rule, so essential in a group, was no longer secured.

She was taken into individual analytic therapy which lasted for eight years. There was active and rewarding cooperation, at times suffused with much suffering since there was so much psychic pain to be faced and to be learnt from her previous strong denial. Often I was confronted with angry members of the clerical staff who saw this "delightful" and "innocent" young woman leaving in tears and in an obvious state of distress. Again the containment provided by the clinic as the third object was invaluable since they were able to provide her with some empathy and support.

It is possible that the "dose" of seeing patients only once a week for analytic therapy is the adequate one. If seen more often, they could feel over-flooded with transference interpretations, which could produce alarming and overwhelming concrete responses. Once-weekly therapy offers a stricter sense of boundaries and helps them in learning to distinguish between reality and fantasy. A strict maintenance of boundaries is imperative since a massive narcissistic transference with the therapist can at times become unbearable. This is the sort of transference that produces a response in the therapist

The psychodynamic meaning of the offence

- The offence is the equivalent of a neurotic symptom, committed clumsily without financial gain and easily detectable
- The offence is "careerist" oriented, committed for financial gain and with care to avoid detection
- The offence is a manic defence against the acknowledgement or recognition of a masked chronic depression
- A criminal action may be the cover-up for a sexual perversion
- A sexual predicament may be the presenting symptom of hidden violence

of the patient getting "under the skin", and that by having such a patient in analytic therapy, the therapist is no longer alone in the world. The patient "remains" with the therapist regardless of place and the passage of time. It is with these thoughts in mind that it is necessary to make a brief and not too detailed report of the years of treatment. Suffice it to say that time after time she has surprised me by getting in touch with me when she has got to "know" that circumstances have been difficult for me.

The first period of treatment was characterized by intense idealization, dependency, and a strong "positive" transference. Soon after she established a pattern of daily nocturnal "dialogues" with me, which later on, when she was temporarily forced to move away, materialized in weekly letters to me.

After one year in treatment, her husband was sent to prison. She resented the fact that she had to miss sessions because she was forced to leave London with her child to be with her family for financial and emotional support. In fact, I think that at this point she felt relieved to be prevented from attending her weekly sessions.

It was agreed that we should meet every three weeks. She never missed a session, despite the financial sacrifices involved. A process of identification began, and as such she started to read psychoanalytic writings and fantasize about my own background. This was clearly the representation of the projections of her own family romance. She believed not only that my accent was authentically Viennese, but that I was also either the illegitimate daughter of Sigmund Freud and Lou Andreas-Salomé, or a Jewish princess!

A few years later she realized that these were delusions to increase her own sense of importance, and that her judgement was not as good as she thought and she must often have been wrong in her life and about many things. I felt rather gratified at the awareness and insights proffered. However, she then revealed she now thought of me as yet another "fairy-tale" character!

Within the next few months she continued to develop a narcissistic identification with what she believed was me. Some of this development was positive, such as the beginning of her self-education. For the first time she started reading in a disciplined way and registered herself in courses to take A levels. Simultaneously she started overeating to excess and as a result felt depressed. She expressed an interest in eventually doing psychotherapy work with children.

By the end of the year she let me know that she had achieved exceptional exam results. Two months later she cancelled an appointment because she felt sick about her husband coming out of prison. There were times when she wished she were dead, she wrote, despite all the work I had done on carving her out of a solid block.

She wrote these words just after her first academic achievements—which several years later were further confirmed with her gaining an Honours Degree in Social Science—gave a strong indication that we were in troubled waters, since she was not sure whether her achievements were hers or mine.

She came to her next session, the last before the Christmas holidays, behaving in a rather seductive way. Although she had known for several years that no presents were allowed, she continued to challenge me and my therapeutic stance by bringing small gifts for the secretarial staff, which made me feel tense and uneasy with both her and the staff. Any of my interpretations dealing with her mourning for me during the Christmas holidays met with dismissal and contempt. This time, when I told her that the session was over, she suddenly took out of her bag a large and beautifully wrapped parcel and presented it to me. Tears and indignation were her response to my refusal to accept her present. The gift was placed in a drawer of my desk, and discussion of its relevance was left for the next session after the holidays.

Four weeks later, we explored the circumstances surrounding her Christmas shoplifting expedition. She became aware of her intense anger and envy experienced towards me, since a part of her also became envious of her own achievements and was furious at the thought that I could claim to be the architect of her therapeutic improvement.

Afterwards, she tried a series of "tests" to validate her "sense of trust" towards me by challenging me in different ways. These were designed so that I could have easily felt threatened and ready to be blackmailed. I certainly felt pushed and bulldozed to act as her persecutory superego. We surely were in the midst of a very vigorous negative therapeutic reaction (NTR), and in this particular case I was very much helped by Rosenfeld's concepts of the infantile self and the narcissistic self, where he locates the capacity for love as dependence in the infantile self, in which there is an acknowledgement of a love object on which the infantile self depends. Meanwhile, he locates envy and destructiveness in the narcissistic self. This duality is painfully present during psychoanalytic psychotherapy in a permanent struggle: the patient experiences the psychotherapist as an object on whom he can depend and cooperate with his infantile-sane part, but he simultaneously experiences envy and wants to destroy the source of help with his narcissistic self.

> For Rosenfeld, the narcissistic self appears highly organized as a delinquent and powerful gang who, with threats and propaganda, keeps the infantile self enslaved. Each time the latter wishes to express himself or tries to liberate himself, the gang that dominates and squashes him appears again. This is how the dramatics of NTR take shape, and how the relationship of dependence and love of the infantile self with the analyst is checked. [Etchegoyen, 1991, p. 742]

I want to explore and share with you something in relation to the above linking it with the portrayal of the stereotype version of the genders in gangster films. If the struggle between the narcissistic self and the infantile self is neatly split in genders, obviously the gang takes the macho overtones and the infantile the endearing female role.

In this particular case it becomes more poignant because this woman was herself in reality a victim of the gang and was operating with all sorts of manic defences. However, initially she was the victim of a familial female plot when she was brought up as her aunt's daughter. This prepared her for a life of being somebody else and ready to acquiesce in any role to make everybody believe she was somebody else. Only with her own pregnancy—again, a life factor available only to women—was she able to become aware of her masked, chronic depression, hence her only suicidal attempt.

Again in Rosenfeld's words: "It is essential to help the patient to find and rescue the dependent sane part of the self from its trapped position inside the psychotic narcissistic structure as it is this part which is the essential link with the positive object relationship to the analyst and the world" (1971, p. 175).

That is exactly what I attempted to do with her trying to reconstruct her remembering of her own suicidal attempt. So many positive changes had been achieved which she was actively trying to destroy in a most consistent and insidious way. Her attack on me and all that had been accomplished with her infantile-dependent self was in real jeopardy. After a painful session in which her acting-out was interpreted as her attack on me and her own improvements, she wrote expressing her frustration at me for throwing her into confusion and for not understanding that she would do anything for me. She was really angry at me and had felt that I hated her. She was now nothing like her old self, a reformed person, trying her best to become a useful citizen—what more did I want, and didn't I realize how being overweight made her feel?

My countertransference reaction was one of frustration, helplessness, and anger. Feeling at the end of my tether, in the next session I said to her: "Why are you trying to kill our child?" She first sat there motionless, then later began to cry. She had finally understood in a female-maternal way that this new child was the link between her and me, the new baby of the acknowledgement and understanding of her good and bad bits, being allowed to be herself and not somebody else—not me, not my child, but a new emerging born self.

She made many more attempts to spoil her own achievements, but to no avail. By now, she had gone through difficult and painful times and was beginning to accept me in a different light; she gave up her fantasies of divorcing her husband and becoming a child psychotherapist. With her treatment, a great distance between herself and her husband had been created and a new situation emerged. Her relationship with her husband became more peaceful and eventually, under her influence, he gave up his criminal ways of living. They started a joint business which brought them together again in a different, more down-to-earth way. She began to take pride in her child's school accomplishments.

She had successfully achieved the capacity to promote separation and individuation with her child rather than seeing her as an extension of her libidinal narcissistic self. Thus, the cycle of perversion had been broken.

She had now become the middle-aged mother and wife that she, in reality, was. Both of us felt the time had come to terminate therapy, although it was painful for her to accept that reality, and how much an achievement it represented. It was clear that not only had she internalized the therapist as a "good-enough" maternal figure, but she had also developed the capacity to experience pain, to reflect on it, to integrate it into her experience, and to grow.

As Minne (1997) poignantly and accurately describes: "The process of treatment appears to require a complicated and lengthy transition period from not knowing anything about themselves to becoming more aware and dealing with the consequent profoundly traumatic effects of this."

The difficulties and pressures of working with such patients should not be underestimated. The therapist must beware behaving in ways that could easily and reasonably be interpreted as neglectful or seductive.

There are immense rewards at knowing that one has contributed to the process of maturation, which includes both freedom from the suffering inherent in perversion and the opportunity for these patients to develop their neglected potential. The long-term intergenerational benefits of interrupting the cycle of perverse motherhood that in turn produces future perversion cannot be overestimated.

Category 3:
The offence is a manic defence against the acknowledgement or recognition of masked chronic depression

Mr A was referred by the court on charges of fraud and deception. He was wealthy, titled, homosexual, a lawyer by profession, who effectively used manic defences against any emotional suffering or lack of care during his early years. His parents were wealthy and completely indifferent towards him. He was hated from the beginning of his life. In a way that was obvious from his very deformed teeth, which could have been easily repaired as a child, especially since his mother was a specialist in orthodontics. Actually he was born as a "replacement" child, as a way to escape any process of mourning for a baby girl who had died of cot death a year before he was conceived.

He had attempted suicide a few times but never succeeded, so in a way he was still in hope of a better life, but his actions were filled with self-contempt. His relationships were characterized by his subjecting himself to much physical and emotional pain that others inflicted on him.

In his early life, the only consistent and caring figure had been his maternal great-aunt, who had developed a soft spot for him; he was a regular visitor to her home from his very early years. She had a beautiful home filled with precious adornments and was surrounded by loyal servants. During the course of his visits to her he always felt the overwhelming desire to "nick"—as he referred to his actions—various belongings of hers. These objects were used daily by her, and their loss would produce an awful sense of alienation and distress in her. For example, as a hobby she used to knit scarves and sweaters for all family members; on one occasion he stole one of her knitting needles, which made her upset, confused, and suspicious of her servants, until then considered to be completely trusted. Such incidents continued. In a rather uneasy way she confided only in him, ironically the guilty party (then a little boy of 8), about her feelings towards her servants. This was met by his gleeful response, because he felt so much in control, though at times he also felt uncomfortable. A change came when he stole one her Fabergé eggs. Just as in the previous case of Mrs D, in which she changed from a flamboyant style to a "simple" shoplifter, Mr A changed from stealing valueless but needed objects to a priceless one. His unconscious was at work and felt too much guilt at continuing being the "innocent" one, so he "gave himself away" by stealing a very expensive object.

This time his great-aunt's response was quite different. She was so distressed that she was now prepared to call the police and to have her "disloyal" servants arrested. In fear of being confronted with the law, he decided to confess to her his present and past stealing. Faced with this admission, she was in terrible suffering—she had never imagined he would be able to deceive her in this awful way. She told him she never wanted to see him again. That was the last time he saw her.

All this happened thirty years ago, and he had obviously dealt with this tremendous emotional loss through a complete denial, only becoming aware for the first time during treatment. The one person who had ever shown concern and care for him was the recipient of his denigration, mockery, and deceit. Depression came to the fore, since he became aware of how effectively, from early life, he had been made so undeserving of any love.

In the course of group analytic psychotherapy, he spoke of a recent trip abroad. The account concerned his tremendous sense of embarrassment at having being questioned by Customs on his return because of his large and overweight bag. This was filled with silver cutlery from the very luxurious hotel where he had stayed with a man he had picked up from one of the toilets he frequently visited. A paradoxical problem arose from the fact that the hotel was part of a chain belonging to his own family. In other words, he was stealing from his own hated wealth that had brought only suffering to his life, and then he was detected as being his own thief—such was the intense degree to which he despised himself because of his inherited unearned wealth, considering himself not to be worthy of any goodness. Interpretations were made to these aspects of himself, and other members began to be aware of this man's suffering, first inflicted by others but now by himself in a most sadistic way. Whereas at the beginning he was cruelly mocked by others and not taken seriously because of his belonging to an upper-class family and having had the benefits of an excellent formal education, fellow members were now ready to accept this man's suffering as genuine and were able to come to his help.

Category 4:
A criminal action may be the cover-up for a sexual perversion

Mr B, 28 years of age, was referred by his employers, a City bank. This in itself was a revelation, that a City bank could be so perceptive of the possibility of unconscious motivations, which speaks to the sense of bewilderment he had caused with a puzzling offence. He was the bank's "bike" man, responsible for carrying money from and to different places. So although his job was rather menial, his responsibility was huge. He had been through years of employment without a complaint, being a most reliable employee. Then he was detected stealing spanners from the boxes of other bikes. Alarm grew to great dimensions when police found 3,000 spanners he had previously stolen. During the interview with me, he tried unsuccessfully to make sense of his unlawful actions by explaining that he was a handyman and that the price of tools was subject to inflation. Obviously, such a clumsy and inadequate explanation pointed to other motivations. In describing his actions, he talked with a great deal of embarrassment mixed with excitement: "I'm on my bike. Suddenly I see another bike being parked and I feel taken over by an extreme curiosity to look at its box. I know this is wrong but cannot help myself. I start sweating. I feel my heart pumping and I just have to do it. I have to take the tools. Then I feel at peace, a great sense of relief surrounds me. I feel great. On my way home I start feeling confused, ashamed, guilty. I don't know any longer what to do with yet another spanner, and I take it to the garage where I keep them all."

His statement is similar to that of a person suffering from sexual perversion, showing the same quality of urgency and the identical cycle, which involves growing sexual anxiety, the fight against it, eventually giving in and succumbing to the action, the sexual relief, and the subsequent sense of shame and guilt.

This was a young, well-groomed man who was still living with his mother, a domineering woman who had never allowed him to lead his own life. When the police came to get him, her first reaction was: "What shall I do if you take him away. I can't be on my own." Apart from his mother, he had never had any relationship of any sort and lived in complete isolation.

The psychiatric court report briefly indicated that this man's criminal offences were the expression of his tremendous sense of social and sexual inadequacy, which in turn was the product of a deprived and depraved early childhood. His father had been absent in the war, and his mother had a severe narcissistic borderline personality. The magistrate found not only the report but also the recommendation useful.

It is possible to deduce from his mother's only reaction when the police arrived at their home that she was highly narcissistic. She was also still very angry with her oldest son for having got married. She told us that she kept his room available, waiting for his divorce. Our patient, who had always been treated as the underdog, had to sleep in a box room. It was obvious that their relationship was of a suffocating nature, in which she was unable to provide him with any warmth or care but was always expecting him to care of her.

With this family history in mind we had no doubts about recommending group analytic psychotherapy, which was immediately implemented. He was introduced into an already-established group where other patients were able to link the chain of events to their own scenarios. For example, a woman shoplifter saw a duplication of herself: the stealing was compulsive, but it also represented an act of revenge against a careless husband (representing an uncaring mother), but in the "spanner man" his mother was still his object of revenge for the dreadful way he felt used by her. The spanner represented the father-phallus, the masculine power that he experienced his mother had always emasculated, trying to keep him as a little baby who had to mother her. Another patient saw himself picking fights whenever possible to discharge his violence for the way he felt abused as a child. The work of psychotherapy consisted of Mr B's growing awareness of the unconscious links between the sexual symbolisms and the enactment of his irresistible impulses. This unravelling made it possible not only for the patient to free himself from these urges, but also for others to exert some mastery over their own aggressive impulses.

Category 5:
A sexual predicament may be the presenting symptom
of hidden violence

Sometimes sexual predicaments and hidden potential violence over-lap. For example, a young man of 23 first came to treatment because of fears of being homosexual. After a year of individual psychotherapy he left, having overcome that particular problem. A few years later he was back, this time because he had suddenly experienced violent fantasies against all women, but particularly against his mother and, later, his girlfriend. On one occasion, during a recent holiday trip with his girlfriend, he felt a compulsion to throw her from a high cliff but was just able to contain this terrible impulse. Another time, at his mother's home, he had a strong urge to plunge a kitchen knife into his mother's back while she was cooking.

During group analytic treatment it became clear that his fear of homosexuality had been a protection—replaced later by a deeper fear, expressed through violent fantasies—against women whom he felt had previously damaged him, indeed almost emasculated him. Again, what appears superficially to be plain violence against women is actu-ally born of great feelings of insecurity, uncertainty, and inability to act as a "man"; more importantly, this violence is the "just" reaction to an earlier, primitive feeling of suffering humiliation from those he considered to be in control and power. After a while he talked about having achieved an intimate situation with his girlfriend but was painfully aware of the urge to hurt her. In an obvious attempt to do so, he had had a one-night stand with another woman. He told us how, despite himself, he had experienced a great sense of elation at his girlfriend being first so worried about his disappearance and later very angry that he had spent the night with another woman. In the fol-lowing group session, he described to us a recent dream: *he had his fist inside a woman's vagina and was punching it vigorously. When he began to enjoy this process he became aware that he was disintegrating—first the hand began to dissolve and later the whole body was annihilated.* He described this dream with such intensity that another patient, a transvestite, reacted as if touched with physical pain in his sexual area, as if he had a real vagina. This dream represented his fears of being destroyed by a woman if he became close to her. The transvestite became aware of his urge to hurt a woman in her identity core since he experienced such tremendous envy towards all women, including his wife. After this session his urge to cross-dress began to diminish and his relationship with his wife got better. This is yet another unexpected turn of events that can only come about because real human interactions take place and are bound to have a strong impact on others in most unpredictable ways. An analytic group process can provide us, the therapists, with most unusual insights, if we are prepared both to be attentive to not only what is being said but also what is *not* being said, and also to observe the body language, which also plays a most important role in how people react to others.

CHAPTER NINE

From the court to the couch

INITIAL ASSESSMENT OF THE FORENSIC PATIENT

Given that forensic patients present serious personality disorders and are unable to form relationships, it is obvious that some are more suitable than others for group treatment. To assess whether individual psychotherapy or group psychotherapy is indicated for offenders, it is vital to look closely at particular psychopathologies and needs. The selection criteria include their family structure, their living circumstances, and certain factors in their personalities.

Selection criteria for individual analytic psychotherapy

Root-family influence: early life

Patients who have never experienced satisfactory relationships in early life—for example, those who come from very large families with financial deprivation and emotional overcrowding—are likely to do better in individual treatment than in group treatment. Patients who are adopted or fostered who join a group with previous history and traditions will feel "on trial" and closely observed by others, who are perceived as "the old", "legitimate", "real" children. Patients who had been evacuated during the war tended to react with fears of rejection and despondency if they joined an already established group.

Other patients likely to do better in individual treatment than in group treatment are those whose families—and especially mothers—

had suddenly rejected them because of a sibling death, leaving them with unresolved bereavement about sudden deaths of siblings.

For example, I went to a custodial institution hospital to assess James, aged 38, to see whether he was suitable for treatment in our clinic. He had spent eighteen years in that prison after being sentenced for killing his best friend. The inmates were treated as a therapeutic community, and all therapy was done in groups. He was a regular attendee at all groups, taking leadership in many issues. He was the sixth child of a family of seven. When he was 3 years old, his younger brother died aged 10 months, and his mother became not only emotionally absent to the patient but also extremely hostile. His mother used to make deprecatory remarks about him, unfavourably comparing him to his dead brother.

During the interview he was proud to show off his "psychological insight", making all sorts of appropriate remarks. This attitude towards community tasks, it later transpired, had been his survival mechanism, but it was just a veneer. Despite his extreme willingness to attend group sessions, I offered him individual therapy instead, which I thought would be best for him considering his struggles about his dead brother. His reaction was one of intense fear and panic; all sorts of phobic problems emerged about the one-to-one situation in relation to dependency on a parental figure. I assessed his predicament as not having had the chance to have some good-enough mothering for himself as a child in a large family, with intense problems of loneliness and feeling unwanted and rejected. His previous success in the therapeutic community at using a false self, to avoid the unmasking of his real self, left him without the chance to change.

Present family structure and living circumstances

Serious criminal patterns are not reasons in themselves for exclusion, provided that the delinquency does not preclude the personal disclosures required for therapeutic progress. An assessment of patients' present living circumstances is crucial. Were they to open up and talk of their own, their partner's, or their associates' criminal activities, the confidentiality rule would be impossible to sustain.

This is what happened with Susan, whom I saw for a psychiatric court report on charges of being the receiver of stolen goods; she had also previously been charged with prostitution and possession of cocaine. Brought up as an only child, she had been the victim of sexual molestation by different family members. This had left her in a state of complete confusion, unsure as to whether she was very special and favourite or just merely being used and abused.

I initially thought that group treatment would be absolutely ideal in this particular case since Susan had always lived in isolation without the benefit of siblings or a peer group. Her own self-assessment would be much better ascertained in a situation with her peer group, and the elements of being so unique and special would have been dealt with in a much quicker fashion. However, I then realized that this woman, who was married to a criminal, was still keeping associations with other criminals. The possibility that in group treatment she might leak information regarding those criminals made that option impossible. The clinic could have easily been a target of attack and open provocation by the people associated with her outside the clinic.

Personality and capacity for insight

The importance of patients' personalities and capacity for insight is basic for both individual and group treatment, but initial strong reluctance to accept the offer of group analytic therapy during the assessment period may denote a need for further exploration in more individual sessions. These could then lead to an eventual understanding that it may be best to examine themselves in a group setting supported by others who share similar predicaments.

Psychopathology

Whereas most perversions are well suited to group analytic psychotherapy, voyeurism and some forms of paedophilia are not. Actually, their inclusion in groups may interfere with the dynamic changes of other fellow patients, who get very frustrated at their stuckness into denial and rationalization.

An awareness that group sessions are used by voyeurs as a captive audience for the concrete acting-out of their perversion is counterproductive to any positive development in them or in the rest of the group. They become in reality "peeping toms" who are very inquisitive and appear superficially to be "insightful" in their questioning of female patients' sexual lives. Their inclusion in these groups could prove to have deleterious effects on the other members and hinder the development of trust and cohesiveness in the group process.

Similarly, with some paedophile patients of the schizoid type, their extreme externalization and denial of their own problems in relation to the children are not only a proof that they would not be touched by the group approach, but any group development into insight would be impossible. Most paedophile patients behave in rigid patterns, very different from incest perpetrators, who are able to do extremely well when treated in groups (see chapter 7).

Selection criteria for group analytic psychotherapy

I have felt the need to challenge both my own previous selection criteria for group therapy and those of others, the most obvious being those of Yalom (1975), who advocates group treatment for the Young, Attractive, Verbal, Intelligent, and Successful—so called YAVIS people. In fact, I believe that often the opposite holds true. Those who are considered old, ugly, illiterate, nonvocal, dull, and failures can do extremely well in group therapy.

Jimenez's (2004) way of conceptualizing perversion based on inter-subjectivity is useful in the recommendation for group analytic treatment, in which different hearings are taking place simultaneously and entrapment is not easily achieved in the transference, which is functioning on many different levels. According to Jimenez: "When the analyst tries to put his mind in touch with the mind of the pervert, time and again the analyst will end up trapped in a dual relation. . . . Perverse collusion is paradigmatic of the situation of unconscious complicity against the analytic work", later adding that "in a first *moment, perverse collusion is inevitable.* Only a second hearing makes it possible to emerge from the entrapment."

There is a growing general consensus regarding the crucial importance that interpretation of transference and countertransference has in the understanding and treatment of patients affected by perversion.

The clinic-father-institution is expected to provide a good supportive system in which the mother-group-therapist can feed the baby (group) adequately. The institution extricates both parties from the possibility of a perverse, unhealthy association. This is, of course, a crude metaphor, to illustrate a dynamic interplay of all players, with kaleidoscopic aspects of the transference. At different times and at any given time, the institution could become the good–bad mother; the therapist, the cruel, penetrating father; the group, the supportive–persecutory target; the mother-therapist, fragmented, splitting between the group and the clinic; and so on.

This patient population presents a worthwhile challenge, given the potential benefits of group analytic treatment for such "antisocial" and "asocial" people. All share an intense sense of shame and despondency about the activities in which they are involved. Effective treatment requires adequate selection criteria, a well-thought-through composition of the group, and modification of technique according to the patients' particular psychopathology. The price paid for effectiveness is to give up rigid ideological psychotherapeutic principles.

Early life

Patients who have been subjected to an intense, suffocating relationship with one parent are suitable candidates for group therapy. Groups provide them with a much warmer and less threatening atmosphere than in one-to-one therapy, in which the sense of authority would be so intense. They can also share their experience with their peers. Often these people are still subjugated to an over-possessive mother, who will not allow them to develop any independence or individuation. Others have left home only to find themselves extremely isolated. In the group, with the help of fellow patients, they begin to express openly some rebellious, anti-authority feelings and eventually some self-assertion.

As discussed earlier, it is important to assess certain factors in the parents' root family to help determine which group is more appropriate for each specific history. If adopted or fostered out, it may be preferable to place them in new rather than already established groups.

Social predicaments: deception and fraud

Deception and self-deception are features often present in the forensic patient. These are deeply interlinked with identity confusion and an inability to see oneself from another's point of view. A sense of false self accompanied by low self-esteem, with an impaired capacity for thinking processes and impulsive action, are present. These characteristics are delicately contained and understood in groups, where confrontation with other patients presenting similar symptoms in a mirroring process is the rule and is responsible for dynamic changes affecting all those with this particular problem. They are able to "read" one another and to offer the most insightful interpretations about their inner and external cheating.

For example, A 34-year-old man referred himself for treatment because he was fed up with the "image" he felt forced to produce to get approval from his peer group. He had spent most of his life in and out of prison for petty delinquency. He was notorious for his criminal activities, which were at the service of the enhancement of his *false self* and involved excellent performances on his part. For example, after weeks of wearing a stolen uniform at an airport and posing easily as a captain, he was caught because the uniform belonged to an officer of a much higher rank than his appearance suggested. On another occasion, noticing a vintage Rolls Royce in a repairer's garage, he rang the garage and, in an upper-class accent, told the manager he would be sending his chauffeur within the next few hours to collect the car. Afterwards he took on the chauffeur role himself, wore a cap, and adopted his best Cockney accent and drove away the car. However, mixed in with his drive for perfection was a little boy who very much wanted to show off, and he started to parade the car up and down his local high street. It didn't take too long for the police to notice and recognize him as one of their regular petty thieves.

Sexual perversions: exhibitionists

Most of the time, exhibitionists are very conservative in their lifestyles, very respectable and very orthodox. Their urge to expose themselves to unknown persons is the only thing that they keep hidden. They go through such a degree of anxiety when these urges appear that sometimes the act is quite an obvious attempt at being caught. So, from being careful to begin with, they might later become neglectful, taking more and more risks—for example, from exposing themselves in remote empty, dark roads, they might start getting closer and closer to the place where they either live or work. These are people who, in a group situation, will tend to show a very inconsistent, double-stand-ard attitude, with an apparently strong superego regarding everybody else's actions in an attempt to cover up their own feelings of shame and guilt. The group can help them face up to this denial.

Violence

Violent behaviour seems better contained and even better understood within the framework of group therapy. Freud points out that the mechanism of identification is a basic one in group formation: iden-tification not only helps to further positive feelings within the group, but also helps in limiting aggressiveness—since there is a general tendency to spare those with whom one is identified. The presence of other participants who may notice hostility before it is overtly expressed (often against the therapist) gives the group a capacity to confront violent behaviour and to deal with it openly and honestly. James Gilligan's (1996) basic concept regarding violence is that it is always preceded by a subjective feeling of humiliation. This is most noticeable in group dynamics when observing incipient violence. As Yakeley (2010) reminds us: "Verbal insults, which most of us would be able to ignore, may be experienced as deeply traumatic and threatening to someone with fragile self-esteem, causing feelings of shame which may precipitate a violent reaction." For example, a comment from a fellow patient—or, more often, an interpretation from the analyst—could be made, and suddenly and completely unexpectedly the patient would feel extremely angry. His anger is always out of proportion to what had been said, but he finds understanding from his fellow patients. He is responding to a primitive echo of an early trauma, an old wound inflicted when he was helpless to defend himself. Other fellow members are able to identify with the patient and to fully understand the origins of that "inexplicable" rage and will effectively sort this out, not allowing any physical violence to take place.

Take the case of a very anxious woman, Miriam, aged 42 years, who had spent many years in a special hospital because of two different charges of actual bodily harm. Trained as a nurse, she admitted she often had intense crushes on middle-aged women in positions of authority. Some years ago, she become very infatuated with a ward sister. One evening, after drinking heavily, she became angry at being told off by the sister and stabbed her several times. She then drove to another neighbourhood and deliberately stabbed an absolute stranger. Both victims were in a serious condition for several days but did eventually survive the attacks.

It took me little time to make up my mind about the course of therapy: group analytic therapy was of course the choice. I was not going to offer myself on a plate for her to develop an intense transference towards me and then run the dangers of her extreme violence. I thought that this violence could be much better contained in a group situation.

Multiple transferences within a group provide patients with the possibility of more than just one target (as would be the case in one-to-one therapy) for their anger, which they find highly reassuring. A detailed example demonstrating these theoretical points of group processes with violent patients is given at the end of the chapter.

Secretiveness

The same presenting or accompanying symptom could be considered either an indication or a contraindication for treatment choice according to the specific context in which it is it is found. Extreme secretiveness could sometimes constitute a contraindication. For example, John, who came to the clinic because of frotteurism, was a shy, awkward, married man with children, who had never confessed to anyone about this perversion. At the first session, when he admitted to his problem, the group's reaction seemed one of anxiety, covered by laughter. Everyone tried to minimize his symptom to such an extent that he felt humiliated, whereupon he became very flushed and left, never to return.

This example provides us with unsuspected insights about reactions to different perversions. Frotteurism is such an unexpected and bizarre action, so very difficult to understand, that it creates a great sense of disbelief and high degree of anxiety. A similar response would be impossible to evoke at the admission of a paedophile to be compulsively attracted to young children. The response would be an immediately judgemental one of indignation and shock—is this because everyone does, in different degrees, share the paedophile instinct?

Whereas I once thought that extreme secretiveness was in itself a contraindication, clinical evidence has proved that group analysis can be the treatment of choice in cases of incest, as discussed in chapter 7.

GROUP ANALYTIC THERAPY

The beginnings of group psychotherapy at the Portman Clinic

In 1971, I joined the staff of the Portman Clinic, where analytic psychotherapy was used exclusively with patients who engaged in acts of delinquency or criminal behaviour or who suffered from sexual perversions. Group analysis was not yet applied there, and there were considerable resistances to implement that sort of treatment. These resistances were subsequently shared for different criteria at both the Portman Clinic and the Group Analytic Society.

I believed that group analytic therapy could offer a different scenario where these patients could explore a new style of peer relationship, offering an alternative way of relating where for the first time a climate of trust could prevail. In such a relationship they might begin to feel somewhat safe in identifying with others. There is always the possibility that one-to-one therapy will be felt as a replacement of an earlier engulfing, neglectful, situation, and a transferential process could develop with both parties unable to think.

From the very start I had to contend with many difficulties involving Portman colleagues who were extremely cautious about, if not openly resistant to, using this therapeutic approach since putting together such "untreatable", troublesome, "impossible" patients would be just like playing with dynamite (see chapter 10). Also, colleagues from the Institute of Group Analysis (IGA) often referred to the "facts" that either these patients do not respond to this type of therapy or that it may be effective only if one such patient is integrated into a "neurotic" group. These "facts", however, were myths and did not derive from experience. Moreover, these myths contained prejudices that could easily produce serious consequences. First, these patients are left without the benefit of being able to interact with the social microcosm that occurs in group therapy and could afford them a much better understanding of their problems, which are so deeply related to antisocial actions. Second, these prejudices professionally isolate the therapist who works with this type of patient, since critics assume that these patients cannot be treated in a group setting. I was at first inclined to explain these myths by relating them to unconscious mechanisms arising from the critic's enormous fear of the inner emergence of the same mental mechanisms in themselves.

Actually if only one of these patients is incorporated into a group of neurotic patients, he or she may never be able to openly talk about tormenting problems and would actually feel isolated and unable to participate or to share with the "alien" others. In groups with others with whom they share a compulsive element—be it exhibitionism, fraud, fetishism, violent acting-out, and so on—careful preparation to enter into these groups can produce a positive outcome.

Bion (1967) says that communication develops into a capacity not only for toleration by the self of its own psychic qualities, but also as a part of the social capacity of the individual. "This development, of great importance in group dynamics, has received virtually no attention; its absence would make even scientific communication impossible" (p. 118).

Clearly patients of the sort described present great difficulties for group analytic psychotherapy. It was feared that not only this type of patient but also their therapists would be split off from society, both through fear and as means of punishment. However, it could just as easily be claimed that individual therapy deprives these patients of the benefit of being able to interact with the social microcosm provided by group therapy, which can afford them a much better understanding of their problems since they are so deeply related to antisocial actions.

At that time there were very few colleagues with whom to share the richness of material emerging from working with "antisocial" patients who have problems related to violence and secrecy in the family—for instance, incest cases. In the early days, in view of so many patients not returning after their first session I almost joined the rest of my colleagues in giving up hope. It was necessary to think again about the whole approach. This initial sense of frustration, disillusionment, hopelessness led to gradual changes regarding selection criteria, preparation, composition of the groups, and leadership techniques (Welldon, 1984).

It was indispensable to examine the patients' psychopathology, the therapists' technique, and the function of the institution, since in forensic psychotherapy three different but interrelated structures are involved: the individual/offender; group analytic therapy; and the society/criminal justice system, by providing and implementing proper treatment programmes through adequate institutions.

Analytic group analysis not only survived but has thrived due to the changes mentioned above and to colleagues who were ready to implement this treatment programme. All the old attitudes have now completely changed, and it is widely accepted that these patients respond very well to the group analytic approach. In treating sexual and social deviant patients together, it has become evident that group analytic therapy may often be the best treatment for severely disturbed patients suffering from sexual perversions. This conclusion was reached after much careful thought.

I feel it is my duty here to acknowledge my debt of gratitude to the IGA and the Group Analytic Society (London) when I was invited in 1996 to deliver the Foulkes Memorial Lecture. This was an unexpected honour that renewed and confirmed my vigour and enthusiasm in working with this patient population. A consolidation of the work had been created. As a result, other colleagues wanted to join our team of group analysts, not just the young, enthusiastic ones but also well-qualified psychoanalysts who also began to refer more patients to be assessed for suitability for group analysis.

Caroline Garland (2010a) has written in a most comprehensive and clear way about group psychoanalytic psychotherapy for borderline patients. In a sensitive manner she reminds us that "the theoretical background and experience of the therapist are crucial" and that "the therapist needs to be able to identify the childhood origins of troublesome and fluctuating states of mind" (p. 81). This will help to frame interpretations for patients to tolerate contact with earlier childhood anxiety situations. (For a more detailed explication of this, see *The Groups Manual*: Garland 2010b.)

Types of group therapy

Modified heterogeneity

Groups are composed of both social and sexual deviances, which allows for a more comprehensive understanding of all dynamic processes involved, especially those related to the patients' inability to think and their identification with the aggressor, actually present in their early lives. Patients become aware of the reasons for their lack of trust and their intense need to be in control of all situations.

One characteristic that is extremely positive but frequently not acknowledged about heterogeneous groups is that of the differing social classes they contain. Whereas the usual attitude, outside and inside groups, is that the show of empathy and a degree of sympathy is very much on the side of those who obviously belong to the "have-not" category, the same cannot be said about group members who are thought to be either too sophisticated, too educated, too wealthy, or too "classy". In fact, the opposite is true: they are subjected to scornful and malicious comments devoid of any empathy. Other fellow members find it very difficult to try to understand their predicaments and to be in empathy with them. The contrary is the rule: they are usually confronted with angry and indignant claims such as: "Why are you here, you have spent so much time at school" or "Why are you here, you are from a good family"—as if the belonging to a "good family" would be a guarantee against earlier deprivations, ill treatments, or lack of essential care. This has been described in chapter 8 in the case of Mr A.

Slow-open group

A slow-open group offers different developmental stages, from dependency to self-assertion, giving opportunities for senior members to take more caring roles confronting newer members in therapeutic ways. It also provides evidence of emotional growth, which is acknowledged by other members and by the therapist facilitating the individuation/

separation never allowed by uncaring, neglectful parents and never observed in individual therapy. *Time* is the key to opening areas of the most primitive defence mechanisms—"short, sharp, shock" treatment of such complex patients is doomed to failure.

Single therapist

I have always worked in groups on my own, without a co-therapist. Two therapists re-create the primal scene in its most concrete terms, which is potential dynamite for our patients who often experience the parental coupling as associated with extreme sadomasochistic behaviour. Given the nature of our patients' early deprivation and broken homes, the response to co-therapists would be one of provocation and humiliation. These patients have more skills in breaking up "parental bonding" than co-therapists have in containing the primitive anxieties, intense envy, and destructive impulses within the group.

There are many positive features to the single-therapist group. For example, patients take issues of seniority very seriously; this is related not just to the time they have been attending the group but also to the inner changes they have been able to achieve, which have been recognized and acknowledged by fellow members. So, at times a "senior" patient-group member could become a "helper" to the therapist. However, some patients are prone to take these "helper" roles only as a consequence of repeating patterns that they might have experienced in the past, such as parenting their own parents. Therapists need to recognize that these are patterns learnt very early in life and that they replicate painful experiences; the possibility of a vicious cycle has to be avoided. So, what may appear superficially as a sign of a maturing process might only be a repetition of their roles in early traumas, as opposed to a real dynamic change.

Our groups are composed mostly of people who see themselves as victims, experiencing the world as divided into the "haves" and the "have nots". Although the therapist holds the authority, by working alone the therapist is seen as unsupported, almost a "have not", and is implicitly trusted by the group.

Preparation for therapy

Before effective group therapy can begin, it is of crucial importance to prepare the members for it, which is done on an individual basis. This introductory work of engaging with prospective group patients through individual alliances with the group analyst is a vital aspect of the treatment. The patients' inability to tolerate time-lapses, and the likelihood of their experiencing reality-testing work as a provocation, establishes the need for brief, irregular, and low-key introductory sessions without interpretations, from which nutritious and holding experiences might then be transferred to the group.

Patients are warned that, whereas at the start they might feel tempted to drop out, it is worthwhile to persevere with continuing attendance because they will soon develop a sense of belonging to the group and feel more at ease about it. The emerging sense of commitment, belonging, and responsibility—in maintaining rules, for example—would continue with the holding aspect of the work.

In these individual sessions, they are informed of the rules and regulations and of the necessity for a serious commitment to group treatment, which will take years as opposed to weeks or months.

They are told that punctuality and regular attendance are essential. If circumstances make attendance impossible, the patient should let us know about this beforehand, because unexpected absenteeism creates disturbances in the group. After six consecutive missed sessions without prior notice, the patient would be removed from the group and the place offered to another patient on the waiting list. In other words, commitment and responsibility towards themselves and the group are fundamental and provide patients with a sense of continuity for which they are responsible. Messages about absenteeism or lateness will be given to the group, who are expected to take action—for example, writing letters to absent members via the clinic. No group session takes place unless at least three members are present on time. They should also avoiding meeting with other members outside the group, since to do otherwise could easily jeopardize the treatment.

They are told that once group therapy started, no more individual interviews would be given to members of the group, so that all new and old conflicts would have to be dealt with entirely within the group. This also applies to requests for information from the outside, such as from GPs or probation officers, and for court reports or reports to other pertinent professional bodies. All members are expected to express their opinions regarding such requests and to give some consideration to the progress and changes happening to the particular patient about whom information had been requested. They and their referral agencies are told that all communication is confidential and is the property of the group.

In the case of a relapse, which might result in a member's court appearance (which often happens either at the beginning of therapy or when confronted with holidays), a colleague of the group's therapist would be responsible for the preparation of the new court report requested. This avoids the possibility of collusion and acting-out behaviour in which patients might feel themselves to be a "favourite" or "special" with their group analyst.

Patients are told that no one outside the group can come to the clinic's waiting room to wait for them until the end of the session, since this could breach the rule of confidentiality as members might be identified by a stranger.

Although giving rules is not entirely helpful, on balance it is considered to be essential, because rules create a sense of belonging and of responsibility for the development of the group. Some members who have strong tendencies for acting out could consider these rules a challenge, which they might meet by breaking them; nevertheless, it is important to make the limits clear—there will always be time to work through acting-out propensities and expressions of anti-authority, rebellious feelings while in treatment.

Since the introduction of this preparation period, patients have been far more consistent in their attendance and the number of "casualties" (i.e., drop-outs) has diminished to a minimum. These sessions promote the bonding between themselves and the therapist, as well as to the clinic. If patients decide to leave their group they can get in touch with the clinic again, instead of hiding away forever as they used to do.

Techniques and other considerations

Leadership techniques

I have already indicated that the group analyst stance of conducting a group should be neither too democratic nor authoritarian, since in the transferential process they will resonate with the patients' own family backgrounds where they did not feel safe since there was no containment or a sense of boundaries.

At times therapeutic interventions involving a very active response from the therapist are needed, rather than a well-prepared interpretation. I think of them as therapeutic because they derive from experience only acquired by treating this patient population.

For example: a therapist vigorously tells a patient to "Shut up" at exactly the right time, when the patient has provoked a great sense of fear and insecurity in the whole group (including him). The fact that the whole group feels contained, including the member who was threatening the cohesiveness of the group, provides us with the evidence that this intervention has been effective. Not only has it provided containment but it has also stopped a process of escalation to enormous acting-out including both the inner and the outer worlds. Hence, this could never be termed as the therapist's "acting-in" or "acting-out".

I also discussed earlier the importance of remaining silent. Nothing is as rewarding as to have the patients' themselves verbalizing their ways of finding out areas of insight. I remember a patient who, at the time of leaving the group, was extremely grateful for everybody's help and acknowledged it personally in different ways. Somebody pointed out that he had omitted me as a group conductor. He immediately answered: "That's exactly what she would like. Through her silences, we became aware of ourselves."

Power and authority

At the start of a group, both authority and power reside within the therapist and institution. From the preparation time, patients become aware of their own participation as essential for the group' survival and development. If there are no patients, there is no group. The patients' anti-authority feelings are so *deceitfully present* and their vulnerability so *apparently absent* that for them it is excruciatingly difficult to be aware of their own sense of power, in which they experience the group as theirs and not the therapist's. It is only when *power* is located in the *patients' membership*, and *authority* is located in the *therapist*, that gaining insight and real changes can take place. This provides the right balance for them to exercise their power in attending or not, in being late, in producing havoc during group sessions, and in challenging the therapist's authority—challenging, in Freud's words, "the dreaded primal father". Members have intense oral needs and want the therapist to be available at all times. They find it very difficult to adjust to the "weekly feed" and cling to it in a very infantile manner. Holidays are always determined by the therapist and are very much resented by patients, who tend at the beginning of treatment to relapse into a lot of acting-out, sometimes in relation to their own previous offences which are perhaps recurring after a long period of time. They fantasize about the therapist's wonderful holidays involving great sex and are outraged at missing the group because of the therapist's perfect family lifestyle. The group analyst has to use his authority in offering the necessary ingredients for patients to feel contained and able to express their anger, which facilitates the relocation of power in patients. The group analyst will also offer links that will make it possible for patients to learn about thinking.

In this way each and every member experiences a powerful sense of belonging to the group. Throughout treatment, patients gain a capacity for self-assertion, emotional growth, independence, and individuation. They see themselves and others developing into respected individuals with self-esteem, which is acknowledged by others and by themselves. They are not only allowed but *encouraged* openly to express anger and frustration that has been kept hidden for lengthy periods. This encouragement comes especially from other "old" members who have gone through similar predicaments and who are now ready to leave the group.

Avoidance of casualties by modification of technique

The group technique that I originally used closely followed Bion's idea of a work group and the basic assumptions; in other words, I gave group interpretations of the here-and-now dynamics as the instrument of therapy and learning. However, slowly but steadily I began to change my approach, since I realized that a technique that provided these patients with only group interpretations seemed to reinforce their feelings of dehumanization and alienation, increase their insecurity, and lower their self-esteem further. In some cases, confusion and anxiety about their own identities were so intense they were forced to suddenly leave the group.

It was not unusual in the early sessions for members to cluster themselves into subgroups, to avoid the fear of becoming individuals who would be liable to be rejected or not understood. For example, during one session people were saying that I devoted Mondays to shoplifters and homosexuals, Tuesdays to psychopaths, Wednesdays to child molesters and burglars, etc. In so doing perhaps they were hoping—dreading—that I could see them all as subgroup types without "individual" characteristics. They were forcing on me a role like that of the head of a penal institution where inmates are depersonalized by numbers and criminal classification. This defensive attitude against being seen individually in the group was fostered by giving group interpretations at a transferential level, so I was colluding with their particular psychopathology.

I realized it would be far more efficacious after giving a group interpretation to link this with individual-patient characterizations of pathologies. Thus, I was able to learn from Foulkes's (1945) more liberal use of the group situation, his profound respect for the interpretations that might emanate from other members of the group, and his belief that such comments could be more effective than the therapist's. I also found useful his remarks about the therapist's attitude: "If the therapist has overcome in himself the claim to perfection, he is not afraid to be found wanting, imperfect and ignorant, he can allow himself to be honest and sincere and stand firm on the grounds of reality. In doing so he exerts, by his own example, the most valuable and potent therapeutic influence." I was also influenced by his ideas that it is mistaken to think that the therapist is passive when he keeps himself in the background: actually while being receptive, he can be very active in his own mind, listening and devoting himself to understanding what the group is saying or trying to say, very much engaged as to his own interventions. This model helps patients in their process of thinking as opposed to acting. Some identification of group members with the therapist takes place, and they learn to wait patiently for the right time to intervene rather than make impulsive and useless gestures. I also saw the need to become at times more firm and rigorous with these patients. I learned from Maxwell Jones (1953) how to allow active confrontation not only among members but occasionally between them and myself when I felt they needed firm leadership to relieve their own anxieties about ineffectual, uncaring parental figures. If the therapist took a "democratic" attitude, it was experienced by our patients as a seductive manoeuvre. If, on the other hand, the leadership was authoritarian, their persecutory anxieties were reinforced. Both styles deprived patients of a real sense of boundary and provided them with seduction during therapy and deprivation during holidays, thus recreating their disturbing familial pattern.

The technique of discussing group interactions in great detail is of great importance for the development of positive therapeutic insight and also enables them to think about their actions and so take responsibility for the life of the group and its survival. This is essential for a person who is prone to acting-out behaviour to relieve mounting anxiety at times of distress. Patients are seen only once a week, and they are without any support until the following week. They seem very vulnerable to mishaps especially during holidays, when they miss the group attendances and feel themselves rejected. A missed session may provoke a member to embark on all sorts of delinquent activity. It is perhaps a month later, after repeated interpretations and working-through, that it starts to click with the member that there is a link between such activities and missing a session.

Group members noticed my adaptation to their needs rather than clinging to a technique that might provide me with a sense of security but would have left them feeling insecure and anonymous. I began to blend different techniques according to the needs of each patient and what I thought was best for all.

Supervision and intervision of group analysts

I am borrowing from my work as a training consultant the term "intervision": a horizontal, linear process of a peer group, with no one person supervising anyone else. All group analysts are inter-looking at one another, inter-vising one another, scrutinizing their own methods of work, examining their skills and failures. This democratic process is, of course, even more highly developed in therapeutic communities where all patients and staff have the same voting rights, and where all voices are heard with equal seriousness. These intervision sessions provided us with an enormous amount of comfort, safety, and reliance on our own abilities to listen or on attempts to understand and frequently to criticize one another in the most positive and constructive way. It is impossible to learn without listening to the other side of ourselves, which is, of course, reflected in our colleagues' observations of our own work. Often I have been asked, while lecturing, how one can endure working with these patients who constantly present us with the most varied and demanding challenges. I admit that I would never be able to do this without the direct support and reciprocity of our own colleagues. These meetings have been used not only for the discussion of clinical presentations and clinical vignettes taking place in the groups, but also for all sorts of policy-making. Adequate criteria have been adopted for selection procedures for preparation for entering into groups and leadership techniques. Discussion of issues arising from concerns about confidentiality and ethics, as well as relationships with third parties in the outside world and appropriate ways of dealing with different referral agencies, are decided. Despite theoretical differences with colleagues, a great deal of solidarity, cohesiveness, and mutual support is an obvious necessity. A colleague will take over the handling of all the external situations, and everyone is expected to take over colleagues' expected or unexpected problems relating to holidays, absences, and illnesses. The reliance is absolute and total.

Intervision has led to group members filling in an attendance sheet at the start of each session (see below under "Practicalities). Though a small but significant detail of technique, this and others items are all discussed in our intervision sessions along with interpretations to do with the here-and-now, the technique of writing reports for outside agencies, and so forth, as well as the patients' own evaluations and thoughts about themselves and others.

In other words, intervision is a constant process of learning, including from the patients, and then sharing this new learning with colleagues to create a continuous process of taking in and modifying ways of working successfully with groups.

Composition of groups

I became aware of the importance of a thorough study of the composition of each particular group, using Foulkes's description of the heterogeneous group as a "mixed bag of diagnoses and disturbances which are blended together to make a well balanced and therapeutically effective mixture . . . the greater the 'span' between the 'polar' types, the higher the therapeutic potential, if the group can stand it". Pichon-Rivière (personal communication in 1961), too, said that the more heterogeneous the group, the more therapeutic it becomes.

Ideally, the group should contain equal numbers of each sex, but in practice this proved to be difficult, since women are referred much less often than men. On the other hand, I was able to mix patients who had sexual perversions with those who suffered from social deviancy or criminal behaviour. So, people with a history of violence, shoplifters, flashers, fetishists, fraudsters, and those with other social and sexual predicaments had to contend with one another, with the usual comparison of who was worse than the other, coming eventually to the painful realization that they were all driven from within to do things they could not really understand the meaning of nor why they were so strongly subjected to reinforce the same scenarios.

This internal look at the possibilities of different meanings inevitably leads to self-respect and to respect towards others. A real interplay and exchange of ideas takes place instead of the easy blaming attitude so usually found outside in society. No wonder that they first appeal to ease the pain and feel temporarily better by judging themselves superior to those outside the groups. I learned that there was no particular law about these matters, but that it was best to err on the side of caution.

The one element common to almost all of them is that they have indulged in actions that are in conflict with the law. In some cases, this conflict has led to its disclosure, with pertinent legal implications such as appearing in court, and they have had to face the outcomes of their actions; in others, it is still a private, encapsulated action of which nobody is aware, and they have never been identified, except by their victims. I remember a group started in the early 1970s that was very heterogeneous from the very beginning. It was composed of two heterosexual paedophiliacs, an exhibitionist, a promiscuous girl unable to reach orgasm, a delinquent mother who had deserted her children and forged cheques, a young man seeking his sexual identity, and a young girl who, despite a stable but sadomasochistic relationship, had never been sexually penetrated. All were highly intelligent and from differing backgrounds. Some occupied responsible situations in society. Some were sent to the group by court orders, on probation or from hospitals; others were self-referrals. In fact, they constituted a rare assembly of the extremely inadequate and disturbed who, brought together, responded quite differently from any apparently similar group of neurotic personalities. This difference of response was conditioned by an equally shared, intense fear of being humiliated, hurt, or tortured and anxiety about any form of coercion and rejection, such as blackmail or arrest. Importantly, they were all sharing something that was either punishable by the law or of which they were extremely ashamed. This put them together, and they felt a sense of comradeship for being in this predicament.

Transference situation

The characteristics of a group composed of members who share the belief that they are unacceptable to society because of their actions are quite different from those groups composed of neurotic patients. It is crucial to deal with deep anxieties about being persecuted, tortured, blackmailed, and thrown out. Indeed, this very explosive material can be used to the best advantages. These characteristics give the clues to their tremendous sense of lack of trust, especially were they placed in a one-to-one situation with a therapist who, in transferential terms, would immediately assume the role of the authority/parental figure.

It is essential to be consistent with regard to the interpretation of negative transferences. As discussed later, interpretation of the negative transference should be present and active from the very inception of the group, since this would be the only effective way to deal with "unhealthy solidarity" and with all attempts to resist the development of group cohesion. Whenever patients get extremely angry with each other, it should be included in interpretations to do with their care, which is present in this emotional response—in other words, that anger may convey concern.

Practicalities

On arrival, patients go to a waiting room adjacent to the receptionist's area. Exactly at the time for the session, patients who are in the waiting room are invited to go to the group analytic room downstairs, where the therapist is waiting for them.

Group members are expected to set out a number of chairs to sit on, arranged in circular fashion but not in any perfect order. There may be more chairs than patients.

There is table in the middle, and on it is a weekly attendance sheet, with blank spaces and dates of sessions. Members write their own names in the first session and tick their attendance in the corresponding blank date, using their own pens. This procedure was adopted after careful study of the circumstances involved: had their names and surnames already been typed down before the meeting it might be thought to denote a faulty sense of confidentiality, hence it is left open for them to write whatever name they want to be identified by.

Not only is it useful for us to have this record of their attendance, but it also increases their sense of commitment and responsibility towards the group. It also creates a fixed sense of belonging and a sense of care and responsibility for those absent. It is revealing to see that some patients try to mark other patients' attendance in the group, trying to take control, or checking the absences of other patients when they are in the process of writing letters to absent members.

If letters have been received, it is best to leave them on the same table for them to read.

At the Portman Clinic, auxiliary devices such as a one-way screen or video-recording are never used. Obviously something of value for training and teaching purposes is missing, but the first priority is given to the patients and their sense of well-being. They have already experienced rejection, humiliation, and isolation and might find unacceptable any devices that increase a sense of distrust and fears of being persecuted or blackmailed.

Letter writing

As soon as the group begin to express concern for an absent member, it becomes part of the philosophy of treatment for them to write a letter to the absentee, which the clinic forwards. It is most rewarding to see patients composing letters, from the moment one of them is selected or volunteers to write them—so much is involved in this process of identification. Different members each dictate a sentence, which is accepted or rejected, until eventually the letter is ready. However, it is the group analyst's responsibility to take the letter and have it posted, since patients have no access to any of the other patients' addresses.

To write a letter, the group members get the stationery from the receptionist, write it, and sign it themselves (never expecting staff members to sign the letters). This in itself is a rather revelatory maturational stage that they have reached; now the roles and areas of responsibility are clearly defined. They feel in full possession of power about themselves as a group and different from the group analyst, who is in charge of the authority and is not included within the patients "membership".

The beginning stage of therapy

Initial resistance to therapy

There are obvious idiosyncrasies with a group composed of members who because of their actions share the view that they are unacceptable to society. They automatically assume, in view of past experiences, that they will not be understood by people but only condemned by them, and they view their prospects of getting into a group with dismay and intense fear.

For instance, in a first group session, Morris, withdrawn in manner and isolated, was able to admit, in a determined but fairly anxious way, being attracted to little girls. To his surprise, Michael immediately confessed to a similar problem. The group reaction varied between shock and complete denial. It was clearly evident that if any of them chose to talk openly about their problems, they had to face one or all of three responses: rejection, persecution, being reported to the authorities. This produced a deeply threatening internal situation, which was worked through in transferential terms: I was the "authority", "torturer", "policewoman"—indeed mother, that being their ultimate fear of me—and as such I was someone who would, without granting them the possibility of independence, report them to the highest authority, or father. As soon as this interpretation was made, anxiety was released and a new sense of trust was created. From that time on, an atmosphere of tolerance and acceptance prevailed.

The first session of a newly established group

The first group session is of vital importance for the understanding of the psychopathologies of these individuals who tend to react in a similar manner. Unlike a group of neurotic patients, when they first confront each other there will not be many sticky silences. On the contrary, once somebody starts talking, everybody joins in and the whole atmosphere is enlivened. Often there will be almost simultaneous presentation of two themes. One of these is of minimizing symptoms and seeing themselves as misunderstood victims of society—it will be implied that on the whole they are good, caring citizens, who feel trapped in all the misunderstandings that surround them. The other is of being victims of intense persecution. Immediately an authority figure will emerge, usually a policeman who is just there to humiliate, persecute, blackmail, or torture them. There is an oscillation between these ways of dealing with their predicament.

It is not unusual for members to conjure up an image of a "nagging" or possessive mother of whom they have been both frightened and rather contemptuous. They will tend to agree with each other, thus creating an atmosphere of unhealthy solidarity, with the main object of assigning that image to the therapist. They will try in very devious ways to get the therapist to collude with their perversions, involving him or her in such a way that, unless transferential interpretations are made very early, the therapeutic process will become extremely difficult to handle. The therapist may be trapped with few options, such as becoming the sadistic policeman who every time they talk about their problems will try to moralize, condemn, or put them away, or becoming a nagging mother who invariably will use the group to question every patient in a persistent and repetitive way about their illegal activities, expecting them to conform to society's norms. Patients will display extraordinary cunning in the presentation of their problems, and the other members will react to create a "grand confession". Unhealthy solidarity often appears to condone members' criminal actions. With the utmost fear of pseudo-acceptance, they will try to put all the "blame" outside in society.

It is difficult to convey the amount of fear, rejection, and humiliation that our patients experience when confronted with their "secrets" in a conversation. This fear is greatly multiplied when facing not just one person but a group of, say, six people for the first time. Of course, as complete strangers they are liable to project into the other members of the group their own sense of rejection and fear of being found unacceptable. For example, people involved in crimes against property would immediately compare themselves in a favourable light to those suffering from perversions. This projection, though, will be reciprocated by those who consider their perversions as not harming anyone and will criticize those responsible for stealing or vandalizing property.

Importance of interpreting the negative transference

The group analyst has, or at least must try hard, to be skilful in dealing with such interactions from the outset. Failing to interpret may result in the arrest of therapeutic development. Collusion for the sake of comfort makes interpretation leading to insight unlikely. This same collusion associated with an intense fear of criticism arising from discussion of motivations therefore operates to spare patients and therapist supposed condemnation. In consequence, though, this will create another anxiety because members are aware that covering up brings frustrations when the conductor does not intervene properly by offering adequate interpretations. Unless unhealthy expectations can be interpreted quickly, the therapist and his or her expertise are likely to be immobilized.

Projective mechanisms are well in play in these groups. A patient in his first session said that his main problem was an intense urge to steal female underwear from clothes lines, to take home to masturbate with. Anxiety generated in the group was quite formidable, until another member (a woman with a background of extremely violent behaviour) became extremely "kind and understanding". She told him, "Well, I don't think stealing a pair of knickers is such a serious problem." In this way she was trying to relieve the patient of his anxiety about his compelling action but was doing absolutely nothing to assist him in understanding his motivations for his actions. Actually, she was trying to silence him through fear of being confronted in future about her own violence.

The group analyst has to be extremely skilful in immediately dealing with such situations during the same session, otherwise the therapeutic development of the group will be jeopardized forever. Once the collusion has settled in, it could become almost impossible to make interpretations leading to insight, the group having already gone in the direction of supportiveness. The reason for this maximum collusion is the intense fear of persecution that they all feel by not talking and not taking the vital point of the patient's motivations in those actions. None of them will face their own motivations, and therefore they will be free of being condemned. Simultaneously, such collusion will create an enormous amount of anxiety because they are aware of the covering up, which could be relieved only by adequate interpretation.

That is why, unless unhealthy expectations are quickly interpreted, the group analyst will be trapped, not being able to exercise his own expertise. Of course, many more attempts will be made during the course of the group to try to revive this situation. For example, members will try to use, with great intensity, externalization and intellectualization by having extended, elaborate, pseudo-sophisticated talks about different cultures and what is supposed to be normal or abnormal in them; the therapist might eventually feel submerged by this mass of information and rather confused.

Early stages

The group culture that emerges in working with social and sexual deviants is quite different from that in any group of neurotics. Here, even in early sessions, symptoms are minimized, although difficulties are invariably externalized. Intensely persecutory feelings about the world beyond bind patients quickly and closely together. Projective mechanisms—operating at their most intense, through issues to do with blackmail (real and imaginary), manipulation, and persecution—aim at putting the therapist into a collusive stance, which has to be analysed constantly.

"Acting-in"

In another direction, the group faces a further danger, especially with patients who exhibit sexual perversions. A patient who previously has been quiet and rather secretive about his actions will start talking with constant repetition and great detail about the actions in which he is involved and about which he feels very ashamed. To start with, this might be thought to denote enormous trust in the group. Later on, though—and especially when a few sessions have taken place and the patient carries on talking, giving more and more details—it becomes quite obvious that he is taking the therapeutic situation, the session of the group itself, as a perversion. In other words, by describing his criminal offence in such richness, he is trying to seduce and excite other members and thereby is getting an enormous amount of sexual gratification. Therapy has now been forgotten: the time and the place for therapy have become the time and the place for the perversion itself. The patient might not now do any acting-out, might not indulge in actions outside the group any more, but in talking about it what he is doing is a repetition of the act itself. The conductor has to be very aware of that, because sometimes the environment is charged with such enormous eroticism that it will be very difficult to be able to make an interpretation that will cut through what is going on.

They will try in many other ways to make the therapist part of their perversions. After all, why is the therapist interested in this bizarre behaviour? Is the therapist getting some satisfaction out of it, thereby playing the willing partner to their perverse activities or fantasies? They—especially the exhibitionist and paedophiliac patients—tend to talk a lot about their "willing victims".

All these different attempts to pervert the group therapy strongly indicate their need to be denigrated. Also, they are implying their hopelessness and helplessness, in which they are not expecting anyone to understand them or help them in the process of growing up.

"Positive" acting-out

Sometimes, especially towards the sixth or seventh month of treatment, patients might embark on some sort of acting-out that in itself might be of a positive kind; by this I mean people who have been very secretive about their sexual abnormalities in a much encapsulated manner (see chapters 1 and 8). Initially very careful in looking for the places or "victims" to avoid being caught, they start being far more casual and careless.

For example, Peter had referred himself for treatment because of heterosexual paedophilia. From the start he created a strong dependency on me as he had with his mother, in a very oral fashion, his fantasy being to be fed on demand by an ever-available breast represented by the group. When the dates for the first summer holiday were announced almost two months in advance, Peter was shocked; he had assumed that I was accessible at all times, living in at the clinic. A good deal of interpretive work was done about separation anxieties, but it was dangerously apparent that Peter was unable to accept the reality of the coming holidays. He began to behave like a deserted child.

On return from the holiday, the group received a letter from Peter in prison: he had been caught. He had acted in a most compulsive way, sexually assaulting several girls in a public place without taking any precautions against detection—indeed, quite the opposite. The group reacted with much sympathy and understanding. They saw the episode as an attempt on his part to seek out punishment for behaviour that they considered to be wrong, possibly the expression of a cry for help, and indeed it could be seen as a reduction in the use of schizoid defences and the beginning of the capacity to own his pathological behaviour. They at once wrote letters of a sympathetic character to both Peter and his father, individually and as a group, expressing a strong wish for Peter to come back, since they felt treatment at this point would be invaluable to him. Five weeks later, on release from prison, Peter returned to the group. He looked somewhat hardened by the experience yet was now able to talk about his depression and anxiety fears, for he felt really accepted by the group. He was firmly determined not only to try to understand the motivation of his actions, but also to use some external impulse control—which actually took the form of the group simply asking him every week about his activities. Thus the group was functioning as an auxiliary ego, which Peter began gradually to incorporate. By now, he was making social efforts with people of his own age, albeit in a rather clumsy fashion, by starting dance lessons, visiting pubs, and eventually going to parties. Some internal change had taken place in him: he was able to perceive internal conflict with guilt and to feel the need for help.

Working through the integration of new patients in an already existent group

Our groups function in the slow-open technique, and new members are only incorporated into an existent group when a small number of vacancies are available. New patients are introduced not more than twice a year. This requires long-term work by the group prior to their arrival. Lots of talk takes place, and in fact the old "patients" may be the first ones to bring up the need to "fill up" the group. They have fantasies at all different levels. Sometimes the group will welcome the idea of new arrivals in a most emphatic manner, talking of "new blood" being injected in to resuscitate the group and expressing all sorts of fantasies about new members who will be suitable matches for them. It is not unusual at these times for patients to talk about placing adverts in "lonely hearts columns". They sometimes express in a rather joking way the wish for the conductor to provide them with suitable matches: the paedophiliacs with young beautiful boys or girls, the exhibitionists with willing women to express admiration or intense fear towards the flashers, and so on. At other times an atmosphere of conning develops, and intense fear is created by the thought of new members coming. Sometimes a fear is expressed of being contaminated by people whom they consider to be more ill than themselves, or with more "kinky perversions". There is a recurrent "hope" that everybody else will leave and only one patient will remain who will eventually get individual treatment.

It takes a long time before they eventually start getting feelings of being more grown up and more prepared not only to share but also to give new members a sense of comfort in connection with acceptance of the realities of life. At other times, material that has been hidden away for a long time suddenly emerges under the threatening situation of the new sharing.

For example, Denis came initially with the problem of heterosexual paedophilia, and after being in the group for six years he began to transfer his sexual interest from young girls to women of his own age. He told us how he felt sexually aroused by a woman with whom he began to go out, though he was in conflict because of frequent impotence. Many other positive changes had happened, and he had become far more independent, having left home and found a place of his own.

From the original group, only he and another patient—who was the senior by then and had already warned us he would be away for four weeks—were left. When new patients came to the group, Denis was therefore in the most unexpected situation of becoming a father-figure. He responded to this with great ambivalence, on the one hand expressing great willingness to help new members. This was very difficult because he had and still kept a very submissive and dependent attitude towards a very possessive mother, and his disabled father had died a long while ago; the whole situation of becoming the senior figure in the group therefore became a bit too much for him. But the real difficulty was that this would be the first time he would be on his own with the other original member of the group—that is, with me as the therapist. The session before the new members were coming, he talked about his fantasies of having impregnated his girlfriend, which was met with scepticism. He responded in a very angry way at them not taking seriously this longing to be a father. In the following session he showed his impotence by withdrawing from the group and regressing to talk about his interest in young girls. This was a serious attempt on his part to cling to the position of a little boy in the group.

Normally a most regular attendee, he suddenly missed three sessions without explanation. Four weeks later, following a letter written by all members of the group, he reappeared saying how difficult it had been for him to come back to the group. He had felt extremely confused, switching between his childlike needs and other needs for maturation and self-improvement. Interpretations were made to the effect that he had felt challenged by me to adopt a parental situation in the group and simultaneously he felt mocked by the others in doing so. He felt trapped in a no-exit situation, which was only resolved by the feeling of being missed. He resumed his attendance and was able to give valuable contributions to the new and old members of the group before he finally left.

Middle stages: erotization of the treatment

Separation anxieties can easily produce dangerous acting-out. The therapist's holidays are very distressing for group members since they feel neglected, abandoned, and uncared for, just as they did when they were infants. There are often, however, signals in the sessions leading up to holidays that "something is going on". It is important to recognize these clues, for they form part of this constellation or syndrome responsible for "acting-out" behaviour. It may be seen as the erotization of the treatment as a resistance to the therapeutic process (Welldon, 1982).

Erotization facilitates the process of acting-in, and this easily leads to acting-out. The acting-out usually takes the form of pairing, either homosexual or heterosexual. One of the group members feels in open rivalry and competition with the therapist's authority. This member sees the therapist as ineffectual, uncaring, deserting, and passive, and this makes that member operate in a very active and seductive manner, feeling strong and powerful through becoming the alternative radical therapist. Frequently the acting-out—usually involving an inexperienced and insecure partner—takes place at the same time as a missed session. Following it he or she comes back to the group and eventually reveals the secret acting-out, with the perverse hope of a process of attempted erotization of the group.

This desperation to be in control, though difficult to contain, is deeply linked to the patient's psychogenesis, and therefore it provides a most fertile ground for the experienced therapist to make accurate interpretations. Treatment in its deepest sense, with the emergence of insight and possibility of inner changes, now becomes possible. Thus, this is the ideal time to make interpretations dealing with their infantile needs and their intense fears of being left alone.

Supervision for the therapists is essential in cases such as this, as a means to protect ourselves from the inherent anxiety produced by working with these patients. They often act out very sadistic and intrusive attacks on us and on their treatment in many different ways, including on our own capacity to think, leaving us confused and unable to offer adequate interpretations.

For example, Paul had referred himself for treatment because of heterosexual paedophilia. For a long period of time he kept completely silent regarding being sexual attracted to young girls, fearing becoming a target for attack from the others, especially mothers of young children. He had only admitted to his sexual preference during the first two sessions, when people expressed a strong disapproval. After several months of attending the group and after the Christmas holidays, he started to talk in an open and explicit way about his approaching young girls during the holidays, offering the group much detail regarding his sexual actions. Whereas initially I considered this to denote a degree of great trust towards the group, suddenly I was on the alert that an unconscious group process was taking place and that I was part of it.

I noticed that the whole group had become mesmerized. There were no interruptions, no confrontations, no questioning. Not only was there silence, but the whole atmosphere was charged with electricity, by which I mean that everybody was very excited, actually sexually aroused, so the patient had succeeded in turning the whole group into a "child" that he could molest and was exercising the situation for his own pleasure. He no longer needed to seduce the children outside—he had the group, and in a symbolic way he was displaying his perversion to a most satisfactory degree for his own sexual gratification. The group was behaving like the child described by him, obtaining sexual pleasure with full consent; he claimed he had not forced but only seduced the child.

My style in the interpretation of the here-and-now encompassed the whole group as the "consenting child" and Paul as the instigator, seducer, groomer, of the group and the session as the scenario of the perversion. So, an interpretation of his psychopathology in action was accompanied by the collusive unconscious participation of the group.

My interpretation enabled the group members to become conscious of their own sense of excitement, to gain insight about their own regressive responses, and to understand their own vulnerability to seductive sexual approaches, which produce not only excitement but also a futile, rather banal sense of being alive, wanted and desired as a part-object, a neglected child, an easy victim to a sexual attack devoid of any loving or caring feelings.

Playing the alternative therapist

At times a climate of fear and threat is present, again creating an enormous amount of excitement, as in the case of Miriam, who to start with was rather antagonistic towards me and later developed the most sadistic attacks on me, trying to belittle my function and denigrate my technique. She took a "special interest" in Jason, a young member of the group who had no sexual experience with girls. After a few months of treatment, he began to have explosive outbursts. The first time took place when a new member disclosed that as a teacher he had behaved in an inappropriate way with one his male students. So here for the first time was an acknowledgement of the traumatic experience of being seduced by a teacher that Jason himself had gone through as a child. Slowly these aggressive outbursts were replaced by situations in which he could cry, showing his vulnerability. He had always felt very deprived and had become the child of the group. It was then that he began to get plenty of sympathy from Miriam. He was utterly dependent on me and would take my interpretations very seriously; Miriam felt very angry with me, since in her view it was my responsibility to educate him sexually in a literal way. This situation became an easy target for her rivalry and competitiveness with me, especially since the holidays were approaching and my "lack of concern" for him would be in the open. On return from the holidays, we learnt that on two occasions she had followed him to his bed-sit and forced her way in, trying to seduce him. This acting-out outside the sessions was to do with her attempting to be a sexual therapist for him in intense rivalry with me. He was very frightened and came to the group to explain it.

My interpretation dealing with her enormous envy of my position as a therapist was that because of the holidays and her real concern for Jason she took advantage of feeling in charge to avoid her own feelings of missing the group and myself as the therapist. In so doing she was attempting to become the alternative, "fucking" therapist, devaluing me and placing herself as the perpetrator, to avoid dealing with her own feeling of being an early victim of sexual abuse. All the fear, neglect, and persecution were now placed on Jason as a repetition of the literal abuse. The group members, including herself and Jason, had much to learn from this multi-symbolic, concrete acting-out.

Development of the capacity to think

Psychoanalytic psychotherapy aims to provide patients with the necessary understanding of their chosen symbolisms, and the part that the affect plays in them, but in the instance of the forensic patient this is especially relevant since their anxiety is only relieved by bizarre actions, of whose unconscious mechanisms they are unaware. If they are able to gain the relevant insight, they might then interpose the thought between the urge and the action (see chapter 7).

This process is highly accelerated in group psychotherapy when a member's particular psychopathology is driven by a compulsive need to alleviate the increasing tension and is confronted by other group members at different stages and his condition is understood in some of its intricacies. At this point the rest of the group does the thinking. The learning by experience is then multiplied not only by the actual number of group members but also by their own growing process of maturation, which intrinsically involves the development of their own capacity to think. A slow-open group facilitates this process.

For example, a patient came because of her compulsive shoplifting. At the start she could not comprehend the complicated mechanisms involved in her self-destructive behaviour, despite her deep motivation for important inner change. Eventually she began to learn of her rage against her partner and her desire for revenge, which pervaded the acting-out that took place after rows with him because of her inability to tolerate frustration. It was only when she learnt about it in transferential terms that she told the group how she had been able to resist the temptation to steal a beautiful garment. She had been able to replace authority in her thinking—the loved–hated parents-therapist-husband—by her peer-group members, considering what her fellow patients' actions and feelings would be after her shoplifting. She had first said to herself: "I want this jacket very badly, and it will make me feel great." Immediately she recoiled from that urge by thinking of the "afterwards", having in mind the group process involving both peer group and authority. "I know what I most want in my life is peace of mind and this will never be achieved by this theft, because I'm doing it in order to take revenge. In fact, the opposite will happen—afterwards, I will feel full of shame and self-disgust." She had been able to interpose this thought before the action, using both her newly gained insight and the group as an auxiliary ego, which stopped her, this time, from committing the action. The hope she created lived on for a long time as other members talked of how deeply affected they were by her experience and how much help they had gained from her capacity to learn. Her urge to steal had to do with the aggrandizement of her false self in order to reinforce her omnipotence versus her despondency; her discovery about herself needed to be communicated to the other members because it constituted an important dimension of her recognition of her own true self.

Gaining of insight and its communication are often not that straightforward in working with destructive patients. For example, Anne, notorious for her shoplifting activities, which were at the service of the enhancement of her false self, told the other group members of changes she had experienced: "I am very worried about myself. I am no longer my usual 'cool' self regarding my shoplifting expeditions; I've recently noticed that when I'm about to do some shoplifting I feel anxious that I'm about to give myself away." One member asked, "Do you think you are changing through your attendance to this group?" "Actually I was thinking myself the same and don't know what to do about it since I'd hate to be caught. My husband would kill me", was her response. Other members were able to make interpretations about her acting-out as a symbolic, contemptuous, revenge attack against her husband. She was placed in a difficult situation because her becoming aware of this symbolic attack meant that she had to sort out her marital problems and stop the destructive acting-out. This was an important change that had to do with her criminal activity changing from ego-syntonic to ego-dystonic. In other words, her capacity to corrupt her ego integrity was no longer so easily available, due to the formation of a new ego that had been internalized from the group, with an accompanying capacity for reflection. At the same time, though, perverse mechanisms in other patients were readily available in their "advising" her to stop attending the group sessions since they were interfering with her "professional" gift as a shoplifter. The group was split in two: some accepted the change as a healthy development, but others were not so generous with their response because of extreme envy of the positive changes she had been able to achieve.

Terminating group therapy

The process of termination is of vital importance in consolidating the improvements and changes achieved, though some patients decide— or are asked by other members (discussed above)—to leave before this. A general consensus should be reached among members and the therapist about the date for leaving, and this should be agreed at least three months prior to the actual termination. This gives time to deal with the anticipation of missing therapy for those who are to leave and also for those who are to stay to voice feelings about missing them. In this way, they become aware of previous unacknowledged grief and mourning for many losses in their lives and they start to value what they are about to offer of themselves to others. In practical terms, the three-month period has to comprise twelve or thirteen consecutive sessions and not overlap with holidays.

"Good termination"

Sometimes it is possible to work towards the "good termination"— that is, the patient, after being with the group for a considerable length of time, is able to achieve the desired changes and improve- ment and eventually talks about feeling ready to leave therapy. He will acknowledge his internal and external changes but also express problems related to separation and fears and dependency, so whereas he may wish to leave the group he is also concerned about his stop- ping treatment. This is widely discussed within the group, in terms of whether or not this is an accurate assessment of the situation and whether it is the right time for the patient to leave the group. If a gen- eral consensus is reached in favour of termination, a time is set for the ending and ample space is given for everybody to comment on how much they would miss that particular member and for the member to acknowledge his own fears of leaving such a sheltered situation and of getting on his own two feet in the outside world.

That was the case with Jennifer, who had been referred to the group because of problems of sexual frigidity after being sexually assaulted, which she assumed was divine punishment for allowing her boyfriend of two years to do some heavy petting. She was also terrified of hav- ing babies, for fear of taking revenge on them and had, in fact, begun to feel prone to attack children during school breaks (we took this potential very seriously). Previous sorts of treatment had not been successful. She stayed in the group for over two years, and from being shy, and withdrawn, she began to open up in all sorts of ways, no longer—as the group had previously said—hiding away like a small child, unprepared to face the world. Simultaneously, changes were happening in her relationship with her boyfriend, as well as in her own parental home. She was now able to assert herself more and be more independent, and from being a "little girl" she began to emerge as a grown-up woman. She now talked about the sexual assault and her previous fantasies of being the victim of multiple rapes. Her family members all shared a strong religious alliance where sexual activities were considered to be dirty and only for the benefit of men and the exploitation of women, and sex was only for procreative reasons. She had been completely dominated by her parents, who were very judgemental towards her and blamed her for the attack. She became aware of this intense dependency on her family and began to detach herself completely from them. In her improvement, which included being able to achieve sexual penetration and experience orgasm, she had to deal with very contradictory responses of both envy and extreme hope from the other group members. Such was her improvement that she considered termination, with the consent of the other members. This was a unique experience for her since separating and individuating had been prohibited at home. However, as a preventative measure it was recommended that she stay for a while just in case this was only a transitory phase. She accepted this, and the group set a date for her leaving after a few months. She was able to leave the group in a successful manner.

The tyranny of the repetition of the original trauma does not allow a complete transformation

From a countertransferential viewpoint it is painful to realize that patients we expect to do well and to have a good ending fail to do so. Therapists are left with a tremendous sense of frustration and bitter awareness that the impact of the original traumas has, after all, prevailed.

These are patients who during treatment have been able to achieve many positive dynamic changes, resulting in a much better life quality and the establishment of relationships that are gratifying to themselves and others. They then announce their wish to end their therapy; in the follow-up discussion among the members and just when a general consensus is close to being reached that the patient is well equipped to leave, something happens that obliterates all previous discussions.

Against any expectation of a negative outcome, therapists are taken by surprise to discover that the patients are stuck to the early traumas, which are determining their destinies. Repetition has structured as destiny and the unbinding power of repetition commanded by the death drive, as Marucco describes (2007, pp. 319–320), in that they are bound to repeat themselves, which thus precludes any further positive changes.

For example, Mary's parents gave her away at a very early age, without explanation, to her maternal aunt. She was soon abused by her aunt, being put in charge of all household activities and doing the heavy work. Her severely disabled uncle also began to abuse her sexually, with the full collusion of her aunt. He died when she was 14, and her aunt then threw her out because "she was no longer of any use". She began to live on her own, lying about her age. Later she became involved in prostitution as a means of securing "independence". Through manic defence and denial of all her previous suffering and exploitation she developed an illusory sense of being in control, but very soon a "pimp" took over her life and her earnings. However, a healthy part of her was very much in evidence, and she was determined get out of this trap. This would not be easy, since it involved powerful men who had established a ring of expensive prostitutes, and she was the "English rose", very much sought after by clients. Despite all sorts of threats, she eventually achieved her freedom and decided to become a florist. She obtained the necessary training and was immediately approached to manage the flower shop at a five-star hotel. Soon afterwards she realized that, despite herself, a repetition of her previous life had begun to emerge in that she felt surrounded not by the beauty of the flowers as she had imagined but by superficiality and vanity.

She felt a strong need to change her life, but it should be underlined that she did not seek help during a crisis as a cry for help; it was only once she was established in her new profession that she referred herself for therapy.

During the first session of group analytic therapy, everyone was taken aback when she admitted to having done "some whoring" for some years, since her physical appearance was one of naivety, virginity—the "English rose". From the beginning Mary was a regular attender and contributed exceptionally well to the group, although rather cold and distant, but later she became warm and concerned about the rest of the group. She was able to look into her depression and her low sense of self-esteem. She felt very close to me, and every interpretation she took into herself with an enormous ability to acquire insight. She developed a relationship with a man who wanted to marry her, but she felt unready for this.

After three years in the group she began to talk of leaving it, since she wanted to train as a nurse as a means to add gravitas and a sense of well-being to her "new" life. At this point and without any warning, I got a letter from a director of nurses' education asking for a reference: she had given my name as a referee. In the usual style, I took this letter to the group where we discussed all the implications of this unexpected twist, since she had never asked me to be a referee nor discussed this in the group. A long and positive discussion ensued; the conclusion reached by all, including herself, was that it would not be appropriate for me to write such a letter, as to do so would conflict with my own ethical responsibilities because she was a patient in treatment under my care and not an employee.

In transferential terms, she was stuck in re-enacting her early experience of being an "illegitimate" child living first as a child of her aunt and later as a "lover" of her uncle who had forced himself sexually on her. Through this request for a reference, she was asking me to behave in a fraudulent way. She was also depriving herself of me as her group analyst by making me appear as her boss. This lack of acknowledgement on her part was reproducing her intense confusion regarding her sense of to what or to whom she belonged. A lot of working through was done about her acting-out to make me reject and abandon her just as she had been, first by her mother, later by her aunt, and ultimately even by her uncle's death which left her literally on the street.

Although she became fully aware of all these intricacies through transferential issues, she felt in two minds. Her rational one accepted all interpretations, but psychologically she was in much pain and decided to create a false compromise by attending the group for another month before leaving. We all felt extremely worried about her and thought she should continue attending the group, but to no avail. By refusing to stay and work through all the traumas of her early life, she painfully demonstrated her compulsion to repeat and to re-enact what had happened in her external reality. She was still full of unexplored rage in that she was taking revenge against her mother—now, in transferential terms, myself—by not allowing her own improvement to be consolidated. We all shared a great sense of helplessness and rejection by her leaving the group. A year later we received a letter from her saying she was performing very well in her training as a nurse and offering her apologies for leaving in the way she did. By then we were experiencing feelings of concern, anger, and helplessness. The letter alleviated some of those feelings, but still a sense of frustration and sadness prevailed in the group. This clinical vignette was used by the patients in predicting and effectively helping those who subsequently presented a similar predicament. It was of central importance not to be seduced into offering a false reparation—such as providing the reference for her to try to repair her sense of abuse and betrayal.

LANDMARKS IN THE GROUP PROCESS
Violent behaviour as a defence against separation anxieties

In this final section I offer a clinical account of some landmarks in group process, with particular reference to dependency/separation problems leading to violent behaviour as a means to ward off depressive anxieties. A brief description is given of the characteristics of the early object relationship and its significance in the transference phenomena,

Although at times I describe the full group in action, I will concentrate in particular on three of the patients, who had a previous history of violent behaviour.

Alma, Alan, and Dorothy

Alma, a prostitute, had referred herself because of feelings of despair and a tremendous sense of confusion that she feared would lead her into further violent actions. She had an early history of extreme violence in the parental home. Father was a drunkard who used to beat her mother up. Alma always felt responsible for protecting her mother. She was evacuated at age 6 years because of the war. It was an extremely unhappy time in which she felt an outsider and was not given affection by anyone. Her parents divorced when she was 12. At age 15 a school teacher wanted her to enter drama school, but her mother refused and specified that Alma should leave school immediately to start earning money. She acquiesced to this, and at the time of entering group analytic therapy, aged 46, she was still living with her mother and with her son. She was always over-protective of both. She had become a prostitute at age 15 and soon afterwards married her pimp when she fell pregnant and had a baby boy. From the start of her marriage, she and her husband had constant physical fights. Eventually they divorced, but the sadomasochistic pattern in her relationships continued despite her constant changes of male partners. Even her son was engaged in the same relational pattern with her.

Alan, 40 years of age and of mixed race (father English, mother of Portuguese-Spanish descent) was referred for a psychiatric report on stealing charges. He had a long history of extremely violent behaviour, sometimes picking fights out of revenge and malice, and of stealing cars and large amounts of money and of breaking and entering; he had also been charged with impersonating a police officer. He had spent many years in prison, without any beneficial effects. His childhood was characterized by considerable domestic, geographical, economic, and social changes. He was born in Calcutta, but his mother left her husband, taking 4-year-old Alan with her. She remarried, and Alan regarded her new husband as his father. There were two children from the new marriage. Alan always felt responsible for his mother. His step-father died when Alan was 14, and from then on he developed the ambition to make money so his mother could live well. She died suddenly three years later, and he felt depressed and desperate, making two suicide attempts during the two following years. He began group therapy being recently married, with a pregnant wife. He had never been able to hold a job for long and had casual jobs as a painter and decorator.

Dorothy, 32 years of age, was referred for a psychiatric report on a charge of shoplifting, the fourth such charge in the previous four years. Brought up in East London with high economic aspirations, she was the youngest of four and from birth became "mother's pet" to the extent of creating disharmony between mother and father. She was epileptic and used to be irritable and lose her temper, with a low threshold for tolerance, which led to innumerable incidents of violent behaviour, especially towards her male partners. Four years after her referral, she had been able to control her temper, but this was replaced instead by compulsive shoplifting expeditions, which consistently took place following domestic violence at moments of intense chaos and distress in her marital situation. She had been married three times and had two children from a previous marriage, a girl aged 12 and a boy aged 9.

Suitability for group treatment

One of my selection criteria for group treatment is that patients who have had a suffocating relationship with either parental figure, but especially the mother, are likely to do better in group therapy than in individual therapy. These three patients all had an extremely close and unhealthy relationship with their mother.

Alma fully supported her mother, from whom she never parted, and was overprotective of her to the extent of fabricating for herself a double life in which the mother was not supposed to know of her prostitution. Alma was repeating this pattern with her son.

Alan's relationship with his mother was characterized by collusive attempts to maintain secrecy concerning the identity of his real father and the circumstances of his own birth. When his mother fell ill with cancer and he learned that she was going to die, he started to steal expensive cars and substantial amounts of money, taking his mother for rides and giving her all the luxuries she had never had.

Dorothy was supported by her mother and completely dependent on her for her daily help because of epilepsy. She had never dared to oppose or criticize her. Incidentally, she had managed to keep her mother from knowing about her delinquent activities on the grounds that this "would kill such a sweet and kind creature".

The others in this group

David, 23 years of age, was extremely immature and referred himself because of his compulsion to steal female underwear, which he used for masturbating as his only way to achieve sexual relief. In his child-hood he had attended public school. He was unable to function in any area.

George, a 25-year-old homosexual, a lawyer, who had become involved in fraudulent activities, had referred himself because of intense anxiety in a very depressive personality. He had a history of suicide attempts.

Greg, 47 years of age, married with children, with no previous history of delinquency or criminality, was referred because of exhibition-ism. A conscientious policeman for twenty-five years, he had to resign following his court appearance.

Martha, 25 years of age, with a long history of criminality, was referred by the probation service for a psychiatric report following charges of theft and dishonest handling. She had suffered from bouts of depression, broken sleep, and periods of compulsive eating. Although capable of getting good jobs, she changed jobs frequently. She was then living with her second husband. She had two children from her previous husband, both of whom lived with him.

Tim, a 32-year-old teacher with a history of homosexuality, referred himself because of his compulsion to cruise, which he found demeaning. At the time of referral he was having a relationship with a woman ten years younger than himself.

Group process

Already in the first session the talk was of risks. They spoke about violent and aggressive feelings and how they handle them. They saw some similarities between shoplifting and cruising expeditions, which involve a sense of excitement and inhibition of aggressive impulses. They also talked about their experiences in prison and the security and safety they felt there.

I approached this material with interpretations concerning the here-and-now: the risks here relate to being open about themselves, showing both sides to the group, abandoning splitting processes, and hence the feared consequences of being either rejected or dejected. The fears are increased since it is an outpatient setting, not offering the "safe/secure" conditions of a prison-residential setting.

In the first session, they had confronted each other with their feelings about committing suicide. In other words, they had many serious conflicts in the expression of their bitter disappointment and anger that had to turn inwards, to killing themselves, or the hate that had to be put outside with fantasies of killing someone else.

The fantasy of being fed on demand whenever they feel in a state of distress was eventually given up, and they came to terms with the once-a-week "feed" in the group. This state of affairs is prone to break down when holidays approach, since they regress to feelings of being neglected and abandoned and can quickly resort to dangerous acting-out. This "separation problem", especially at holiday times, is illustrated by the following material. I will take a series of sessions for each of the patients under consideration.

First, Alan. Two weeks after starting group treatment, he became a father. This event seemed to increase considerably his anxiety and confusion about his own identity, which, coupled with the lack of sessions during holidays, drove him to very stormy acting-out.

Following a Bank Holiday weekend, Alan confronted us as follows: "I've felt very lonely while my wife was in hospital having the baby. I couldn't stand the idea of coming back home to find it empty so I began to have this urge to steal a car." He described his very premeditated actions, giving full details of how he managed to take a car and drive it for three or four days, picked up a few "birds", and eventually returned it without anyone knowing about it. He had told no one else about this. Needless to say, the car was stolen at the exact time of the missed session.

Two months later, after the summer holiday, Alan told the group that during the holiday break he had been stealing cars and credit cards and almost got nicked. Alma responded to this in a very angry manner: "You are not even a good thief; you are just a little petty and insignificant thief. You don't care a bit about your family, about the group, about anyone at all. You are a fucking selfish bastard." Other members joined in, asking him about his criminal activities. Alan replied: "In fact, I used to be as cool as a cucumber, a very good con-man, but I have noticed now that I get scared. I know that in a way I am giving myself away."

Other members showed great interest in this statement. Tim asked whether he thought this "consciousness" had anything to do with the group, thereby indicating through his very use of language that he had begun to understand more than might have been thought possible. (I had never used this word, not ever using any jargon.) Alan replied: "Yes, it has all appeared since I came here, and I am very scared."

This acute awareness of his failing as a conman is of basic importance, not only for what it means to himself but also to the group. That statement contains a spontaneous giving up of previous defensive mechanisms that were used to support his criminal actions.

For the first time there was an acknowledgement of guilt, which leads to an acceptance of a need for help. This also includes the beginning of a better use of critical faculties in these patient' views of right and wrong. They can no longer hold the opinion that what they do is acceptable for themselves and for society. They no longer feel justified that their criminal actions are compatible with the ego's integrity and with its demands.

Alan continued: "I had a dream that scared me a lot the week before I came to the group. *I am stealing a compass that children use to draw circles, and the same man who caught me the first time appears in the dream and confronts me with the theft. I just tell him that the value of the compass is so little, it is really insignificant, at which point he tells me 'I am going to punish you, not for the value of what you have stolen, but for the crime in itself which you have committed'.* At that point I woke up in a cold sweat and was very scared."

Members did not respond immediately or directly to the dream but started talking about crime and what they get out of it. They seemed to realize that the element of risk that gives rise to excitement was essential, because all of them were trying to deal with a sense of emptiness and deadness, experienced consciously as a sense of boredom.

The dream was clearly about the group/breast/therapist and shows both the wish to steal it for the holiday period and the fantasy that it was being stolen from mother.

The material led to an interpretation of their intense needs of dependency and how vulnerable they felt about holidays since they felt so let down that they feared not being able to survive the ordeal of being apart from mother, who was not taking care of them, neglecting them. To protect against those very depressed feelings, they resort first to "boredom", "lethargy" (almost dead), and eventually to violent acting-out which makes them feel alive again. I interpreted to the group that they were extremely concerned about the inability they were experiencing in creating meaningful relationships, so they go on about cruising or prostitution. In the case of Alan, having a stable domestic situation makes him feel trapped because he is so scared of losing it; he must take small risks because the biggest risk of all would be to trust his family and himself because he fears that both they and he might let him down at any time.

During subsequent sessions the group discussed their awareness of being quite incapable of having a good relationship with another person. For example:

> George (addressing Alan): "I am extremely worried about you and the effect the group has on you if this means that you are becoming more ineffectual as a thief. Perhaps you ought to do something about that—I don't know whether to leave the group or what, but to make sure that the group is not affecting your skills as a thief."

People started getting very angry with him, calling him cynical. After all, they said, Alan came here in order to deal with his criminal actions.

> George (laughing): "He is not coming here to deal with his thieving problems, he's coming here because of his boredom, looking for excitement, and first he will have to know about this boredom. In the meantime, he has to be careful not to get caught."

I said that it looks as if people like George are getting quite a lot of vicarious satisfaction from listening to someone else committing all the crimes and he can go ahead giving his good advice as a lawyer.

It is important to note that while patients who are severely violent express their aggression in a very straightforward manner with physical gestures and over-abusive language, others do so in a sly and roundabout way, like George. He has become the devil's advocate in a way that essentially makes a mockery of what I had been saying, showing his "concern" for Alan's predicament—for example, advising Alan to stop treatment since "according to Dr Welldon" he is not coming here because of his stealing problem but because of reasons underneath that have to do with his depression and looking for excitement.

Several months later, after the Christmas holiday, Alan began to calm down. Whereas at the beginning he had always referred to his mother as being the most wonderful woman and to his real father as being a bloody bastard, he now began to change this story and could speak about his mother with a sense of disillusionment. For the first time in his life, he talked about how much she had neglected him and the heavy demands she had always placed on him.

A few sessions followed in which other members had been able to express their own sense of being lost during the holidays, with my interpretations of the group members feeling like small children, very neglected by me and not being taken good care of. They were then able to express their hostility towards me, which caused intense relief that I was not being killed off by it. Slowly Alan became much more aware of the intensity of his violent impulses. In one session he was describing an episode in which he had displayed very premeditated and calculated rage towards a man who was going out with his then girlfriend. Later on he began to displace his anger towards the other patients, and he dreamt of exterminating anyone who was not a healthy and good citizen, in a rather fascistic line. He wanted to kill off everybody—Alma because she was living off the dole, others for being homosexual, etc.

Now let us turn to Alma. She started group treatment being punctual and responsive, placing herself in the role of my "assistant", which was a repetition in the transference of her taking care of her mother. She got into a few fights with Dorothy, who was taking rather a jocular line of behaviour in the group (trying to be the mother's pet). Alma began to opt out of the group with several rationalizations and externalizations. This was interpreted as her need to avoid her fears of getting too close to me, with the dreaded consequence of my not allowing her to become independent, as had previously happened with her mother. She began to be extremely demanding on practical requests, such as a letter to the council to justify that she was in more urgent need than others, therefore trying to get me into the unethical position of helping her jump the queue. She talked about her impending eviction and her sense of homelessness. Others joined in her sense of being dispossessed. All this took place around Christmas, and interpretations were being made to the effect that people were feeling homeless, looking for a safe place where they could be taken care of (in a sense being a repetition of the scenario of Jesus in the stable, which is fairly typical of the way in which material that is common to each of the patients in a group is usually expressed collectively—i.e., by way of myth). She got exceedingly angry. Eventually she was in touch with the social worker and was placed in a new flat. Any attempts on my part to interpret her behaviour as one in which she had turned the tables (as opposed to what had happened to her as a young girl, in which she had to provide for mother) were now met with contempt and sarcasm towards me. After missing several sessions she came determined to attract everyone's attention by taking the floor, demanding feedback about the previous missed sessions. The others were very scared of her, letting her do the talking and actually not making any comments that might help her gain some insight about her acting-out behaviour. In other words, under the appearance of being attentive listeners they were giving her nothing to help her own understanding of her hidden violence. Eventually I had to intervene in a very active manner with her, such was the amount of threat and fear she produced in the group. So when I told her that the source of her anger towards me had to do with her own realization of how much she was missing out compared to the others and her need to repeat the situation in which she felt a burden and not being taken care of properly, she dramatically changed and began to cry.

This produced immediate relief in the group since everybody became aware that all this bravado on her part was only to cover up her intense depression, which had made it so difficult for her to take any good nurturing experiences, clinging instead to the early ones in which she felt deprived at home and also very isolated when she was evacuated during the war. Once more the source of extreme violence had to do with the fears of separation that produced in her a sense of imminent death of either her mother or herself—hence the impossibility for them to live apart.

After a flat was found for her she was able to tell both mother and son that they should care for themselves and that she was ready now to live on her own.

Now let us turn to the case of Dorothy and pick up the central themes of the group process. In the first session Dorothy said: "I'm here because of my husband, the third one, and I have the same shop-lifting problems again." She talked of her shoplifting activities and how they take place when she gets upset with her partner. She was very loud, did not listen to anybody else, and persisted in a very jocu-lar attitude. The others found her a bit of a handful and were rather wary of her except Alma, who interrupted her in a threatening way, saying "I think we are going to have lots of fights, you and me", imply-ing that she wanted to take a serious and caring attitude and would not let Dorothy be as casual and cavalier as she appeared to be.

Six months later Dorothy stated: "As a matter of fact every time I get caught I have only been too pleased and I said to myself how this will teach him [her husband] because he will feel humiliated and I know I am getting at him." There was a lot of talk by the group of their violent feelings involved in all these actions in relation to people they felt close to. Dorothy started to gain a sense of insight.

She became aware that she had always managed to maintain "close" relationships at the expense of the change of partners with whom she had been vociferous, violent, and vindictive. Eventually she realized that she stole in order to "punish" her partner, to humiliate him, to make him feel useless, to render him impotent, and also to anger him. She had a triumphant feeling when *he* got to know of her delinquent activities, which was just the opposite of what she experienced in rela-tion to her mother whom she had been extremely careful not to tell about her court appearances since "this would kill *her*".

Dorothy always sat opposite me—as she said, "To keep a check on 'Mum'"—and would scrutinize me constantly and respond to any interpretations of a transferential sort in the most dismissing and contemptuous manner. "It is all nonsense", "You are so bloody bent", "Psychiatrists need psychiatrists of their own". On one occa-sion when she was mad at me about the possibility of seeing me as a mother figure, her immediate reply was: "I want to kill you. How dare you make comparisons with my mother—you are more like my father, so distant and cold." After this angry reply she was able to look into her needs of being dependent on me and how vulnerable I made her by not being always available, just like her real mother. This also led her into the direction that I did trust that she could grow up and eventually grow away without me or the group. She had become very close to her father before he died suddenly, and she was extremely depressed for a long time, unable to accept his death. By telling me this, she was trying to kill me off and still be able to keep mother alive within herself in order to avoid the sadistic attack

towards her. Of them all, she was the one who was able to acknowledge the group's help.

In September, Dorothy told the group: "I am much calmer nowadays, I don't blow my top. I think a lot before I talk and I find myself
much more tolerant." She attributed this improvement to her group
therapy. Actually, her voice had come down a lot in decibels, and
she tended to look at me in a conciliatory manner in contrast to the
previously very aggressive and hostile way. She even talked about me
having big brains, being able to remember everything about everyone.
Before the Christmas holidays she announced to the group that she
would be absent the first session after the Christmas break due to a
hospital appointment for a periodical examination for her epilepsy.
The first session after the break there were a few absentees, and it
was agreed by the group to send them letters reminding them of their
attendance. I took the dictated letters by the patients and sent them to
the absent patients including, inadvertently, Dorothy. The following
session there was a very angry Dorothy, who threatened to kill me. She
was in a very agitated state, walking out of the group several times in
order to control her murderous feelings towards me. With the help of
the other members she was eventually able to explain the source of
her distress. She couldn't believe that I, of all people, had forgotten
her previous announcement of being absent. Actually, the letter had
caused quite a turmoil in the household since she had never told her
husband of her having treatment (in fact, she had never told us that
she had kept it secret from her husband, despite some interpretations
earlier on that she was treating the attendance at the group as an
extramarital affair).

By now they all joined in talking about murderous impulses they
had experienced and began to question each other about these. They
expressed fantasies of killing their partners and also killing me or
running me over because of my apparent lack of concern during the
Christmas break. They continued talking about feelings of revenge,
how they would make sure they paid back anyone who did any small
wrong to them, which took us back to the previous session and the
"mistake" I had made in sending the letter to Dorothy.

I made an interpretation to the effect that how much easier it was
to talk about their hostile feelings as opposed to ones of despair, sadness, and the fact of being let down. Children cannot accept mistakes
grown-ups make because of the extreme idealization they have about
the adult world.

* * *

I wrote this account when the group was in its fourteenth month. The changes they had gone through were quite noticeable, as was their gaining of insight into their unconscious motivations. Our three patients had by then experienced marked changes. They became aware of their feelings of inadequacy in communicating their despair and sadness and how much this had affected them in their expression of rage, appealing to violent and aggressive behaviour against society and themselves in order to "produce some self-justice".

Dorothy not only completely stopped her shoplifting for over a year but was also for the first time able to relate in a meaningful way to her husband (so much so that while initially she had concealed her treatment from him, he now insisted on her continuing group attendance). She was able to listen to other people's suggestions, ideas, and points of view, feeling much more self-assertive.

Alan showed an increasing sense of maturation and responsibility after a very stormy acting-out start in which he indulged on repeated occasions in criminal activities whenever there were holidays. He was also rebellious and irresponsible towards his family, having innumerable extramarital affairs, which led to him facing a lot of anger and contempt in the group, especially from Alma and Dorothy. He stopped his acting-out and developed a sense of limitations about his life, coming to terms with the person he is. He also expressed a wish to stop treatment some time in the future but felt very cautious as to whether this was a transitional phase or a more permanent change.

Alma had resorted to all sorts of externalizations and rationalizations, talking about "real" difficulties like being evicted, fights with her son and other men, and missing sessions whenever she didn't feel "up to it". Nevertheless, she changed her lifestyle in the sense that for the first time she was able to live on her own. She was much more prone to depressive bouts and not so keen on escaping from it all.

As already described, these three patients have in common some characteristics in their early object relationships which were affecting their presenting modes of behaviour. They had intense ambivalence, with masses of splitting processes and intense idealization of the mother figure, which led them into the direction of being unable to express any criticisms or objections to their mother's attitudes. They found extreme difficulties in doing so because their rage, anger, and sense of disillusionment were so strong. They feared that to express such murderous feelings would lead to actual murder. The only way to prevent this was to deny all hostility. They managed to displace this violence from the early maternal object into their present partners or society or both.

Furthermore, it should be clear that such material characterizes the group process insofar as these issues typify both their relationships to one another and their central preoccupations as members of the group.

It is desirable for patients to express their frustrations and anger in an open way, since this will promote maturity, growth, and self-assertiveness. It will also stop any physical violence. However, this requires quite an amount of trust on the part of the group analyst to contain the verbalization of patient's anger and an awareness of his or her dependency needs. Groups can be a great help in this respect because other patients are prompt to recognize violent moods and will protect the group analyst from impending physical attacks. Group members prove to be very efficient and therapeutic in their interventions, especially in helping one another to establish self-control on the basis of an understanding of their violent behaviour.

* * *

In conclusion, when working with criminals and deviants the therapeutic task is to facilitate a movement towards acting less and suffering more, whereas with neurotics it is to help them to suffer less and to act more.

CHAPTER TEN

The Portman Clinic and the IAFP

The Portman Clinic has been at the forefront of forensic psychotherapy throughout its history, dating back to 1931 when a small group of men and women met in London and established the Institute for the Scientific (later, "Study and") Treatment of Delinquency (ISTD) to promote a better way of dealing with criminals than putting them in prison. The clinical arm of the ISTD was called the Psychopathic Clinic, which was renamed the Portman Clinic in 1937.

From the start, the founding members of the ISTD aimed to:

- initiate and promote scientific research into the causes and prevention of crime

- establish observation centres and clinics for the diagnosis and treatment of delinquency and crime

- coordinate and consolidate existing scientific work

- secure cooperation between all bodies engaged in similar work in all parts of the world, and ultimately to promote an international organization

- assist and advise through the judiciary hospitals and government departments

- promote educational and training facilities

- promote discussion among, and educate the opinion of, the general public by means of publications, lectures, etc.

These idealistic and hopeful goals from sixty years ago were adopted in 1991 by the International Association for Forensic Psychotherapy

(IAFP). Until then, not many of these aims had flourished, and it is interesting to speculate as to the factors that prevented natural growth for such a long time—that is, this "failure to thrive" (Pilgrim, 1987).

Of course, we should be aware not only of the lack of "voice" but also of the absence of hearing. Scepticism about the application of psychodynamic theory and treatment of the forensic patient has been common. Eastman (1993), for example, has noted that "in a specialty where there is an extraordinary level of psychopathology, as well as of childhood deprivation and abuse, it seems extraordinary that the [forensic establishment] has paid so little attention to psychopathological understanding and psychotherapy."

During the history of the original Institute and then the Portman Clinic, clinical work has always been the main concern, to the extent that the promotion of ideas and training were neglected or even ignored: so much was this the case that it was commonly assumed that the clinic was "private". Highly trained professional staff devoted their working time to the provision of psychoanalytic psychotherapy but failed to recognize the growth of a new discipline. The provision of proper training for junior practitioners was neglected, and there was accordingly no natural reproduction in outpatient clinics elsewhere. However, some degree of internal consolidation had been necessary before any plans for expansion could effectively be developed. This was especially so since the outside world was cautious and suspicious when faced with the idea of an offender having an "internal" (mental) world.

Such had been the stigma (and eighty years later continues to be!) attached to contact with criminals that it had been difficult to find premises for the Institute in the 1920s and 1930s, and for some years, the medical staff saw the patients in their own private rooms. The Institute was housed under one roof for the first time in May 1937. In 1948, with the National Health Service Act, there was a division of the old ISTD: the Portman Clinic became part of the NHS, concentrating on the treatment of offenders. The Institute for the Study and Treatment of Delinquency continued under that title (now housed at King's College London), taking responsibility for research and the expansion of training programmes. Scientific cooperation between the two had been assured, and it was hoped that, despite the split, the Portman Clinic would become a model of its kind, undertaking specialist teaching, experimental work, and research.

These hopes have only been partly realized. Why?

Projective identification is used by those professionals working with "fringe" patients within a "fringe" framework in a society that operates with splits about "good and evil forces". At times of stress when staff members, in their intense commitment to their work, experience lack of support from those outside, they obtain a sense of solidarity by experiencing the "outside" as failing to understand and threatening—actually as the "bad" ones, for example, ready to close them down. There is also some identification with their patients' anti-authority feelings and rebelliousness.

Consequently an ethos developed at the Portman Clinic where there was a cosy, small-family atmosphere in which unique and optimal psychotherapeutic services could be delivered: this was rarely challenged by the outside world. The Portman did not need to face the difficulties now encountered in trying to promote a wider influence outside a small institution. This feeling of safety and closeness led to the enormous ambivalence and internal tension that characterized both the creation of the Course in Forensic Psychotherapy in 1990 and the founding of the IAFP in 1991. Both, in different ways, did exert some pressure on the Portman to change, by opening their doors to the training of a wider membership. Unfortunately, whereas the IAFP has continued to develop and flourish, the diploma course, which was created a year earlier than the IAFP, has been completely eclipsed. However, I shall give its history and development since it was a most accomplished course and was responsible for the training of distinguished and dedicated clinicians of all professions who are also presently the pillars of the IAFP. Hence, a golden decade was created that was worth all the effort placed in creating the structural and developmental changes required by the academic institutions involved.[1]

The IAFP itself had an interesting gestation. The story began at a meeting in Oxford in 1980, which was sponsored by two organizations: Law and Psychiatry and the charity Mind. A small group of European forensic psychiatrists, trained in analytic psychotherapy, were in the minority at the meeting and felt like outsiders whose views about their own work were misrepresented by the two main organizations, leaving them feeling battered. Thus they decided to have a meeting to discuss and share the difficulties encountered in their daily work, not only the dilemmas of facing patients but also those of working with colleagues from other institutions. With backing from the Portman Clinic, I offered to host such an annual meeting, the first of which was held in 1981. The three-day meetings were structured scientifically but had a friendly atmosphere. Originally it was envisaged that there would be gatherings in different countries, but in the event we always met in London. Although the membership was open to any interested colleague from the Continent, in the UK it was limited to Portman Clinic staff only. The rationale for this was the importance of keeping numbers small to be able to discuss clinical matters in depth. In fact, this meant that some well-trained, experienced colleagues working in other UK institutions were unable to contribute. As time went by it was felt that this European Symposium (with a membership below thirty) was so creative and useful that some of those committed from its inception wanted it to be shared more widely, especially with the younger generation. Also, formal teaching of young colleagues had started at the Portman, making such concerns even more urgent. However, some senior staff believed that the meetings should continue to be closed with no "outsiders" allowed, because the quality of the meetings would deteriorate and confidential issues could not be raised. Others considered that not only was the Portman being ungenerous and elitist, but also that wider aspects with regard to training issues in forensic psychotherapy had been neglected. An open conflict emerged around the fears of corruption and the need for discussion and negotiation of all the unconscious implications.

The next step was taken by some members of the European Symposium at the 17th International Congress on Law and Mental Health in Leuven, Belgium, in June 1991. They formed the IAFP with a truly international character, with eighty delegates as founder members. The rest is history: the IAFP has been holding annual international conferences in Europe and the USA, and it will be celebrating its twentieth anniversary in 2011 in Edinburgh.

The founding of the course and the resultant suspiciousness and conflict within the Clinic were also born out of insecurity and arrogance. The insecurity related to fears of invasion from outside, revealed by the sentiment of "they will take over"; the arrogance was reflected by feelings and expressions of "they will never understand", or "they will corrupt our purity of work". This again reflects the deep splitting processes that characterize the nature of our work, requiring as it does the amalgamation of a positivist forensic psychiatry stance with the understanding and compassion that psychoanalytic psychotherapy can provide.

Philosophy of the course

As stated previously, a crucial point about the discipline of forensic psychotherapy is that it is a team effort, not a lone heroic one. Action begins with the referral agencies, which may include the courts of justice. People from all walks of life are involved, and many of them will have to be part of the successful management and treatment of the forensic patient. Forensic psychotherapists, regardless of their professional background, should be able not only to lead their teams but also to educate others in order to obtain appropriate help and support from the media, politicians, social scientists, and so forth.

The practical approach

There are a few specific features to be considered when teaching a new discipline. First, a fresh approach is needed, which can be extremely difficult to establish since it requires an open mind, free of dogma. Second, being multidisciplinary creates demands and expects cooperation from a variety of colleagues and establishments regardless of their therapeutic/philosophical viewpoints. Third, the range of experience and theoretical knowledge of all trainees may be uneven.

There are basic distinctions between different aspects of a new teaching venture, and all must be carefully explored and examined—namely (a) the institution in which the training occurs, including the teaching staff; (b) the trainees; (c) the working places. The different assumptions, needs, and expectations must be debated and agreed upon before training begins. The offer of a course can only be successful if the final product makes sense to those who demand it.

I will describe the development of the forensic psychotherapy course at different stages by treating it as a clinical presentation, since this may offer insights into some of the complexities that are bound to occur.

Brief history of the course on forensic psychotherapy

In 1988 I was appointed Clinic Tutor at the Portman Clinic, an appointment automatically attached to the British Postgraduate Medical Federation (BPMF) at the University of London. I approached the Director of the BPMF, Professor M. Peckham with an idea, which I had harboured for over twenty years, of creating a multidisciplinary psychodynamic training course for all those who work in different forensic settings. This had always been thought by both sides—that is, psychodynamic and forensic—to be a quixotic, unrealistic, and impractical suggestion. In fact, the idea of integrating both fields met with derision. "How could soft-wet psychoanalytic psychotherapy ever blend with hard, sceptical, cynical 'real-world' forensic psychiatry?"

It was fortunate that Professor Peckham was not a psychiatrist, but a professor of oncology and an artist as well, deeply imbued in both research/prevention and creativity. Also, he was not at all familiar with the different divisions within the psychiatric world and was ignorant of the assumptions and prejudices associated with the various factions. To him, not only did the idea of such a course make a lot of sense, but he was amazed that it did not already exist. In a brief meeting, we reached an agreement for the creation of the course and designed a steering committee with professionals from both the psychotherapeutic and the forensic worlds. Later, the Advisory Group was formed comprised of senior professionals, NHS staff, and senior members of the judiciary. Both professional groups were intensely and emotionally involved with the life of the course and felt part of an innovative, creative, and very much needed resource. They were also responsible for sending us prospective students from their own work places.[2] The BPMF took charge of the administration and academic approval of the course, and a faculty of Portman Clinic staff and other consultants was to be in charge of the actual teaching and syllabus. Both were under the scrutiny of the Steering Committee and Advisory Group. There were many changes under the wise, effective, and neutral leadership of Professor Peckham, who continued in his role as director until the course was consolidated. A tacit awareness emerged that the Portman Clinic had to "open up" and to trust that the intermarriage of disciplines would work—however difficult it was to accept other opinions and other ways of thinking and working. There was no possibility of forcing the issue: adaptation and discussion was the only way. Actually, the bridging had already started, due to the intense involvement of all participants and its neutral base.

Trainees

In the first year there were fifteen trainees, and the combination of homogeneity in professional interests with heterogeneity in experience and background proved to be very successful.

Requirements of the course

Apart from the usual requirements of attendance and academic work (including written papers), there were two other basic requirements that remained a vital part of the life of the course. One was for the trainee to have personal therapy, either individual or group, while attending the course. This requirement was initially objected to by a minority of the Steering Group members. However, in response to the students' course-evaluation questionnaire after the first year, overwhelming support was expressed for the need for personal therapy as an intrinsic part of the personal and training experience. Not only did they acknowledge its personal value, they felt that such an experience was essential for the understanding of their work with forensic patients.

The other requirement was to have a forensic patient in weekly supervised dynamic psychotherapy. Our assumption that the first requirement would be difficult to achieve proved to be wrong; it was the second requirement that caused more problems than had at first been envisaged. It was difficult to find patients. Such difficulties however, provided valuable information about the trainees' places of work as well as their fellow workers' attitudes about their attendance on the course. Cooperation and support from colleagues and superiors was vital, but at times it had seemed that competition and rivalry predominated instead. However, the presence of one or more trainees from the same institution, either at the same time or subsequently, facilitated the trainees' emotional and practical entry in the course.

Structure of the day

The day began with a discussion group in which all trainees presented routine dilemmas from their own working places, the aim being the acknowledgement and recognition of their various professional perspectives. Different philosophical approaches were presented, discussed, and scrutinized. The trainees valued and criticized what they had and also what they had not. The importance was in familiarizing themselves with, and respecting, other viewpoints so that they were no longer in a position of discarding, dismissing, or denigrating the ways others work. On the contrary, they were able to examine their own working scheme and thus explore how best to interact with one another. As a result, a network system was created. It was important that the position of convenor for this meeting was rotated among the faculty member, since there was so much for all faculty members to learn about other forensic institutions.

Lunch followed, in which students felt free to discuss their own experiences with one another, and then there was a supervision group, which was much valued by all students. They seemed eager to present material in their groups of three or four with supervisors who were

Portman staff. It was important that these small groups did contain students from different professional backgrounds and working settings. The more heterogeneous they were, the more successful the integration was.

The afternoon lecture time was met with anticipation, since there were a number of faculty members involved who were non-Portman staff. The syllabus allowed some changes according to the relevance to trainees and solid suggestions to do with their own areas of specializations. Examples were subjects such as adolescents, families, child abuse, learning disabilities, suicide, and murder.

The working day ended with a plenary session. This was unstructured and was convened by the course director who had also chaired the lecture. It is more difficult to convey what happened here. There were many silences containing different qualities of meaning—for example, frustration, dissatisfaction, contentment, reflection. At other times the students expressed a longing for "guidance" and "directives". Perhaps an agenda? And so forth. There were switches between the need for interpretations and the complete rejection of the idea of being an experiential group and becoming "patients". There were comments about how good it was to have some time to think together, rivalries, conflicts, attempts at scapegoating, coupling, projection of unwanted bits into others or other institutions, composition of poems, rebelliousness against authority (especially against the Portman Clinic, who were "unable to understand the hardships of their own forensic settings"), denial, mourning, grief, idealization of the training, and feeling deskilled by it. These were a few of the themes the students faced, talked, or got angry or sad about. Occasionally mischievous suggestions were put forward, as well as moving statements that drew people together. Altogether the plenary provided an intense experience of sharing powerful emotions, which was not to be missed or cut off—a suggestion often made during the first term because of the intense anxieties emerging from these meetings.

Staff meetings

The staff members met regularly to discuss different issues related to week-to-week events. During the students' lunchtime, the teaching staff met to discuss the happenings of the previous week, supervision issues, the lecture aspects, the plenary, and the discussion group of the day. Our interaction was rich and made us see not only the interwoven connections of the students but also our own, which offered insights regarding splits and projections. For example, our own disagreements about structures were at times taken up concretely by our trainees: we were in a constant process of learning, and many changes were implemented since it first started. The survival and success of the course largely depended on the faculty members from the Portman Clinic who generously gave of their time and tremendous efforts. At times, it was difficult for them, too, to envisage this "cross-fertilization", and its achievement was due to their consistent trust in this exciting new venture. Week after week we struggled with vigour in the process to teach and to learn from new situations, and we were rewarded with new insights and knowledge.

During the very first year, the composition of the student group included not only professionals from both the forensic and the psychotherapeutic worlds, but also those working privately in their own rooms as psychotherapists, with no forensic experience at all, and some forensic professionals in possession of minimal psychodynamic understanding and no experience of personal therapy. This, as we painfully learnt, presented everybody—students and faculty members—with innumerable problems and clashes, although with an eventually enriched experience. Portman staff members conversely had little if any background in dealing first hand with some of the forensic settings of the students. Some forensic colleagues considered it unnecessary for trainees to undergo personal therapy, and paranoid anxieties were generated, with everyone wanting to demonstrate how much better they were doing. Tegwyn Williams, one of our first students, describes in *Forensic Psychotherapy: Symbiosis or Impossibility* (1991) an account of difficulties encountered.

Prejudices and assumptions ran high and were supported by everybody's lack of experience in the first year. During the first term the different groups disowned, consciously or unconsciously, parts of their own working situations, which they projected onto the other group. During the plenary sessions there were jokes representing either "soft" or "hard" responses according to which "group" someone belonged. Sarcastic and cynical remarks were the rule when the "forensic team" attacked the "psychotherapeutic team" for their gullibility, softness, and lack of awareness of the conditions in which they themselves were working. The "psychotherapeutic team" counter-attacked with subtle but sadistic interpretations regarding lack of sensitivity, style, and over-simplicity. At this time, the faculty members, according to trainees, were mostly faultless and beyond criticism. Hinshelwood (1996) has clearly defined this particular phenomenon as "the culture clash", meaning that the two different groups take opposite polarizing situations. Our aim was for the two cultures to come and to work together harmoniously.

At the beginning of the academic year, students meeting for the first time felt insecure and inadequate, and they tried to compete from their own position. For a long time those from the same place sat together, and then regrouping took place. Students working in forensic settings showed off their toughness and reality sense in dealing with all sorts of terrible crimes and predicaments. They were not aware of being used as "protective containers" by the psychotherapeutic team, who experienced them as completely devoid of any capacity for empathy and compassion. On the other hand, the psychotherapy team appeared to be rather naive and acted as irritating and nagging "do-gooders". Both groups felt deskilled in their own areas of expertise, and it took quite a while for them to find not only their voice, but also an empathetic hearing. This only happened when they were ready to look at their own areas of "not knowing" what to do with the forensic patient. In fact, both groups experienced these mixed feelings of harshness and compassion, but they were split into the different factions in order to avoid facing confusion.

These anxieties were vividly present usually during the first term and were especially prominent in the first year of the course. From the other side, faculty members were also able to express openly some degree of frustration with their students for not knowing all about psychodynamics. At the same time they themselves demonstrated some degree of insensitivity, rigidity, and intolerance about the extremely difficult forensic settings. At times they were somewhat rigid and inflexible in their assessments of the quality of their own work with the students, as was discovered at moderation by the External Examiner. During the second and third terms, both faculty and trainees began to work more effectively together, with some degree of integration and reparation.

Development of the trainees' and faculty members' attitude in the life of the course

The trainees' attitude changed altogether during the second and third years of the course as a result of changes both in the composition of the trainees group and in our own role. The fact that the trainees all worked in forensic settings facilitated the understanding of the specific difficulties encountered in the functioning of their work. Earlier mechanisms that involved splits in the patient population were no longer available. Similarly, there were no easy targets for the derision and contempt that had been easily projected into "the other student population" available in the first year.

The split between soft and hard had worked so effectively that our own faculty members had been left almost beyond criticism or fault. Indeed, on their part, the faculty members were understanding and rather tolerant of the divisions. This began to change when the composition of the trainees' group became more homogeneously forensic. To start with, the supervisors who had previously been seen as "soft", "humane", and "wet" became suddenly and unexpectedly seen as "hard and brutal, judgemental, tough and controlling". Faculty members began to notice "tremendous" changes occurring in their students, and a sense of pride and achievement began to emerge. They themselves began to change their own stance from being somewhat analytically omnipotent to being more understanding of the hard, difficult circumstances of the forensic setting.

It was only possible as the year progressed for trainees to start introjecting the knowledge of "bad bits" and thus to make sense of the requirement for personal therapy. They also became aware of the tremendous limitations of the work and how much more they did need to know. In other words, a little knowledge lead to a thirst for further training. Goals became more limited and more realistically based, a realization that was of great importance bearing in mind the severe difficulties in dealing with our patient population.

My own role as a founder course director also developed and changed over time. In our third year, I ceased supervising a small group, since this was experienced by the faculty members as implying that the trainees in my supervision group were "favoured", thus increasing splitting mechanisms. On reflection, after this change was introduced, I realized that boundary issues for both students and staff were at stake. It appeared that my role was much more one of container of anxieties for both groups. Stricter use of boundaries was included, and more time was allocated for the teaching staff to get together, especially for supervision issues.

The Diploma Course in Forensic Psychotherapy

As a direct result of achieving diploma status, many changes were implemented.

The knowledge among students of the third year that a second year leading to a diploma was in existence created renewed enthusiasm but also much competitiveness and rivalry. The fact that the additional year offered only nine places, and that a backlog of students from three previous courses would be applying, increased anxieties and created much tension. Students tended to be more open in their disagreements with one another, and more demanding with faculty members. Still, they did participate and created an effective network with a high degree of involvement and, with the odd exceptions, better attendance than in previous years.

* * *

In summary, there were difficulties in the development of the training of forensic psychotherapy, but these were outweighed by the long-term advantages and great rewards encountered in establishing a new model of training in a field traditionally ambivalent/hostile towards psychoanalytic psychotherapy.

Someone might have once said: "So what's all that about—mixing up the hard and the wet together? Please, I don't want to be part of it. Can you imagine forensic psychiatrists admitting to any unconscious motivations? This sounds bizarre."

Well, not any more, I am happy to say.

Notes

1. The development of group psychoanalytic therapy at the Portman Clinic is also discussed in chapter 9 and in the final interview.

2. It was most unfortunate that, after my retirement, people left in charge of the course decided to remove themselves from this academic structure. The course became an unidentifiable Tavistock-Portman Trust course called P2. This eventually led to the disappearance of the course because of too few applicants, which was obviously linked to its insularity and its lack of a working and academic network with the academic bodies that were essential for the course's great success.

An interview with Estela V. Welldon, November 2010

B RETT KAHR: *Greetings, Estela. It is a very great pleasure to talk to you again. I'm shocked to discover it was back in the mid-1990s that we conducted the first interview about your professional life, your career, and your contributions to mental health. It seems like only yesterday, but here we are fifteen or so years later and I certainly wanted an opportunity to find out what has happened in your professional career as well as in the field of forensic psychotherapy, which you pioneered during the 1990s and the 2000s. So, thank you so much for agreeing to speak to me.*

ESTELA V. WELLDON: Always a pleasure to meet you again, Brett. You have been very much part of all the developments in forensic psychotherapy, so let's share some of what has taken place so far. Since 1995 much has been happening in two different directions. One, of course, is the International Association for Forensic Psychotherapy, which gives me great pride. But it also gives me much pride to acknowledge the enormous work that all my ex-students—including you—have done in this field and continue to do, in exciting and remarkable ways. So many are now teaching and in charge of educating all sorts of people and professionals about this new branch of mental health, as well as being involved directly.

Q: *And there are the books—actually, how many have been published?*

A: Yes, many of the students have published books describing the way they feel and dealing with sexuality and perversion. The number of books being produced is quite extraordinary, as you know being the editor of the Forensic Series at Karnac. Another ex-student, Gwen Adshead, is currently the President of the International Association and also the editor of a series of forensic books published by Jessica Kingsley.

Q: *Is the list now so long it's hard to be comprehensive?*

A: Exactly. In addition there are all the conferences, in many places. I think you and I had our previous interview the year before the conference in Boston. We have had a wide range of contributors and organizers, including Professor James Gilligan, with his important work on violence, who has also been President of our International Association. We have been approached by many different associations who want to work with us. So, we've met in many locations, including all over Europe, and in 2008 there was the very successful joint meeting in Venice with the Psychotherapy Faculty of the Royal College of Psychiatrists, followed by the equally successful meetings in Konstanz in 2009 and Oxford this year.

Q: *And next year it's the anniversary conference . . .*

A: Absolutely, and we decided to have our celebration and consolidation of our work at the twentieth anniversary in Edinburgh. There have been changes in legislation, and recognition of the field by the Royal College of Psychiatrists. Many of our students are working in different organizations, in a range of different special hospitals and medium-secure units. Some have posts, jobs, situations, in Germany, as Professors of Forensic Psychotherapy. We are very proud because of the number of ex-students of the course that I began, in 1990 at the Portman clinic, with the help of an advisory group and then a Steering Committee, which gave us access to the advice of Professor Michael Peckham. In a way, the course very much owes its foundation to him, because he was impressed with the creation of this new discipline. As a scientist and painter he was used to mixing ideas. And so, for him, it was not a crazy idea to combine psychoanalytic thinking and forensic psychiatry, psychology, and psychoanalysis, even though many colleagues from this country were quite resistant because they felt it was trying to mix the "soft" with the "hard" (see chapter 10).

Q: *Can we just pause to think about that? Because what you're telling me is that when you started the course, and also the IAFP, and these organizations developed together, you had resistance not only from the broader psychiatric and medical field, who thought that psychoanalytic science was a soft option, and not really helpful for treating forensic patients, but you also had resistance from long-standing colleagues?*

A: It's very interesting you should say that, because a colleague, Dr Cleo van Velsen, suggested to me that the Portman Clinic was rather like a psychic retreat, not wanting to be too involved with other associations or organizations. It would not have been possible for me to create the course on my own, that's for sure. I'm very grateful that there were the ten years that I call the golden decade. In those ten years we produced many wonderful students, and the course went from strength to strength, from being a sort of one-year probationary course to a two-year diploma course. And then Professor Peckham was awarded a professorship at the University College Hospital (UCH). We worked extremely hard at that point, I remember, with my colleague and member of the steering group Bruce Irvine, to meet all the conditions required to be part of UCL, which is, as you know, one of the most important colleges in England, with substantial financial resources. All this was available to us and was ready, with Professor Peckham's help, to become a university course—an MA and perhaps even a PhD. At that point, suddenly, I was forced to retire because of my age.

Q: *After thirty years on the staff.*

A: After thirty years of being there, yes. We had a fantastic weekly course consisting of a full day at the Portman clinic, starting at 9 o'clock in the morning with a large group including all the students and a member of staff, followed by clinical cases in supervision in small groups of three or four. In the afternoons, there was a lecture by outside speakers, with the Course Director present throughout the lecture and question time, first to make the necessary introductions to the students and later on to lead the discussion with the lecturer. Obviously the attendance and activities, developed by staff members, meant quite high costs. However, the professional gains were necessary for the proper training of responsible and conscientious colleagues. It also meant there was considerable interaction and exchange of ideas, among the students, from all different disciplines working with the forensic patient which allowed and facilitated mutual respect and reciprocity for their own roles. Also, the invited speakers, whose work was valued by us, would refer potential students because they in turn valued the course. From the beginning it was essential to recognize the value of multi-professional working within the field of forensic psychotherapy. Psychotherapists, music therapists, nurses, psychologists, probation officers, social workers, psychiatrists—everybody was recognized. It was very important to recognize both internal and external negotiations. So this I called the golden decade.

Q: *May I make an observation? It's useful to hear you talk about the history of both the International Association on the one hand and the Diploma Course in Forensic Psychotherapy, which you founded and directed for many years at the Portman Clinic. It's important, historically, to remember that both* *of these developments took place at the same time, and there was a great synergy between the organization and the course. They developed simultaneously and fed into one another really nicely. I certainly remember, as a student of yours, many years ago on the diploma course, what a privilege it was to be able to attend the international conferences and start presenting at them—how one felt part of a bigger international network. As students we were privileged not only to meet the local experts and senior clinicians who practiced in London, but when at the international conferences we met the Germans, the French, the Danish . . . it was very, very exciting. It seems to me that what characterizes your work, not only as a clinician, but also as an organizational leader, and a field developer, is that you drew together a very large group. Perhaps your large, and small, group experiences in analysis have been pivotal because you knew how to create a course that was multidisciplinary, that drew from inside the Portman Clinic and from outside resources within other branches of mental health organizations and the international field. You invited people from every country, every discipline, and threw a big party that made everyone feel included. I wonder if you can tell us how you managed to achieve such a big undertaking.*

A: This is a paradoxical situation. As I've already said, I did meet colleagues, in 1981, at that conference in Oxford, and we were all feeling rather despondent about the way our psychoanalytic understanding was treated. So I asked whether they would like to have a yearly symposium. I raised the suggestion at the Portman Clinic, which did then host for some years what was called the European Symposium, but other people from this country were not allowed to attend.

Q: *So it was very exclusive?*

A: Exactly—and ten years on we had to go international to find the support with colleagues from so many places, like Canada and Italy— and from here too. Then we had the meeting in Leuven and I came forward with the idea of creating an international association. Then the Law and Psychiatry group immediately wanted us to be a part of them, which we didn't need to because we had our own membership now, ready to start an international organization.

Q: *What was the reluctance from the staff members in the Portman Clinic to inviting other English people, other British people? Was there a fear of contamination?*

A: It was fear of contamination of pure psychoanalysis. I remember asking Portman colleagues why we couldn't invite somebody like Murray Cox and others, from Broadmoor and so forth, and they just replied, "no—they're not psychoanalytically trained". It was very backwards and a real shame.

Regarding the course, the most shameful part happened after I retired. I behaved in a bloody naive and overly generous way when I decided to step down as leader of the course a year before I retired, in order for the course to survive. I knew that there had been, and, would be, resistance within the clinic, but I assumed that the course would continue in the format as it was. But within two or three years the Portman Clinic withdrew the course from UCH, which was a terrible thing to do. There was no alternative association with the Tavistock Clinic or the University of East London . . . nothing. The clinic attempted to run a Portman course on its own, which eventually had to be cancelled because there weren't enough applicants. How could there be trainees when the course lacked connections with the outside world? That was forgotten. Not only did those managing the course sever themselves from others, but the others grew hostile towards the course at the Portman, knowing that they were no longer seen as contributors to the field by being part of the teaching staff or anything like that. So, it was unable to continue, and grow, any more. That the course didn't continue is the one regret in my life, and I feel very bitter about it. By now it could have been a university course, perhaps even with a professor at its head.

Q: *And all this has gone completely . . .*

A: Yes.

Q: *As one of the many people who had the privilege of being a student on the course, I know how much I learnt from you and the other staff members and what an impact learning psychodynamic forensic work has had on every branch of my clinical practice, whether it's forensic work or not. For example, I've taken the knowledge and applied it in the field of marital psychotherapy. I often say to marital psychoanalytic colleagues that had I not studied with Estela Welldon at the Portman Clinic, I would not be able to tolerate the violence of the warring marital couple that one sees in the room, so it's heartbreaking that the course has stopped. What happened? Was it your retirement as the loved and cherished leader?*

A: No, I just feel that the Portman Clinic didn't have the wisdom to continue. I think some staff there didn't want to be bothered with outside links and relationships. There was a supervising authority in academic terms, and they couldn't stand the idea that they had to submit themselves and their teaching to an outside authority. The people just felt they were too big—the problem with some small places is that they consider themselves to be big because they are small and unique.

But it was a very precious course, as you know, and I want to dedicate this book to all my students of the golden decade, because I feel extremely proud of them all, and it's such a shame—we could have had another decade by now of students from the course. There are a few people around whom I see sometimes in conferences, and other colleagues who ask me where can they send their trainees for training, which does exist now in many other countries . . .

Q: *It's a great loss to the field that the course that you established, the diploma course, no longer exists. Hasn't anybody else attempted something comparable in Great Britain?*

A: I don't think so. I approached a few people some years ago, but it was acknowledged that the apparently grandiose ideas of the Portman Clinic have, in a way, been responsible for the termination of this project.

Q: *It is a sadness that, partly because you had to retire, the course stopped at the Portman Clinic, but you did not, have not, retired from the International Association. In fact, you are the Honorary Life President, and under your leadership it has continued to grow. What, beyond your tremendous energy and creativity, has allowed the International Association to become an organization that has not withered but has actually taken off in exciting directions?*

A: Many people who work in the field today have an enormous amount of courage, resilience, enthusiasm, and hope. They are working under such difficult circumstances, with sometimes awful things happening, and yet, despite the tribulations, difficulties, traumas, they are still creating and creating and creating. And I think this is part of the ethos of our organization that we all share regardless of which nationality we are—a strong sense of being on the same kind of exciting professional journey.

Q: *But it also seems to me, Estela, that your work as a group analyst and aspects of your personality, which are very much about welcoming and including people, have had a big impact on the furtherance of the International Association, because rather than regarding people as suspicious if they've had a training or a background different from yours, you've embraced the difference and realized that these serious workers all have something interesting to bring to the party. There was a generosity of spirit, I remember very clearly, in terms of people helping one another.*

A: Well, I think you may have overstated it, but I think that it's true. For example, in the diploma course there was a large group at the end of the day comprising all the students and the Course Director as its conductor or convener. This was an hour for the students to digest all they had learnt and also to explore, experientially, their own relationships with one another, including rivalry, jealousy, and competition.

We also had a few students pairing, and some "Portman children" born out of the course. At times emerging relationships were obvious to the Course Director but were denied and unacknowledged by other students. Life was working at its full.

The International Association is easier in a way because there are people coming from everywhere—it's an umbrella organization. And, as soon as we know that somebody is working with the forensic patient, there is considerable respect. We believe that those who have less say, perhaps, at work, should be allowed more say and encouraged to contribute and participate, since they often are the ones who get little recognition during the year. There are some people who also have much creativity in this field, people who also present plays or musicals—as you know yourself, with your forensic cabaret.

Q: *Yes! We've had twenty years of forensic psychotherapy in terms of its formal institutional setting, and I do think that enormous changes have taken place among the attitudes of mental health professionals. I find mental health professionals are less frightened by forensic patients and are more willing to take on the more challenging patients and seek consultation and supervision where appropriate. And I think they are treating the forensic patient with more compassion. I certainly remember that when I began as a student in this field, analysts and therapists of a certain seniority were very, very quick to label everything perverse or psychopathic . . .*

A: The other important word that was used all the time was "manipulative", reflecting a lack of respect and a derisive element. I agree that there has been a huge attitudinal shift. I see this in younger colleagues who, while not condoning crimes, are at least not so punitive and sneery towards the patients; they are trying to understand patients' predicaments, and not just to judge all the time.

Q: *I think also we have to acknowledge that, through your efforts and those of colleagues, in terms of developing the course and the International Association, there are now, as you've said, not one but two monograph series from major psychoanalytic publishers devoted specifically to forensic psychotherapy. I estimate that, altogether, between the Jessica Kingsley series and the Karnac series there are about fifty volumes of literature specifically on forensic psychotherapy.*

I also remember when Gill McGauley was appointed as the first Consultant Forensic Psychotherapist, as opposed to Forensic Psychiatrist—that was symbolic of the opening up of the field at a very important institutional level. There has been a great deal of interest developing in the field, which is very exciting. So I want to ask you: what is your hope for the future of forensic psychotherapy? We've got a platform but we haven't done all the work we need to do yet. If you had to draw up a blueprint for the next twenty years, what would that include?

A: First, I think this means creating more training posts. Carine Minne was the first to complete dual qualification as a forensic psychiatrist and psychotherapist. Others have now followed her, including Cleo van Velsen from very early on. But we are only speaking about medically trained forensic psychotherapists, whereas I believe that the richness of the field resides in the fact that this is a multi-professional area and many books have been published by all professionals involved, including art therapists, music therapists, forensic psychotherapy nurses, psychologists, etc. The problem about training is that a multi-professional course, such as the one created in 1990 at the Portman, has been eliminated and not replaced in this country. As I have always stated, forensic psychotherapy is not the heroic work of one person or profession, but is the action of a multi-professional team. More books by different professions will also be written and published. But I think we also require changes to legislation and more liaison with the official governmental organizations that produce the legislation. For example, in the diploma course, His Honour Judge Stephen Tumim led the advisory group. At that time he was head of the HM Inspectorate of Prisons. We need more affiliations of that sort . . . I don't mean just politicians, because that can be difficult and complicated, but certainly with the House of Lords and other independent institutions. The country requires legislation not to operate in a hopeless way with people who commit crimes or act in a violent way. Understanding, although not collusion, is important.

Q: *Yes. Over the period of time you've been working in this field, have you come to feel that forensic psychotherapy is—how can I put this—an easy option? And are there times when you even feel that some crimes are so horrific that people should not be given psychotherapy but total custodial care—end of story?*

A: It is very important to differentiate between those who can respond to psychotherapy and those who can not. We cannot dispense psychotherapy as if it were a pill producing a miracle cure. No. Many people do not respond to psychotherapy, but the staff working with them can try to understand these people who have committed these awful crimes, so as to help in their management. We have to always remember that people have an internal world with internal objects, and it is possible to facilitate some modifications and dynamic change. I mean that most people have enough good objects to be helped, even though, at times, they have acted and reacted in ways that we consider to be irrational and destructive. A psychodynamic model may help treating staff to formulate why the irrational may make sense in the unconscious or preconscious.

There have also been creative projects—for example, taking theatre to special hospitals like Broadmoor. These are more than gestures, because people are promoting understanding of criminal behaviour so as to embrace and comfort the patients in their daily lives.

Q: *And what about what people from the outside think . . .?*

A: It's very important, of course, to be able to cooperate and collaborate with, for example, the media, in the form of reporters and journalists, politicians, legislators—people from all different parts of society. The field needs their support and understanding, and we cannot just sneer at them. We have to cooperate and work with them. We have to educate the public too.

Q: *Estela, let's return to your own personal journey over the last fifteen years since we last spoke. What was it like to retire from the Portman Clinic? Was it a great sadness, or was it a great relief after having worked there for thirty years?*

A: Well, it was a bit of a mix of everything, I must say. In a way, it has allowed me to visit, and teach, in different countries and has given me flexibility. It has meant I could buy a place in Venice and have a different sort of life there too. And I have been very active in various conferences to do with forensic work and also with COWAP (Committee on Women and Psychoanalysis, sponsored by the International Psychoanalytical Association), which is extremely active and concentrates on what appeals to many women, including in the forensic field. Through COWAP I have been invited to many parts of the world, and the people seem to respect my work very much.

Mother, Madonna, Whore—my book that created such an upheaval over twenty years ago (and which was recently acknowledged as a "Medical Classic" in the *British Medical Journal*: Ashurst, 2011)—has been published in many different languages, including recently in Polish. It gives me great satisfaction to have visited—and still to go to—so many such countries and make a contribution. People always feel, as do I, very grateful for the work at the Portman, over thirty years, which allowed me to understand so much about the clinical situations I have experienced. Many people do not get near to any of these patients, and I feel privileged to have had this access. Whenever I give a lecture, I welcome discussions with the audience, because I always have at hand multiple clinical examples that come to my mind as soon as somebody raises a question. So it's alive in my mind and feels as if I were still working there. People are always impressed by the detail in the clinical vignettes, some of which I have not considered for many, many years. In this way I offer a degree of solidity about my work, which is quite considerable in comparison to, say, colleagues who are working privately and perhaps have had one or two patients with this sort of predicament; they may know somebody very well in depth, but their familiarity with these sorts of problems is limited.

I never wanted to leave the Portman Clinic because of the patient population; they, I think, made the Portman. Sometimes colleagues worked there, and even though they might have been good in different ways, they could not put up with the place. Partly this is because some of us had problems with other colleagues there. I felt that you had to put up with it and carry on doing the work because of the patients. In a way, one could argue that there is a voyeuristic element, but there is also a sense of excitement about trying to formulate problems that are so difficult to understand. There is a degree of excitement but, at the same time, also a degree of fear or resistance. If it is possible to consider all these elements together, it is an incredibly rich field which can offer much satisfaction and many rewards. And today whenever I go abroad, whereas before they used to say: "Oh, this only happens in England", now it is present in their own local newspapers, confirming all that we know.

Q: *I suppose having retired from your consulting post in the NHS has, as you say, given you freedom to travel, to lecture internationally, to do more writing, to do more teaching, and so on, but it's also allowed you to do non-forensic work, because you've kept up a very active clinical practice both privately and in consultation. I'm just wondering how your forensic work has helped you in work with non-forensic patients, who are, after all, the majority of mental health patients.*

A: Well, as you said before, it's not just forensic patients who suffer from perversions and delinquency, we all have these tendencies and can see them in other patients. There are situations in which we are invited to collude, and patients expect a degree of secrecy or whatever. I always remember, for example, that it used to be said that training with children could help therapists to understand more about adults. It's the same with forensic work, which enables awareness of situations that could appear, on the face of it, to be rather innocent. Making this innocent façade explicit means patients are not "getting away" with anything, and this helps them feel understood in all their totality. So, like you, I feel that this is a gift.

Q: *And of course you've now reached a point in family and domestic life where you have become a grandmother, to a beautiful granddaughter. And it occurs to me—since your students are now twenty years in the field—do you feel you are a professional grandmother as well?*

A: It gives me a lot of pleasure to observe that I do feel very close to my own professional children. To a degree, with grandchildren, it's a space for playing, but I feel like, professionally, I rely more on my children, my students like you, than on the other ones, who are much more for playing or for other tasks. With all the work that you—all of you—have been doing, it is a great honour and privilege . . . to think that my contribution is very rich because of what I get back from you all.

Q: *Lovely. I think that's a very nice place to stop.*

REFERENCES

Abraham, K. (1920). Special pathology and therapy of the neuroses and psychoses. *International Journal of Psychoanalysis*, 1: 280–281.

Abraham, N., & Torok, M. (1986). *The Wolf Man's Magic Word: A Cryptonomy*, trans. N. Rand. Minneapolis, MN: University of Minnesota Press.

Adshead, G. (1991). The forensic psychotherapist: Dying breed or evolving species? *Psychiatric Bulletin*, 15: 410–412.

Adshead, G. (2009). Women and evil [BBC Radio 3 series episode]. *Night Waves*, 26 October.

Aiyegbusi, A., & Clarke-Moore, J. (2009). *Therapeutic Relationships with Offenders: An Introduction to the Psychodynamics of Forensic Mental Health Nursing*. London: Jessica Kingsley.

Alizade, M. (2005). Incest: The damaged psychic flesh. In: G. Ambrosio (Ed.), *On Incest: Psychoanalytic Perspectives* (pp. 101–114). London: Karnac.

Amon, M., & Bihler, T. (2007). *Transgenerational Transmission in Schizophrenia*. Paper presented at the 15th World Congress of the World Association for Dynamic Psychiatry, St. Petersburg, 15–17 May.

APA (1987). *The Diagnostic and Statistical Manual of Mental Disorders* (3rd edition, revised). Washington, DC: American Psychiatric Association.

APA (1994). *The Diagnostic and Statistical Manual of Mental Disorders* (4th edition). Washington, DC: American Psychiatric Association.

Appignanesi, L. (2008). *Mad, Bad and Sad: A History of Women and the Mind Doctors from 1800*. London: Virago.

Argentieri, S. (1988). Incest yesterday and today: From conflict to ambiguity. In: G. Ambrosio (Ed.), *On Incest: Psychoanalytic Perspectives*. IPA Committee on Women and Psychoanalysis. London: Karnac, 2005.

Argentieri, S. (2007). *Erotic Playthings or Little Perverse Polymaths?* Paper presented at the 3rd COWAP (IPA Committee on Women and Psychoanalysis) European Conference on Incest and Paedophilia, Lisbon, 26–28 January. [Published as: "Pedofilia. Giocattoli erotici o piccoli perversi polimorfi?" *Psicoanalisi, 11* (2007, 1).]

Arlow, J. A. (1971). Character perversion. In: I. M. Marcus (Ed.), *Currents in Psychoanalysis* (pp. 317–336). New York: International Universities Press.

Ashurst, P. (2011). Medical Classics: *Mother, Madonna, Whore: The Idealisation and Denigration of Motherhood* [Book review]. *British Medical Journal, 342* (4 January): c7155.

Ashurst, P., & Hall, Z. (1989). *Understanding Women in Distress*. London: Tavistock/Routledge.

Aston, G. (2004). The silence of domestic violence in pregnancy during women's encounters with healthcare professionals. *Midwives, 7* (4).

Bacchus, L. (2004). Domestic violence and health. *Midwives 7* (4).

Bak, R. (1953). The schizophrenic defence against aggression. *International Journal of Psychoanalysis, 35* (1954): 129–134.

Barnett, M. C. (1966). Vaginal awareness in the infancy and childhood of girls. *Journal of the American Psychoanalytic Association, 14*: 129–140.

Bartlett, A. (2010). Introduction to social policy and the mentally disordered offender. In: A. Bartlett & G. McGauley (Eds.), *Forensic Mental Health: Concepts, Systems, and Practice* (chap. 11). New York: Oxford University Press.

Bentovim, A. (1976). Shame and other anxieties associated with breast-feeding: A systems theory and psychodynamic approach. [Breast feeding and the mother.] *Ciba Foundation Symposium, 45*: 159–178.

Bentovim, A. (1991). Children and young people as abusers. In: A. Hollows & H. Armstrong (Eds.), *Children and Young People as Abusers* (pp. 5–54). London: National Children's Bureau.

Bentovim, A. (1995). *Trauma-Organized Systems: Physical and Sexual Abuse in Families*. London: Karnac.

Bentovim, A., Kolvin, I., & Trowell, J. (1993). *Child Psychiatry and Child Sexual Abuse*. Unpublished manuscript, Royal College of Psychiatrists, London.

Berkoff, S. (2001). *Shakespeare's Villains*. Play performed at the Haymarket Theatre, London (October).

Bion, W. R. (1959). Attacks on linking. In: *Second Thoughts* (pp. 93–109). London: Karnac, 1984.

Bion, W. R. (1961). *Experiences in Groups and Other Papers*. New York: Basic Books.

Bion, W. R. (1967). A theory of thinking. In: *Second Thoughts* (pp. 110–119). London: Karnac, 1984.

Bion, W. R. (1970). *Attention and Interpretation*. London: Tavistock Publications. [Reprinted London: Karnac, 1984.]

Black, D., & Newman, M. (1996). Children and domestic violence: A review. *Clinical Child Psychology and Psychiatry, 1*: 79–88.

Bluglass, R. (1990). The scope of forensic psychiatry. *Journal of Forensic Psychiatry, 1* (1).

Bonner, S. (2006). A servant's bargain: Perversion as survival. *International Journal of Psychoanalysis, 87*: 1549–1567.

Bowlby, J. (1980) *Attachment and Loss, Vol. 3*. New York: Basic Books.

Brierley, M. (1932). Some problems of integration of women. *International Journal of Psychoanalysis, 13*: 433–448.

Brierley, M. (1936). Scientific determinants in feminine development. *International Journal of Psychoanalysis, 17*: 163–180.

Bronfen, E. (1992). *Over Her Dead Body: Death, Femininity and the Aesthetic.* Manchester: Manchester University Press.

Brunori, L. (1997). *Gruppo di fratelli, fratelli di gruppo.* Rome: Borla.

Carloni, G., & Nobili, D. (2004). *La Mamma Cattiva. Fenomenologia, antropologia e clinica del figlicidio.* Rimini: Guaraldi.

Chasseguet-Smirgel, J. (1983). Perversion and the universal law. *International Journal of Psychoanalysis, 10*: 293–301.

Chasseguet-Smirgel, J. (1984). *Creativity and Perversion.* New York: W. W. Norton.

Chasseguet-Smirgel, J. (1985). *The Ego Ideal.* London: Free Association Books.

Ciba Foundation (1984). *Sexual Abuse Within the Family.* London: Tavistock Publications.

Cox, M. (1983). The contribution of dynamic psychotherapy to forensic psychiatry and vice versa. *International Journal of Law and Psychiatry, 6*: 89–99.

Cox, M. (1992a). Forensic psychiatry and forensic psychotherapy. In: M. Cox (Ed.), *Shakespeare Comes to Broadmoor.* London: Jessica Kingsley.

Cox, M. (1992b). *Forensic Psychotherapy: An Emergent Discipline.* Paper presented at the 17th International Congress of the International Academy of Law and Mental Health, Leuven, Belgium.

Davies, R. (2007). The forensic network and the internal world of the offender: Thoughts from consultancy work in the forensic sector. In: D. Morgan & S. Ruszczynsky (Eds.), *Lectures on Violence, Perversion and Delinquency: The Portman Papers Series* (pp. 221–237). London: Karnac.

Deb, S. (2006). *Children in Agony.* New Delhi: Concept Publishing Company.

de Smit, B. (1992). The end of the beginning is the beginning of the end: The structure of the initial interview in forensic psychiatry. In: *Proceedings of the 17th International Congress of the International Academy of Law and Mental Health.* Leuven: International Academy of Law and Mental Health

Deutsch, H. (1942). Some forms of emotional disturbance and their relationship to schizophrenia. *Psychoanalytic Quarterly, 11.*

Devereux, G. (1954). Perversion: Theoretical and therapeutic aspects [Scientific Proceedings Midwinter Meeting, 153. Panel Report 3]. *Journal of the American Psychoanalytic Association, 2*: 336–345.

De Zulueta, F. (1993). *From Pain to Violence: The Traumatic Roots of Destructiveness.* London: Whurr.

Doctor, R. (2008). *Murder: A Psychotherapeutic Investigation.* London: Karnac.

Eastman, N. (1993). Forensic psychiatric services in Britain: A current review. *International Journal of Law and Psychiatry, 16*: 1–26.

Edleson, J. L., & Syers, M. (1990). Relative effectiveness of group treatments for men who batter. *Social Work Research & Abstracts, 26*: 10–17.

Eshel, O. (2005). Pentheus rather than Oedipus: On perversion, survival and analytic presencing. *International Journal of Psychoanalysis, 86*: 1071–1097.

Etchegoyen, A. (1997). Inhibition of mourning and the replacement child syndrome. In: J. Raphael-Leff & R. J. Perelberg (Eds.), *Female Experience: Three Generations of British Women Psychoanalysts on Work with Women*. London: Routledge.

Etchegoyen, H. (1978). Some thoughts on transference perversion. *International Journal of Psychoanalysis, 59*: 45–53.

Etchegoyen, H. (1991). Reversible perspective. In: *The Fundamentals of Psychoanalytic Technique* (revised edition, pp. 772–778). London: Karnac, 1999.

Evans, H. (2009). *My Paper Chase: True Stories of Vanished Times—An Autobiography*. London: Little Brown.

Fantuzzo, J. W., & Lindquist, C. U. (1989). The effects of observing conjugal violence on children: A review and analysis of research methodology. *Journal of Family Violence, 4*: 77–94.

Filippini, S. (2005). Perverse relationships: The perspective of the perpetrator. *International Journal of Psychoanalysis, 86*: 755–773.

Finkelhor, D. (1983). Common features of family abuse. In: D. Finkelhor, R. Gelles, G. Hotaling, & M. Straus (Eds.), *The Dark Side of Families: Current Family Violence Research*. Beverly Hills, CA: Sage.

Foulkes, S. H. (1945). *A Memorandum on Group Therapy*. Mimeograph, British Military Memorandum ADM 11 BM, July.

Foy, R., Nelson, F., Penney, G., & McIlwaine, G. (2000). Antenatal detection of domestic violence. *Lancet, 355* (9218): 1915.

Freud, S. (1905). *Three Essays on the Theory of Sexuality. Standard Edition*, 7.

Freud, S. (1916). Some character-types met with in psycho-analytic work. *Standard Edition*, 14: 311–333.

Freud, S. (1920). *Beyond the Pleasure Principle. Standard Edition*, 18.

Freud, S. (1923). Two encyclopaedia articles. *Standard Edition*, 18: 233–239.

Freud, S. (1924). The economic problem of masochism. *Standard Edition*, 19: 155–170.

Freud, S. (1931). Female sexuality. *Standard Edition*, 21: 225–243.

Freud, S. (1933). Lecture XXXIII: Femininity. *Standard Edition*, 22: 112–135.

Gallwey, P. (1991). Social maladjustment. In: J. Holmes (Ed.), *Textbook of Psychotherapy in Psychiatric Practice*. London: Churchill Livingstone.

Gamman, L., & Makinen, M. (1994). *Female Fetishism*. New York: New York University Press.

Ganzarain, R., & Buchele, B. (1993). Group psychotherapy for patients with a history of incest. In: H. Kaplan & B. Sadock (Eds.), *Comprehensive Group Psychotherapy* (3rd edition, pp. 551–525). Baltimore, MD: Williams & Wilkins.

Garland, C. (Ed.) (1998). *Understanding Trauma: A Psychoanalytic Approach*. London: Duckworth.

Garland, C. (Ed.) (2010a). *The Groups Book*. London: Karnac.

Garland, C. (2010b). *The Groups Manual: A Treatment Manual with Clinical Vignettes*. In: C. Garland (Ed.), *The Groups Book*. London: Karnac.

Gillespie, W. H. (1940). A contribution to the study of fetishism. *International Journal of Psychoanalysis, 21*: 401–415.

Gillespie, W. H. (1956). Experiences suggestive of paranormal cognition in the psycho-analytic situation. In: G. E. W. Wolstenholme & E. C. P. Millar (Eds.), *Ciba Foundation Symposium on Extrasensory Perception* (pp. 204–214). Oxford: Little, Brown.

Gillespie, W. H., Pasche, F., Wiedman, G. H., & Greenson, R. R. (1964). Symposium on homosexuality: I–IV. *International Journal of Psychoanalysis, 45*: 203–219.

Gilligan, J. (1996). *Violence: Reflections on Our Deadliest Epidemic*. New York: Grosset/Putnam Books.

Gilligan, J. (2009). Sex, gender and violence: Estela Welldon's contribution to our understanding of the psychopathology of violence. *British Journal of Psychotherapy, 25* (2): 239–256.

Glasser, M. (1979). Some aspects of the role of aggression in the perversions. In: I. Rosen (Ed.), *Sexual Deviation* (pp. 278–305). Oxford: Oxford University Press.

Glover, E. (1944). The diagnosis and treatment of delinquency. In: *Mental Abnormality and Crime* (pp. 269–299). London: MacMillan & Co.

Glover, E. (1949). Outline of the investigation and treatment of delinquency in Great Britain: 1912-1948. In: K. R. Eissler (Ed.), *Searchlights on Delinquency: New Psychoanalytic Studies* (pp. 433–452). New York: International Universities Press.

Glover, E. (1960). *The Roots of Crime*. London: Imago.

Gordon, J., & Kirtchuk, G. (2008). *Psychic Assaults and Frightened Clinicians: Countertransference in Forensic Settings*. London: Karnac.

Granoff, W., & Perrier, F. (1980). *El problema de la perversión en la mujer*. Barcelona: Editorial Critica.

Green, A. (1972). Aggression, femininity, paranoia and reality. *International Journal of Psychoanalysis, 53*: 205–211.

Green, A. (2002). A dual conception of narcissism: Positive and negative organizations. *Psychoanalytic Quarterly, 71*: 631–649.

Greenacre, P. (1950). Special problems of early female sexual development. *Psychoanalytic Study of the Child, 5*: 122–138.

Greenacre, P. (1968). Perversions: General consideration regarding their genetic and dynamic background. *Psychoanalytic Study of the Child, 23*: 47–62.

Hanson, M. (1988). Into inner space. *The Guardian*, 15 November, p. 21.

Harding, T. (1992). *Research and Evaluation in Forensic Psychotherapy*. Paper presented at the 1st International Conference of the International Association of Forensic Psychotherapy, London.

Hinshelwood, R. D. (1996). Changing prisons: The unconscious dimension.

In: C. Cordess & M. Cox (Eds.), *Forensic Psychotherapy* (pp. 465–474). London: Jessica Kingsley.

Hollender, M. H., Brown, C. W., & Roback, H. B. (1977). Genital exhibitionism in women. *American Journal of Psychiatry, 134*: 436–438.

Hopper, E. (1991). Encapsulation as a defence against the fear of annihilation. *International Journal of Psychoanalysis, 72* (4): 607–624.

Hopper, E. (1998). On the nature of hope in psychoanalysis and group analysis [Keynote speech at the 13th Congress of the International Association of Group Psychotherapy]. In: *The Social Unconscious: Selected Papers.* London: Jessica Kingsley, 2003.

Hopper, E. (2001). On the nature of hope in psychoanalysis and group analysis. *British Journal of Psychotherapy, 18*: 205–226.

Hopper, E. (2003). *Traumatic Experience in the Unconscious Life of Groups: The Fourth Basic Assumption: Incohesion: Aggregation/Massification or (ba) I: A/M.* London: Jessica Kingsley.

Horney, K. (1924). On the genesis of castration complex in women. In: *Feminine Psychology.* New York: W. W. Norton, 1973.

Horney, K. (1926). The flight from womanhood. *International Journal of Psychoanalysis, 12*: 360–374.

Horney, K. (1932). The dread of women. *International Journal of Psychoanalysis, 13*: 348–60.

Horney, K. (1933). The denial of the vagina. *International Journal of Psychoanalysis, 14*: 57–70.

Hughes, R. (1993). *Culture of Complaint: The Fraying of America.* New York: Oxford University Press.

Iacuzzi, A. B. (2009). *Los enigmaticos laberintos carcelarios. Un itinerario psicoanalitico.* Buenos Aires: Ediciones de las Tres Lagunas.

Jacobs, A. (2008). *On Matricide.* New York: Columbia University Press.

Jaffe, P. G., Hurley, D. J., & Wolfe, D. (1990). Children's observations of violence: I. Critical issues in child development and intervention planning. *Canadian Journal of Psychiatry, 35*: 466–470.

Jasinski, J. L., & Williams, L. M. (Eds.) (1998). *Partner Violence: A Comprehensive Review of 20 Years of Research.* Thousand Oaks, CA: Sage.

Jimenez, J. P. (2004). A psychoanalytical phenomenology of perversion. *International Journal of Psychoanalysis, 85*: 65–81.

Jones, E. (1927). The early development of female sexuality. *International Journal of Psychoanalysis, 8*: 459–472.

Jones, M. (1953). *The Therapeutic Community: A New Treatment Method in Psychiatry.* New York: Basic Books.

Joseph, B. (1981). Towards the experiencing of psychic pain. In: *Psychic Equilibrium and Psychic Change: Selected Papers of Betty Joseph* (pp. 88–100). London: Routledge, 1989.

Joseph, B. (1994). *Where There Is No Vision: From Sexualization to Sexuality.* Paper presented at the San Francisco Psychoanalytic Institute, San Francisco, April.

Kahr, B. (2007). *Sex and the Psyche*. London: Penguin.

Kaplan, J. (1991). *Female Perversions: The Temptations of Emma Bovary*. New York: Doubleday.

Karpf, A. (2008). Our first step towards understanding the death of this child should be not to blame social workers but to face the mother's experience of childhood. *The Guardian* [Online], 15 November. Retrieved 30 January 2011 from www.guardian.co.uk/society/2008/nov/15/child-protection-social-care-babyp

Kaufman Kantor, G., & Jasinski, J. L. (1998). Dynamics and risk factors in partner violence. In: J. L. Jasinski & L. M. Williams (Eds.), *Partner Violence: A Comprehensive Review of 20 Years of Research*. Thousand Oaks, CA: Sage.

Kennedy, H. (1992). *Eve Was Framed: Women and British Justice*. London: Chatto & Windus.

Kennedy, H. (2009). Mythologies and stereotypes- A woman's lot? *British Journal of Psychiatry, 25* (2).

Kernberg, O. F. (1991). Aggression and love in the relationship of the couple., *Journal of the American Psychoanalytic Association, 39*: 45–70.

Khan, M. M. R. (1965). The function of intimacy and acting out in perversion. In: R. Slovenko (Ed.), *Sexual Behaviour and the Law*. Springfield, IL: Charles C Thomas.

Khan, M. M. R. (1979). *Alienation in Perversions*. London: Hogarth Press.

Klein, M. (1932). The effects of early anxiety situations on the sexual development of the girl. In: *The Psycho-Analysis of Children* (pp. 268–325). London: Hogarth Press.

Kohon, G. (2010). *Jokes and Perversions: The Question of Symbolic Impoverishment*. The Birkbeck Institute for the Humanities Autumn Lectures, London, 9 November.

Kureishi, H. (2011). *It's a Sin: the Kama Sutra and the Search for Pleasure*. Manuscript in preparation.

Leader, D. (2008). *The New Black: Mourning and Melancholia*. London: Hamish Hamilton.

Lewis, E. (1979). Two hidden predisposing factors in child abuse. *Journal of Child Abuse and Neglect, 3*: 327–330.

Lewis, E., & Page, A. (1978). Failure to mourn a stillbirth: An overlooked catastrophe. *British Journal of Medical Psychology, 51*: 237.

Limentani, A. (1984). Toward a unified conception of the origins of sexual and social deviancy in young persons. *International Journal of Psychoanalytic Psychotherapy, 10*: 383–401.

Mahler, M. (1963). Thoughts about development and individuation. *Psychoanalytic Study of the Child, 18*: 307–324.

Mahler, M. (1979). *The Selected Papers of Margaret S. Mahler* (2 vols.). New York: Jason Aronson.

Malcolm, R. (1970). The mirror: A perverse sexual phantasy in a woman seen as a defence against a psychotic breakdown. In: E. Bott Spillius

(Ed.), *Melanie Klein Today, Vol. 2* (pp. 115–137). New York: Routledge, 1988.

Marucco, N. (2007). Between memory and destiny: Repetition. *International Journal of Psychoanalysis, 88*: 309–328.

Mathews, R., Matthews, J. K., & Speltz, K. (1989). *Female Sexual Offenders: An Exploratory Study*. Brandon, VT: Safer Society Press.

Matthews, J. K. (1993). Working with female sexual abusers. In: M. Elliot (Ed.), *Female Sexual Abuse of Children: The Ultimate Taboo* (pp. 61–78). London: Longman.

McCarthy, B. (1982). Incest and psychotherapy. *Irish Journal of Psychotherapy, 1*: 11–16.

McDougall, J. (1978). Primitive communication and the use of countertransference. *Contemporary Psychoanalysis, 14*: 173–209.

McDougall, J. (1980). Plea for a measure of abnormality. In: *Plea for a Measure of Abnormality* (pp. 463–486). New York: International Universities Press.

McDougall, J. (1984). The "disaffected" patient: Reflections on affect pathology. *Psychoanalytic Quarterly, 53*: 386–409.

McDougall, J. (1986). Identifications, neoneeds and neosexualities. *International Journal of Psychoanalysis, 67*: 19–31.

McDougall, J. (1989). *Theaters of the Body: A Psychoanalytic Approach to Psychosomatic Illness*. New York: W. W. Norton.

McDougall, J. (1995). *The Many Faces of Eros: A Psychoanalytic Exploration of Human Sexuality*. New York: W. W. Norton.

McGauley, G., & Bartlett, A. (2010). *Forensic Mental Health: Concepts, Systems, and Practice*. Oxford: Oxford University Press.

McGee, C. (2000). *Childhood Experiences of Domestic Violence*. London: Jessica Kingsley.

Meltzer, D. (1973). *Sexual States of Mind*. Strath Tay: Clunie Press.

Menninger, K. (1967). The injustice of justice: Who is to blame? *Bulletin of the Menninger Clinic, 31*: 325–333.

Mezey, G. (1997). Domestic violence in pregnancy. In: S. Bewley, J. Friend, & G. Mezey (Eds.), *Violence against Women*. London: Royal College of Obstetricians and Gynaecologists.

Miller, P. (2011) The Mother of invention: Turner Prize-winning artist Martin Creed. *Herald Scotland*, 21 January. Retrieved 28 January 2011 from www.heraldscotland.com/arts-ents/more-arts-entertainment-news/the-mother-of-invention-turner-prize-winning-artist-martin-creed-1.1081172

Milton, J. (1996). Technical problems in the psychotherapy of perverse female patients. In: E. V. Welldon & C. van Velsen (Eds.), *A Practical Guide to Forensic Psychotherapy* (pp. 188–193). London: Jessica Kingsley.

Minne, C. (1997) Forensic psychotherapy assessments and the legal system. In: E. V. Welldon & C. van Velsen (Eds.), *A Practical Guide to Forensic Psychotherapy* (pp. 246–252). London: Jessica Kingsley.

Minne, C. (2009). Infanticide, matricide or suicide. *British Journal of Psychotherapy*, 2: 194–202.

Mitchell, J. (1997). Sexuality, psychoanalysis and social change. *IPA News Letter*, 6 (1).

Mitchell, J. (2000). *Madmen and Medusas: Reclaiming Hysteria*. London: Basic Books.

Mitchell, J. (2003). *Sibling*. Cambridge: Polity Press.

Moguillansky, R., Szpilka, J., & Welldon, E. (2007). *Perversion: Performance, Memory, Repetition?* Panel discussion, IPA Congress, Berlin, 25–28 July.

Motz, A. (2001). *The Psychology of Female Violence*. Hove: Brunner-Routledge.

Motz, A. (2008). *The Psychology of Female Violence: Crimes Against the Body* (2nd edition). London: Routledge.

Muller, J. (1932) The problem of the libidinal development of the genital phase in girls. *International Journal of Psychoanalysis*, 13: 361–368.

Nobus, D. (2006). Locating perversion, dislocating psychoanalysis. In: D. Nobus & L. Downing (Eds.), *Perversion: Psychoanalytic Perspectives/Perspectives on Psychoanalysis* (pp. 3–18). London: Karnac.

Ogden, T. H. (1996). The perverse subject of analysis. *Journal of the American Psychoanalytic Association*, 44: 1121–1146.

Orbach, S. (2005). *Hunger Strike: The Anorectic's Struggle as a Metaphor for Our Age*. London: Karnac.

Pandolfi, A. M. (1999). *Le perversioni relazionali nella coppia e nella famiglia*. Paper presented at Convegno Internazionale CeRP, "Lo psicoanalista con e senza divano. Individui, famiglie, istituzioni tra psicosi e perversioni", Verona, 12–13 November.

Parsons, M. (2000). Sexuality and perversion a hundred years on: Discovering what Freud discovered. *International Journal of Psychoanalysis*, 81: 37–51.

Payne, S. (1935). A concept of femininity. *British Journal of Medical Psychology*, 15: 18–33.

Perelberg, R. (1999). *Psychoanalytic Understanding of Violence*. London: Routledge.

Person, E. S. (1994). Corpo ridotto al silenzio, corpo nemico. Una fantasia di percosse. In: F. Molfino & C. Zannardi (Eds.), *Sintomi Corpo Femminilita* (pp. 305–325). Bologna: CLUEB.

Person, E. S., & Klar, H. (1994). Establishing trauma: The difficulty distinguishing between memories and fantasies. *Journal of the American Psychoanalytic Association*, 42: 1055–1081.

Pfäfflin, F. (1992). What is in a symptom? A conservative approach in the therapy of sex offenders. *Journal of Offender Rehabilitation*, 18: 5–17.

Pilgrim, D. (1987). Psychotherapy in British Special Hospitals: A case of failure to thrive. *Free Associations*, 11: 59–72.

Racamier, P. C. (1992). *Le génie des origines. Psychanalyse et psychoses*. Paris: Editions Payot.

Raphling, D. (1989). Fetishism in a woman. *Journal of the American Psychoanalytic Association, 37*: 465–491.

Rascovsky, A., & Rascovsky, M. (1968). On the genesis of acting out and psychopathic behaviour in Sophocles' *Oedipus*. *International Journal of Psychoanalysis, 49*: 390–395.

Reed Report (1992). *Report of the Academic Advisory Group*. London: Department of Health/Home Office.

Resnik, S. (2005). *Glacial Times: A Journey through the World of Madness*. Hove: Routledge.

Richards, A. K. (1989). A romance with pain: A telephone perversion in a woman? *International Journal of Psychoanalysis, 70*: 153–164.

Richards, A. K. (2003). A fresh look at perversion. *Journal of the American Psychoanalytic Association, 51*: 1199–1218.

Riviere, J. (1929). Womanliness as a masquerade. *International Journal of Psychoanalysis, 10*: 303–313.

Rosen, I. (1979). *Sexual Deviation* (2nd edition). Oxford: Oxford University Press.

Rosenfeld, H. (1971). A clinical approach to the theory of the life and death instincts: An investigation into the aggressive aspects of narcissism. *International Journal of Psychoanalysis, 52*: 169–178.

Rosenthall, J. (2009). Perversion as protection. In: C. Clulow (Ed.), *Sex, Attachment and Couple Psychotherapy: Psychoanalytic Perspectives*. London: Karnac.

Roth, P. (2000). *The Human Stain*. Boston, MA: Houghton Mifflin.

Royal College of Midwives (1999). *Domestic Abuse in Pregnancy*. Position Paper 19a. London: Author.

Sachs, A. (2008). Infanticidal attachment. In: *Forensic Aspects of Dissociative Identity Disorder*. London: Karnac.

Sachs, H. (1923). The tempest. *International Journal of Psychoanalysis, 4*: 43–88.

Sanchez-Medina, A. (2003). Perverse thought. *International Journal of Psychoanalysis, 83*: 1345–1359.

Scott, A. (1996). *Real Events Revisited: Fantasy, Memory and Psychoanalysis*. London: Virago.

Scott, P. D. (1977). Assessing dangerousness in criminals. *British Journal of Psychiatry, 131*: 127–142.

Segal, N. (2009). *Consensuality: Didier Anzieu, Gender and the Sense of Touch*. New York: Editions Rodopi.

Sinason, V. (1991). Interpretations that feel horrible to make and a theoretical unicorn. *Journal of Child Psychotherapy, 17* (1): 11–24.

Sperling, M. (1959). A study of deviate sexual behaviour by the method of simultaneous analysis of mother and child. In: L. Jessner & E. Pavenstedt (Eds.), *Dynamic Psychopathology in Childhood* (pp. 221–243). New York: Grune & Stratton.

Sperling, M. (1963). Fetishism in children. *Psychoanalytic Quarterly, 32*: 374–392.

Sperling, M. (1964). The analysis of a boy with transvestite tendencies: A contribution to the genesis and dynamics of transvestism. *Psychoanalytic Study of the Child, 19*: 470–493.

Stark, E., & Flitcraft, A. (1996). *Women at Risk*. London: Sage.

Stein, R. (2005). Why perversion: False love and the perverse pact. *International Journal of Psychoanalysis, 86*: 775–99.

Stoller, R. (1968). *Sex and Gender: On the Development of Masculinity and Femininity*. New York: Science House.

Stoller, R. (1974). Hostility and mystery in perversion. *International Journal of Psychoanalysis, 55*: 425–434.

Stoller, R. (1975). *Perversion: The Erotic Form of Hatred*. New York: Pantheon.

Stoller, R. (1991). The term perversion. In: G. I. Fogel & W. A. Myers (Eds.), *Perversions and Near-Perversions in Clinical Practice*. New Haven, CT: Yale University Press.

Szpilka, J. (2002). Good in evil and evil in good. *International Journal of Psychoanalysis, 83*: 1037–1049.

Taft, A. (2002). Violence against women in pregnancy and after childbirth: Current knowledge and issues in healthcare responses. *Australian Domestic & Family Violence Clearinghouse Issues, Paper 6*.

Tate Modern (2008). *Juan Muñoz: A Retrospective, 24 January—27 April 2008* [Exhibition guide]. Retrieved 18 October 2010 from www.tate.org.uk/modern/exhibitions/juanmunoz/rooms/room4.shtm

Trowell, J. (1996). The psychodynamics of incest. In: E. V. Welldon & C. van Velsen (Eds.), *A Practical Guide to Forensic Psychotherapy* (pp. 33–41). London: Jessica Kingsley, 1997.

Tuovinen, M. (1973). Crime as an attempt at intrapsychic adaptation. *Acta Universitatis Ouluensis, Series D, Medica No. 2, Psychiatrica No. 1*.

van der Kolk, B. A. (1989). The compulsion to repeat the trauma: Reenactment, revictimization and masochism. *Psychiatric Clinics of North America, 12*: 389–430.

van Velsen, C. (2010). Psychotherapeutic understanding and approach to psychosis in mentally disordered offenders. In: A. Bartlett & G. McGauley (Eds.), *Forensic Mental Health: Concepts, Systems, Practice*. New York: Oxford University Press.

Verhaeghe, P. (2004). *On Being Normal and Other Disorders: A Manual for Clinical Psychodiagnostics*. London: Karnac, 2008.

Warner, M. (1983). *Alone of All Her Sex*. London: Vintage Books.

Welldon, E. (1982). Erotization of the group process used by patients suffering from sexual deviations as a resistance against the therapeutic alliance [Presented at the 5th European Symposium in Group Analysis, Rome 1981]. *Group Analysis, 15* (1): 22–24.

Welldon, E. (1984). Applications of group analytical psychotherapy to those with sexual perversions. In: T. E. Lear (Ed.), *Spheres of Group Analysis* (pp. 96–108). London: The Group Analytic Society.

Welldon, E. (1988). *Mother, Madonna, Whore: The Idealization and Denigration of Motherhood*. London: Karnac, 2004.

Welldon, E. (1996). Contrasts in male and female sexual perversions. In C. Cordess & M. Cox (Eds.), *Forensic Psychotherapy*. London: Jessica Kingsley.

Welldon, E. (1997). Let the treatment fit the crime: Forensic group psychotherapy [20th Annual Foulkes Lecture]. *Group Analysis, 30*: 9–26.

Welldon, E. (2002). *Ideas in Psychoanalysis: Sadomasochism*. Cambridge: Icon Books.

Welldon, E. (2009). Dancing with death. *British Journal of Psychotherapy, 2*: 149–182.

Williams, T. (1991). *Forensic Psychotherapy: Symbiosis or Impossibility*. Address given at the 17th International Congress of the International Academy of Law and Mental Health, Leuven, Belgium.

Winnicott, D. W. (1953.) Transitional objects and transitional phenomena. *International Journal of Psychoanalysis, 34*: 89–97.

Winnicott, D. W. (1955–6). Clinical varieties of transference. In: *Through Paediatrics to Psychoanalysis* (pp. 295–299). London: Hogarth Press, 1975.

Winnicott, D. W. (1956). The antisocial tendency. In: *Through Paediatrics to Psychoanalysis* (pp. 306–315). London: Hogarth Press, 1975.

Winnicott, D. W. (1965). *The Maturational Processes and the Facilitating Environment*. London: Hogarth Press.

Winnicott, D. W. (1974). Fear of breakdown. In: *Psychoanalytic Explorations* (pp. 87–95). London: Karnac, 1989.

Wolak, J., & Finkelhor, D. (1988). Children exposed to partner violence. In: J. L. Jasinski & L. M. Williams (Eds.), *Partner Violence: A Comprehensive Review of 20 Years of Research* (pp. 73–112). Thousand Oaks, CA: Sage.

Yakeley, J. (2010). *Working with Violence: A Contemporary Psychoanalytic Approach*. London: Palgrave Macmillan.

Yalom, L. D. (1975). *The Theory and Practice of Group Psychotherapy*. New York: Basic Books.

Zavitzianos, G. (1971). Fetishism and exhibitionism in the female and their relationship to psychopathy and kleptomania. *International Journal of Psychoanalysis, 52*: 297–305.

Zavitzianos, G. (1982). The perversion of fetishism in women. *Psychoanalytic Quarterly, 51*: 405–425.

Zilboorg, G. (1933). Anxiety without affect. *Psychoanalytic Quarterly, 2*: 48–67.

Zilboorg, G. (1955). *The Psychology of the Criminal Act and Punishment*. London: Hogarth Press & the Institute of Psychoanalysis.

INDEX